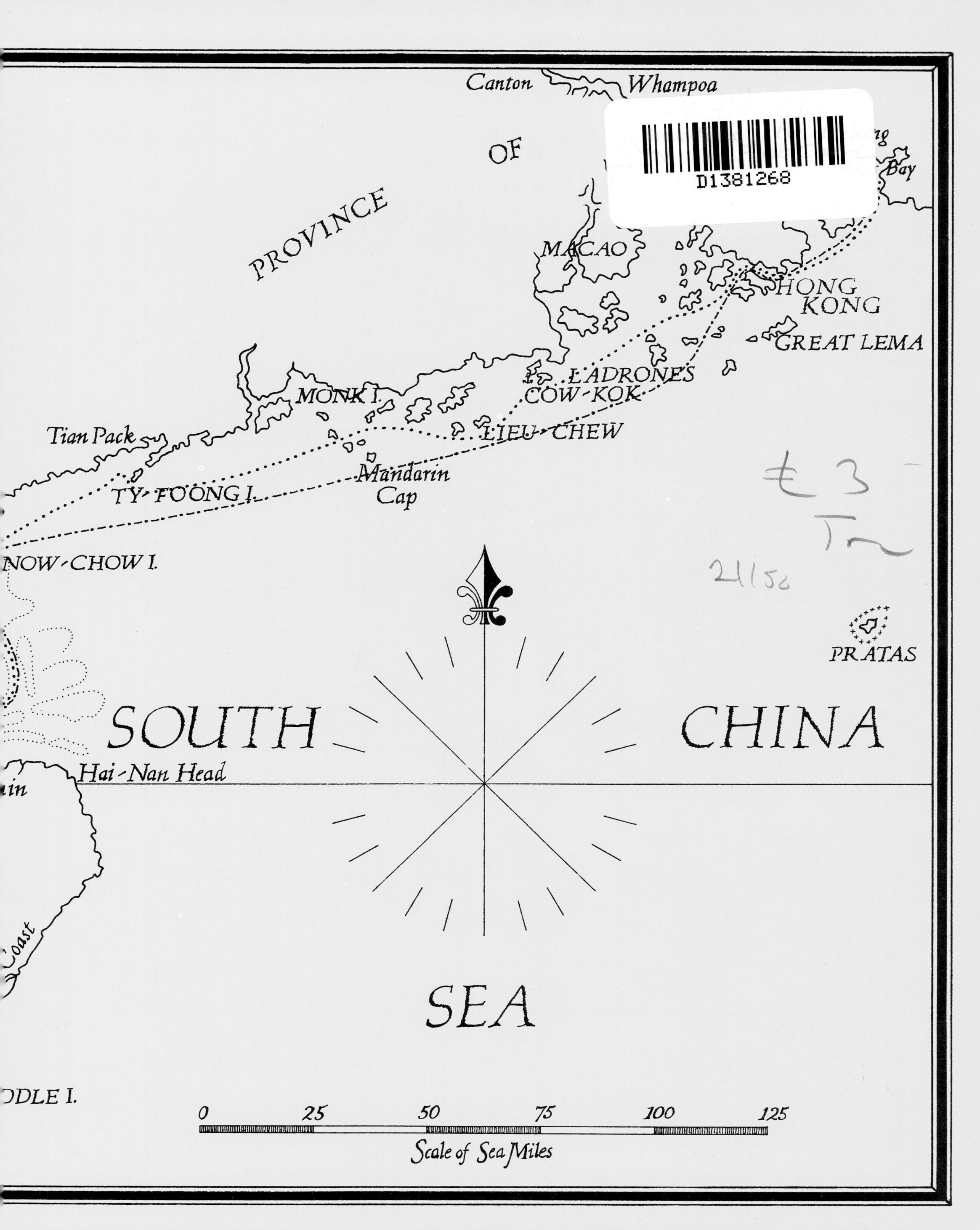

Canton
Whampoa
OF
PROVINCE
Bay
MACAO
HONG KONG
GREAT LEMA
LADRONES
COW-KOK
MONK I.
LIEU-CHEW
Tian Pack
Mandarin Cap
TY-FOONG I.
NOW-CHOW I.
PRATAS
SOUTH
CHINA
Hai-Nan Head
SEA
DDLE I.
0
25
50
75
100
125
Scale of Sea Miles

THE CREE JOURNALS

Edward Hodges Cree at the age of forty-six

THE CREE JOURNALS

The Voyages of Edward H. Cree, Surgeon R.N., as Related in His Private Journals, 1837-1856

Edited and with an Introduction

by

Michael Levien

EXETER, ENGLAND

Published in Great Britain 1981 by
Webb & Bower (Publishers) Limited
33 Southernhay East, Exeter, Devon EX1 1NS

Designed by Malcolm Couch

British Library Cataloguing in Publication Data

Cree, Edward
The Cree journals.
1. Great Britain. Royal Navy – Surgeons
2. Great Britain. Royal Navy – Sea life
I. Levien, Michael
359.3'45'0924 VG265.G7

ISBN 0-906671-36-1

Typeset in Great Britain by Keyspools Limited, Golborne, Lancashire

Printed and bound in Hong Kong by Mandarin Offset International Limited

Contents

APPENDICES

MAPS

Introduction

The Cree Journals is the personal narrative of Dr Edward H. Cree, an Englishman of Scottish extraction who served in the Royal Navy, almost uninterruptedly, from 1837 to 1869. Hitherto they have never been published. The original bound manuscripts, from which the present selection has been made, span Cree's service as a naval surgeon in the period 1837–61 and extend to around a million and a quarter words. Against a background of dramatic historical events they record all his sea voyages, his experiences abroad, his impressions of people and places in days of peace and war, his professional duties, his time spent in England and Scotland among family and friends, his marriage and domestic life. The text in its complete form is supplemented by some seventeen hundred water-colours and sketches, executed by Edward Cree contemporaneously with his narrative.

Edward Hodges Cree was born on January 14th 1814 in Devonport, the son of Robert Cree and his wife Charlotte (née Street). His middle name, Hodges, was that of his paternal grandmother. He was one of five children, one brother dying in infancy and an elder brother and a sister dying in 1829 and 1830, aged twenty and twenty-three respectively. His mother having died aged forty-eight in 1833, Edward became close to his surviving sister, Percy. Robert Cree had served as a Unitarian minister, first for seven years at Preston, Lancashire, and then at Bridport, Dorset, in the period 1828–34. His reasons for leaving the Church are not known. Earlier in his life, however, and at the time of his marriage, Robert had been a mercer, and it was to this profession that he now returned, being based for a while as previously in Devonport. In his later years Robert worked as a commercial traveller, living in various parts of the country – and none too happily, it seems – but he continued to keep in touch with his daughter Percy, and with Edward too, and Edward always writes affectionately of his father.

Edward went to school at Preston and then received private medical tuition at Bridport before going on to university. He studied medicine at Dublin and Edinburgh Universities, graduating from the latter as L.S.A. (Licentiate of the Society of Apothecaries) in 1837. Ten years later he returned to Edinburgh and obtained his M.R.C.S. and M.D. He entered the Royal Navy in June 1837, the same month as Queen Victoria's proclamation, at which point the Journals begin. He continued writing them, without a break, until the end of his last seagoing appointment in 1861.

Edward spent most of his sea service on foreign stations, including ten years (1840–50) in the Far East. By the end of that period he was much troubled by dysentery, and consequently, in December 1850, he was granted a year's sick-leave on half pay, an interlude he turned to good account in a trip to Europe. A year later his father died, and Percy having by then remarried, Edward felt free to find a wife for himself. In September 1852 he married Eliza Tanner Hancock, the twenty-six-year-old daughter of William Hancock of Plymouth and his second wife Eliza (née Teage).[1] Hancock was a successful mercer and friend of the Cree family (Robert had once worked for him), and an early letter shows that as a boy Edward had taken a holiday job in Hancock's drapery business in Catherine Street.

[1] William Hancock's first wife had been Ann Cree, Edward's aunt, by whom he had eight children. He was a widower at the time of his marriage to Eliza Teage, spinster, on May 24th 1825. Their daughter Eliza was born on July 12th 1826.

After service on the Lisbon station (1853–4) Edward served in the Baltic (1854) and in the Crimea (1855–6). From the end of 1856 until 1860 he served in home waters. In June 1860 he took up an appointment as Private Medical Attendant to the invalid Earl of Mount Edgcumbe, being based at the Earl's Winter Villa in Plymouth and accompanying him on various journeys, sometimes in his yacht. He relinquished the post in October of that year, receiving shortly afterwards his final sea appointment, to H.M.S. *Orion*, a 91-gun line-of-battle ship in which he spent the year 1861 cruising in the Mediterranean and revisiting some of his haunts from earlier days – that is, when he was serving in the paddle-steamer *Firefly* (1837–9). He then took up a shore job, being appointed Staff Surgeon in December 1862 and serving latterly in that post at Portsmouth Dockyard, namely from 1864 until 1869, in which year he retired from the Navy with the rank of Deputy Inspector-General of Hospitals and Fleets.[2] Afterwards he went into general practice in Holloway, London.

[2] The ranks of Inspector-General and Deputy Inspector-General of Hospitals and Fleets were created when those of Physician-General and Physician lapsed in 1840. Today's equivalent of Cree's retirement rank is Surgeon Captain. It was not until 1918 that medical officers in the Royal Navy were accorded ranks in line with combatant officers.

Edward and Eliza Cree had eight children, seven sons and a daughter. Edward was keen that all his sons should follow his footsteps and become doctors in the Royal Navy, and thus it was that all of them attended Medical School at the Middlesex Hospital in London. However, only the two eldest, William and Percy, were to join the Navy, each serving abroad as surgeons in H.M. ships. But William resigned after three years and then went into his father's practice, while Percy died of tuberculosis soon afterwards. Of the remaining sons, three joined the Royal Army Medical Corps (two reaching the rank of Colonel and the other becoming a Major-General), one served at sea with the Peninsular and Oriental Steam Navigation Company and other steamship companies before starting his own practice in London, and one, having failed his finals, emigrated to Canada and joined the North-West Mounted Police. He settled eventually in British Columbia, where his descendants remain. For her part, Edward's daughter became a nurse at Great Ormond Street Hospital, London, and married a doctor.

Edward died on January 15th 1901, five years after his wife, with whom he lies buried in Highgate Cemetery.

The Journals were begun by Edward Cree on the very first day he joined the Royal Navy. For the most part, he kept them on a day-to-day basis, especially whilst he was travelling at sea and serving abroad. At certain periods he recorded, as in a ship's log-book, the daily temperature, wind velocity and weather conditions, as well as the position of the vessel in which he was travelling, details it would not have been practicable to reproduce in the present volume. The limp workaday notebooks that Edward utilised, and to which he appended his sketches and paintings, were somewhat cramped, and certainly some were untidy and scarcely legible in places. Hence, about 1887, his eldest son William by now having taken the weight of the family practice on his shoulders, Edward decided to make a fair copy of his entire collection of Journals, rewriting them on sheets suitable for binding in annual volumes.[3] This must have been a laborious task for an elderly man, to say the least, and when he had reached the ninth volume, that of 1845, his handwriting had become so hard to read that his family presented him with a typewriter, which he used to good effect from then onwards.

The completed fair copies of the Journals, bound in twenty-one volumes, were passed on to William and are still in the possession of the Cree family. What became of the original notebooks, however, remained a mystery until their partial rediscovery in the summer of 1980 among various family papers that had been stored away and forgotten about since the time of William Cree's death in 1939. I say "partial" rediscovery because, regrettably, the notebooks are far from complete, only a few portions, together with some additional pictures, remaining intact. Among these is Edward's account of his wedding and honeymoon in 1852, complete with a sprig of heather picked on a drive in the forest of Fontainebleau. Two sketches from that notebook are reproduced in the present selection. A study of the original material against the bound manuscripts has revealed that, as he reread his notebooks, Edward became his own editor, cutting some parts of his narrative and elaborating upon others. This explains why some sections of the bound Journals, such as the opening pages of 1837, are in the form of summaries of certain spells of time, penned by Edward on reflection, rather than in the immediate style he must have used initially.

Apparently Edward had little formal training in art – the earliest sketch-book of his to survive is one he completed on a visit to the Highlands of Scotland about 1834 whilst he was a medical student at Edinburgh. In the Journals, he mentions having private tuition from two men. One was a Signor Schranz who lived in Valletta – "his style is rather too smooth and tame," Edward notes in April 1838, "but there is no better in Malta". But perhaps it was Schranz's niece, Clementina, who inspired Edward to return regularly for lessons, for he found her "a pretty girl . . . who has one of those beautiful oval Italian faces and sunk eyes as one sees in some of the old Italian pictures", and he continued to comment on her charms. Edward's other tutor was R.H.C. Ubsdell (*fl.c.*1809–49), well known in his day as a miniaturist, illustrator and photographer, from whom he took drawing lessons when he was based in Portsmouth in July 1839. Later on, Edward achieved some artistic success through his contributions to the *Illustrated London News*.

[3] About this time Cree wrote an autobiographical piece for *The Cosmopolitan*. It appeared in the February issue of the second quarterly volume, published in London by Digby & Long in 1888. The British Library's copy of that volume lacks the February issue, and efforts to trace it elsewhere have hitherto been unsuccessful.

What kind of a man was Edward Cree? The self-portrait that comes into focus in his Journals is of a genial, outward-looking man with an infectious enthusiasm and great zest for life. Sharply observant of all he encountered, eager to seek out and explore new places, as ready for duty as he was to enjoy himself, he was the ideal messmate and travelling companion. Small wonder he was popular among his comrades – a fact that emerges of its own. Naturally enough he was a product of his age, with some of the tastes and prejudices typical of an educated Victorian. Yet he was never starchy, deflating any show of self-importance with an irreverent dry wit; and though staunchly patriotic, he affirms his regret over the war in China and dislike of "the opium question". In lighter moments, the reward of hard days at sea, he was ever the dashing lady's man, dancing and flirting with the prettiest girls he could find from Alexandria to Hong Kong. He makes no secret of delighting in their company, on country picnics and revelries aboard ship, days of jollity that were followed by tearful partings, as when wistfully he bids adieu at Trincomalee to his favourite "little fairy", Emily Pett, "a cruel fair wind" blowing his ship out of sight of "Fairyland" for all but the last time.

Edward's early naval service in the Mediterranean, chiefly in the mail carrying *Firefly*, was tranquil enough. However, his first long sea voyage in the troop-ship *Rattlesnake*, which he joined in September 1839, was to take him into the heart of the First China War. Some background guidance concerning that conflict, first of the so-called "opium" wars, is necessary for an understanding of the events in which Edward became involved.

The quarrel between Great Britain and China was essentially over trade, in particular the restrictions imposed upon British merchants. Like all foreign merchants, the British were from 1750 onwards restricted to the port of Canton, situated 2,000 miles from Peking and out of touch with the main production centres of silk and tea, the principal Chinese exports. No less a thorn in the flesh of the British merchants were the restrictions on their personal freedom, subject as they were to the arbitrary exactions of Chinese officialdom and against which they had scant hope of redress. Furthermore, Chinese and Western ideas of justice and standards of behaviour were poles apart, and the Chinese embargo on communicating in the vernacular with foreigners stunted the development of relations between the various parties no less than it was the cause of persistent misunderstandings. While the disparity between host country and foreign guests was on the British side the source of mounting distrust and resentment, this was compensated by the handsome profits accruing from importation of the drug opium. In its early stages there had been considerable imbalance in trade, Chinese exports being far in excess of imports, but that imbalance came to be checked by the huge growth of opium imports. It was the prodigious increase in opium traffic, and the outflow of Chinese silver to pay for it, that was to strain Anglo-Chinese relations to breaking-point and pitch the two countries into war.

Since the previous century, the British East India Company had enjoyed a monopoly in trade with China, and by the 1830s its merchandising in opium from Bengal was providing a rich source of revenue for the government of British India. Company ships had been forbidden from carrying the drug following a ban on its importation by the Chinese (in 1796), since when the opium traffic had been conducted by licensed private traders, who unloaded their illicit cargoes on the island of Lintin. There the Indian opium changed hands, being transported deviously by swift-moving Chinese craft on the last leg of its journey to the mainland.

The prickly question of the contraband trade aside, relations between the British and Chinese had never been happy, and the official structure set up by the Chinese for supervising trade in Canton was none too satisfactory, certainly from the British viewpoint. The exclusive commercial right to deal with the British was held by a guild of Chinese business men, known as the *Co-hong*, or Hong merchants, who acted under the authority of an Imperial Commissioner of Customs. In cases of dispute there was no diplomatic channel through which the British could appeal, and their only means of referring to a higher authority was by petition through the Hong merchants. In the circumstances, commercial dealings came to be tainted by bribery and corruption, trade with the British "barbarians" continuing to be concessionary, with the Chinese always holding the whip hand. This was still a period of Grand Isolation in China, the Chinese having a contemptuous attitude towards all Westerners, begrudging them even their single trading-post. Thus the city of Canton itself was pretty well barred to Europeans and Americans, the mixed foreign community leading a stifling existence in the small area allotted to them beside their factories. On the British side, ignorance of China in general and of the Chinese character in particular, by the Foreign Office as well as by the Admiralty, was to hinder subsequent negotiations with the "inscrutable" mandarins who took it in turn to deliver the arrogant and intractable "chops" issuing from the Imperial Court in Peking.[4]

In 1834 the East India Company's trade monopoly was revoked, an event that heralded a hardening of attitude towards the Chinese. In place of the Company's Select Committee, under whose direction dealings with the *Co-hung*, which if tinged with appeasement had at least been peaceable (largely in order to maintain the valuable trade in tea), came a Superintendent of Trade, appointed by the British Government. The "velvet glove" policy towards the Chinese was to all intents and purposes pursued, though not without humiliations, by a quick succession of chief superintendents, and by the time Captain Charles Elliot took over the post in 1836 there were still hopes for the legalisation of restricted opium imports, a measure that would certainly have taken some of the heat out of the air. However, these hopes were dashed to the ground when in March 1839 the Emperor sent to Canton an abrasive Imperial Commissioner called Lin Tse-hsü. Lin's uncompromising demand for the surrender of all the European opium stocks was met, 20,000 chests valued at £3 million being thereupon destroyed. The British merchants then took

[4] An excellent guide through the tangled web of Anglo-Chinese intercourse is given by Gerald S. Graham in his book *The China Station: War and Diplomacy 1830–1860* (1978).

refuge in Macao, where more trouble followed after a drunken fight involving British sailors in which a Chinese was killed.

Even now, it was hoped to bring the Peking government to the conference table in order to conclude a satisfactory trade agreement. Meanwhile an expeditionary force was assembled in Singapore. Its task was primarily to show the flag, to demonstrate the strength of British naval power, of which the Chinese were as yet unaware. In pursuit of this policy, the initial plan was to blockade the Canton River and then to proceed northward in order to sever communication between Amoy and Formosa, blockade the estuary opposite the Chusan Islands leading to Hangchow, blockade the mouth of the Yangtse as well as the Yellow River, and establish a firm headquarters in the Chusan Islands. All Chinese vessels that were encountered were to be seized and detained.[5] The expedition set forth from Singapore on May 30th 1840 under the temporary command of Commodore Sir James Gordon Bremer. The troop-ship *Rattlesnake*, with the young assistant surgeon Edward Cree aboard, sailed with the armada, and here the Journals take up the story.

The series of battles that followed, it should be noted, were staged in the first place to draw the attention of the Emperor. But the Emperor was deliberately kept ignorant of events by officials who feared that to bring him news of defeat would mean the loss of their heads – until the capture of Chin-kiang-foo in July 1842.[6] This unequivocal British victory secured the Treaty of Nanking.[7]

There were serious problems in the way of prosecuting a war in China. Communications were slow, coastal waters and rivers were incompletely charted, maps of the country were inadequate, disease and sickness were rife. Sea journeys were made doubly hazardous by monsoons and typhoons, and the sheer magnitude of the country ruled out all but limited land penetration by military force. The unique feature of the nineteenth-century campaigns, by which means the capture of Peking in the Second China War of 1856–60 was ultimately to be achieved, was the successful use of the steam vessel. For the first time the steamers made it possible to launch an amphibious operation far inland, able as they were to guide or tow warships hundreds of miles up a grand river like the Yangtse, as in 1842, or act in support of troops, as in the Peiho in 1860. This maritime mobility was to have far-reaching consequences, for it was to lead to the opening of China to the West.

Among the other Far East expeditions in which Edward Cree participated was the pursuit of pirates who operated along the southern coast of China and beyond, killing and plundering as they went. More often than not their victims were village fisherfolk, and it was with the co-operation of such people that in October 1849 the British were able to root out and destroy the fleets of the two arch-scoundrels Chui-apoo and Shap-'ng-tsai, in which engagements more than 1,700 pirates were killed.

In the nineteenth century, piracy persisted also in the Malayan seas, the Archipelago still being divided into numerous petty kingdoms, many of

[5] The emphasis was on blockade not bloodshed. However, if Peking obdurately refused to come to terms, hostilities were to commence. In the event, that is what transpired, as becomes apparent in Cree's account of subsequent naval and military actions.

[6] The Chinese took withdrawal, however successful a British attack may have been, as a sign of weakness. In their reports to Peking, the high mandarins went a stage further, claiming Chinese defeats as glorious victories. At the fall of Chin-kiang-foo, however, trade (via the Grand Canal) came to a virtual standstill, and Nanking, one-time capital of the Ming Empire, was threatened. These facts could not be concealed from the Emperor.

[7] Under the main terms of the treaty Hong Kong was ceded to Great Britain and the ports of Canton, Amoy, Foo-chow, Ningpo and Shanghai were to be opened to foreign residence and trade. No mention was made of the opium traffic.

whose rajahs boasted their own pirate fleets. These marauders preyed not only on native craft but on European and American ships alike. Edward Cree tells the story of the downfall of two notorious piratical characters, Pangeran Usop and Serip Usman, though piracy was to continue in those waters for several years to come.

Cree's experiences in the war against Russia of 1854–6, during which he served in the Baltic as well as the Crimea, speak for themselves. The causes of the war were complex, the chief one being Russian expansionist ambitions in the Balkans and Eastern Mediterranean. This was linked with the weakness of the Turkish or Ottoman Empire, whose integrity was vital as a buffer against Russian territorial aspirations. On the one hand, Russia sought to gain access to the Mediterranean by the occupation of Constantinople; and on the other, to assert a protectorate over Christian Slavs in the Balkans, as well as to preserve the special status enjoyed by Orthodox Christians in the Holy Places of Palestine. In July 1853 the Russians crossed the River Pruth and occupied the Danubian principalities of Moldavia and Wallachia. As a result, in October of that year Turkey declared war on Russia. In March 1854 Great Britain and France also declared war on Russia[8] (later allied support came from Piedmont-Sardinia), and by concentrating their armies at Varna in Bulgaria, safeguarded Constantinople. By July, the Turkish forces had driven the Russians back across the Pruth, and hostilities might then have been brought to a satisfactory conclusion. However, the allied governments felt moved to continue the war, and in September Anglo-French forces, taking advantage of their naval superiority, invaded the Crimean peninsula. Their aim was to capture the Russian naval base of Sebastopol and vanquish the Russian navy in the Black Sea. Some of the main events that followed in that war zone are touched on later.

[8] Britain sought to protect her interests in India, which were threatened by the Russian advance into Central Asia, and also by possible Russian control of the Eastern Mediterranean, which eventuality would mean their gaining command of the short overland route to the East. France was drawn into the war through a dispute concerning the claims, which she supported, of Roman Catholic orders in the Holy Land, and through the *folie de grandeur* of the new Emperor, Napoleon III.

In making my selections from the Journals I have been influenced by two main factors: to include as broad a coverage as possible, both textual and pictorial, of Edward Cree's eventful life, within the strict limitations of space, and at the same time to exclude nothing of major significance. Selections from his most exciting voyages – in *Rattlesnake* (1839–43), *Vixen* (1843–6), *Fury* (1847–50) and *Odin* (1852–6) – are the key links in the ensuing narrative. Major omissions of text are signposted by linking passages. These pinpoint what has occurred in the interim, though obviously it was not feasible to explore each and every event that has been bypassed. In the interests of clarity and consistency, I have updated spellings, corrected spelling errors and introduced some punctuation. Certain idiosyncrasies, such as Cree's almost consistent misspelling "under weigh", have been left alone. Wherever possible, I have checked and amended as necessary the names of ships as well as of individuals. In the period covered by the Journals, the transliteration of Chinese names into English was a somewhat hit-or-miss affair. Moreover, in the intervening years many names, such as those of Chinese towns and villages, have been superseded. But, with a few exceptions, I have not attempted to modernise Chinese and other place-names or to introduce their present-day variants (e.g. Manila for Manilla, Valletta for Valetta). Notes appended by Cree are indicated by an asterisk. Those that I have introduced are numbered. A superior letter B against the name of an individual (e.g. Major-General Gough[B]) denotes his inclusion in the Selected Biographies section at the end of the book. Occasionally the reference is repeated. Editorial insertions in Cree's text are in square brackets, and cuts within the journal entries are indicated by ellipses. The maps, together with the track-chart, all specially drawn for this volume, are based on Cree's own sketch-maps.

Whilst preparing this book for publication I consulted a number of people, to whom I wish to record my appreciation.

First of all I should like to thank Brigadier Hilary Cree for the invaluable advice he has given me concerning his grandfather and other members of his family, and for his helpful comments and suggestions on reading the edited typescript. I am also indebted to him, and to his wife Joan, for the hospitality they extended to me during the months I worked on the Journals in their delightful house.

I should also like to thank the following for various services: Surgeon Captain J. Cox and staff of the Royal Naval Hospital, Plymouth; Dr A.L. Furniss, Director, Public Health Laboratory, Preston Hall Hospital, Maidstone; Dr J.T.D. Hall, Keeper of Special Collections, Edinburgh University Library; Mr Alan Pearsall of the National Maritime Museum, and the staffs of the Reading Room and Pictures Department at the Museum; Mr Robin Price, Deputy Librarian, The Wellcome Institute for the History of Medicine; Mr Brian Thomson, Secretary, Royal United Service Institution; Mr N.E. Upham, Department of Ships, National Maritime Museum; the staffs of the British Library, India Office Library and Records, National Army Museum, Public Record Office, Kew, and of the Central Libraries of Exeter, Plymouth and Torquay; and the National Historical Museum, Moscow.

Finally, I wish to express my thanks to Mr and Mrs Peter Snape, through whom the Journals first came to my notice.

MICHAEL LEVIEN

THE JOURNALS

H.M.S. *Adelaide* – 104 guns

1837

Entrance into the Navy

Having finished my medical studies for the present, I had a great desire to go into the Navy. Therefore Sir George Grey,[B] M.P. for Devonport, was applied to by my father to use his influence with one of the Lords of the Admiralty to give me an appointment as Assistant Surgeon. My father had wished me to go as Assistant to a friend of his, a country surgeon in Cornwall, but that I utterly repudiated. I got an order from the Admiralty to Sir William Burnett,[B] Physician-General of the Navy, as the Medical Director-General was then styled. I was then sent up to the College of Surgeons for examination, and afterwards passed Sir William Burnett's examination. I was an L.S.A. before.

First Appointment – Royal Naval Hospital, Stonehouse

June 8th I received my appointment from the Admiralty as Assistant Surgeon a few days before the accession of Queen Victoria. I was appointed as additional Assistant Surgeon to H.M.S. *Royal Adelaide*, flagship at Devonport. On joining her I was ordered to do duty at the Naval Hospital, Stonehouse,[1] where I was under the Physician Sir David Dickson.[B] The other Assistant Surgeons were Weale, an excellent artist in water-colour, an Irishman from Cork. He inspired me in my love of drawing. He was kept at the Hospital principally for pathological drawings. Easton, an Edinburgh man. McDougall, also a Scotchman, and Oman, an Irishman. The three latter were on the surgical side under Dr Armstrong, a Scotchman. Browne, a big, fat Irishman from Derry, and Slight, an Englishman, were also on our side of the Hospital. Our pay was 6/-6 a day and 1/-6 in lieu of provisions.

[1] By the beginning of Queen Victoria's reign the three adjoining maritime towns of Plymouth, Devonport and Stonehouse had begun merging together into one city. They were eventually amalgamated under the name of Plymouth in 1914. Devonport, the youngest of the three, had until 1824 been called Plymouth Dock.

All the Assistant Surgeons messed together in a room in the Chapel Building, had a ward to sleep in. We kept a pretty good mess and got on very well together. Our duties were not arduous: at 8.30 a.m. to attend the Physician round his wards, afterwards to the Dispensary to assist in making up medicines with the Apothecary. Generally nothing more till the evening visit,

The Royal Naval Hospital, Stonehouse. The sketch, probably drawn from memory, is not quite accurate, e.g. the various blocks should not be joined together. The sundial in the foreground is by J. Gilbert.

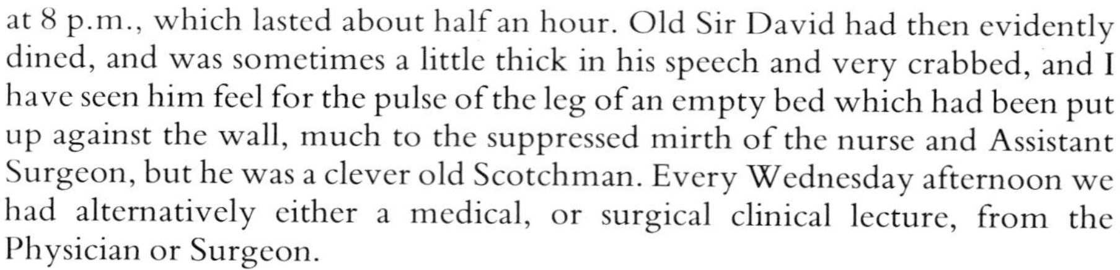

at 8 p.m., which lasted about half an hour. Old Sir David had then evidently dined, and was sometimes a little thick in his speech and very crabbed, and I have seen him feel for the pulse of the leg of an empty bed which had been put up against the wall, much to the suppressed mirth of the nurse and Assistant Surgeon, but he was a clever old Scotchman. Every Wednesday afternoon we had alternatively either a medical, or surgical clinical lecture, from the Physician or Surgeon.

The old King, William IV, having died, Queen Victoria was proclaimed at the Hospital gates on Saturday, June 24th, and we were all summoned to attend in uniform. I had scarcely worn mine, and was hardly familiar with the cocked hat and sword. It being a very windy day, my big cocked hat was like a fore-and-aft sail, almost carried my head away, and the sword would endeavour to get between my legs. All the Hospital authorities, both male and female, were there. We wore crape round the left arm for the old King. Of course, I thought I looked particularly fetching in my new blue and gold uniform.

Sir David Dickson on his evening round

Proclamation of Queen Victoria at the Hospital gates

" The veil was carried right across my head."

The buoy-boat, Falmouth (*right*)

On returning to the Hospital quarters, I followed one of the lieutenants of the Hospital, with two of his pretty daughters. The day being very windy, the veil of one of the young ladies, which was blue, was carried off her bonnet, and right across my head. I had to take it back to the owner and present it with as pretty a speech as I could think of. I was invited to tea next day, and my visits were frequent afterwards.

A raw-boned, red-headed Scotchman, Alexander, joined us, with more shrewdness than manners, but he was very amusing at times, and one day, dining with Sir David and Lady Dickson, he kept the table in a roar of laughter, relating his experiences of Canadian society. He had lately returned from Canada.

Leave Plymouth Hospital

I was not allowed to remain much longer at Plymouth Hospital, as on July 28th I received an appointment as additional Assistant Surgeon to H.M.S. *Princess Charlotte*, flagship in the Mediterranean. Easton and McDougall also received similar orders. Cholera is raging at Malta and more medical officers are wanted for the ships.

Sun., July 30th We waited on Lord Amelius Beauclerk,[B] the Port Admiral, who ordered us a passage to Falmouth to join the packet going out to Malta, as we were also to take out a quantity of medical stores. The buoy-boat was to sail for Falmouth next morning, so I had little time to prepare for my voyage. However, I managed to get a big sea-chest, and as much of the necessaries as I could collect, and wish my numerous friends farewell.

Falmouth

Got on board the buoy-boat next morning at 8, and soon after Easton and McDougall came on board in the hospital launch laden with beds and bedding and other hospital stores. We soon afterwards left the Hamoaze and stood out to sea. We got to Falmouth in the evening and after going alongside the *Volcano*, paddle-steamer, where we deposited the medical stores, went on shore, as she was not going to sail for a few days.

We called on Captain Plumridge,[B] the Superintendent, for our appointments, and I met a few old friends at Falmouth, and my father came to see me before I left, but he had to go on to Plymouth by the *Sir Francis Drake* steamer. I put up at the Green Bank Hotel, a comfortable house. What strikes one most at Falmouth is the everlasting clatter of women's pattens about the streets. They say a Falmouth girl's fortune is an umbrella and a pair of pattens.

AUGUST *Thur. 3rd* Green Bank Hotel. We took a stroll through Falmouth to take a last look at the English girls. We dined at the Royal Hotel and were going on board the *Volcano* but found she was detained on account of bad weather. However, in the evening it cleared and she fired a signal gun and hoisted the Blue Peter, so we went on board and found all confusion – ladies and luggage, and bags of mails, all being hurried on board. However, we got down to the gunroom with our future messmates, and soon after put to sea, and bid adieu to the shores of old England, which soon grew dim and I seasick.

At Sea

I am not used to sleeping in a hammock, but I found mine, slung on the main deck, very comfortable.

We had the weather tolerably fine in crossing the Bay of Biscay, but I did not get over my seasickness till we were running down the coast of Portugal on the 7th. Amongst the passengers is a son of Lucian Bonaparte,[2] very like the pictures of the great Napoleon; Sir Thomas Fellowes, Captain of the *Vanguard* at Malta, and his son Charles, a mate; Lady Woodford, wife of Sir George Woodford,[B] Governor of Gibraltar, and their son and daughter; [Robert W.] Campbell, Surgeon R.N., going to Malta on the same errand as ourselves; Hassen Medina, an Egyptian youth who has been studying in England by order of the Pasha; and many others.

[2] Lucian Bonaparte, Prince of Canino, was a brother of Napoleon. Cree meets his son Prince Pierre Bonaparte once again in May 1838, en route from Malta to Gibraltar, and then writes: "He is from Corfu where he found it prudent to quit, as he had unfortunately shot an Albanian in a dispute while out shooting in Albania."

Tue. 8th Passed down to Cape St Vincent – glorious weather, hot and fine. Splendid sunset.

Cadiz

Wed. 9th–Thur. 10th Running along towards Cadiz, where we arrived Thursday, August 10th. An old Spanish pilot came on board and took us into harbour. The view of the city is pleasing. The dome of the new cathedral and the buildings all so white and the sky and sea blue. The bright boats with their painted, butterfly sails. We found H.M. Steamer *Blazer* here, in quarantine from Malta, on her way to England, and by her we sent our letters. I went on shore with some of the others in a native boat, quite delighted to land after our voyage, everything one sees so new and interesting. The streets are narrow but clean and shaded by the projecting balconies. Went into a fruit shop and indulged in luscious grapes and figs, bananas, peaches, &c., for which I only paid twopence halfpenny. We paid a visit to the English Hotel and then found our way to the new cathedral, a fine building of white marble with elaborate carving both outside and in. In the interior fine polished marbles of various colours with lapis lazuli and other valuable stones. It is not yet finished, although it has been 170 years in building. A lot of boys are employed polishing. The roof is exquisitely sculptured.

Pilot boat, Cadiz

. . . We got a capital dinner at the hotel – vermicelli soup, boiled and fried fish, fowls and a stew of veal and vegetables, very good withall, with just a flavour of garlic. Afterwards delicious fruit and good claret and light sherry – but we had been at sea, not on luxurious fare, and our appetites good! We returned to the ship with reluctance about 3.30 p.m. after a pleasant, but too short, visit to Cadiz. An American frigate and a French brig-of-war were in the harbour as well as H.M.S. *Trinculo*, sloop.

Gibraltar

We left Cadiz about 5 p.m. and arrived at Gibraltar at 2 the next morning. I remained on deck nearly all night, the air was so delicious and sky and sea beautiful.

Our appointment was to the *Princess Charlotte* which had gone to Barcelona, but we were intended for work at Malta. M'Ilwaine, the Captain

Gibraltar – the town

of the *Volcano*, was acting up to the letter, but not the spirit, of the order when he sent us to the *Medea* steamer, starting to join the Admiral. We left and had got round Europa Point when the Captain of *Medea* examined our orders and found we were intended for Malta. Therefore he put back and returned us to the *Volcano*, much to the disgust of M'Ilwaine. As she was not going to sail till next day, we went on shore to have a look at the place. Landing at the new mole, we walked to the town, about a mile. The narrow street was gay with crowds, people of various nations in their native costumes – Moors, Spanish, Greeks, &c. Brenan, Assistant Surgeon of *Volcano*, was with us. He took us to the shop of an old Moor called Zanut, where we got dates and cool water, but did not buy any of his slippers. We then went into a store kept by Rowswell, an Ilminster man, with whom I had a chat, and as he is a wealthy man, with three daughters that he wants to send to an English ladies' school, I recommended Miss Baker's.[3] After coffee at the hotel we went out to listen to the military band, in the Alameda Gardens.

[3] Cree's sister, Percy, had attended Miss Baker's Ladies' Boarding School, at Ilminster, Somerset, in 1833–4.

Fri. 11th . . . After dinner landed again and went to Rowswell's, where we were regaled with cigars and champagne, but soon had to go, as the Skipper called in and told us we should lose our passage if we delayed, as he intended to start before dark.

Algeciras from Gibraltar

Mediterranean

We were soon off and steaming round Europa Point and in the Mediterranean. A lovely calm evening and so clear I remained on deck till very late watching the fires on the Spanish coast. As we were bowling along with a fair wind and tide, and all square sails set, the water beautifully phosphorescent, saw a beautiful meteor which went away to the NE, leaving a streak of light lasting many seconds.

Sat. 12th Passing Cape de Gattor at noon, therm. 82°. Lord Edward Clinton, a son of the Duke of Newcastle, a mate in the Navy, going to join his ship at Malta.

Sun. 13th Passed in sight of Algiers. Pretty appearance of the white triangular city, set in the dark green hills, dotted with white villas and country houses. We have been running along in sight of the Atlas range of mountains all day. Muster as usual, the men all in white. The Commander read prayers.

Mon. 14th Still running along in sight of the African coast, bold and mountainous, no towns or villages to be seen.

Tue. 15th Some trees and villages and an old Moorish castle in sight, and date palms near the shore. Afterwards passed the entrance to the Bay of Tunis and also the Canes Rocks, a dangerous reef 10 miles from the coast. In the evening passed the Zembra and Zembretta Rocks and near these a Tunisian galley full of turbaned Moors.

Wed. 16th No land in sight in the morning, but at 2 p.m. saw the island of Gozo and were soon running along its rocky shore before a fresh breeze. Passed the straits between Gozo and Malta, where St Paul was shipwrecked.

Malta

Malta, a white rocky looking island with nothing but walls and rocks, and square dice looking houses, also white, to be seen. It looks very hot and dazzling compared with the deep blue of the sea. A lovely morning.

We ran into Quarantine Harbour,[4] but were ordered round to the Grand Harbour by the Port Admiral, Sir Thomas Briggs.[B] At night the scene is very striking, by moonlight especially. The white houses and great fortifications contrast with the deep blue of the water. The perpetual clanging of the bells of the numerous churches, the numbers of white awninged boats flitting backwards and forwards on the calm water of the harbour, make a novel and interesting scene. We anchored in Dockyard Creek. A military band could be heard in the distance, and Maltese music in some of the boats. The Maltese boats are clean and comfortable, sharp at both ends, with high prows and white awnings with curtains round.

[4] The quarantine station was situated on Manoel Island, in the harbour of Marsamxett.

Thur. 17th Very hot. Remained on board till the evening, then took a native boat and landed at the well-known Rix Mangeri Stairs, which we climbed to the centre of the city of La Valette and went to one of the cafés, Joe Maceliffi's, where we had iced lemonade and sweetmeats, then to a hotel and played billiards and slept there, or tried to sleep, for I was melted by the heat and bitten all over by mosquitoes, for my curtains were torn, although the room was large and breezy, with numerous doors opening on to a balcony, and the floor of stone. The balcony surrounded a central court with orange trees and bananas, which gave out a pleasant perfume. Next morning a good bath and a breakfast with plenty of fruit, then returned to the ship.

As cholera had abated, and nearly all the ships were away, Easton and McDougall were ordered to join the *Wolverine* going to Barcelona, where the flagship was. Campbell remains here with one Assistant Surgeon, and he

Rix Mangeri Stairs, Malta

The receiving ship *Ceylon* in Dockyard Creek

chose to ask me, therefore I was ordered to join the *Ceylon*, receiving ship lying in Dockyard Creek. In the night we were visited by a tremendous thunderstorm, which woke me up, and as the natives did not think the thunder loud enough, set all the church bells in the place clanging.

Sat. 19th I went on board the *Volcano* to see my two friends Easton and McDougall, and with them went to Valetta. Some of the streets are not paved but the rock is worn smooth. A shrine with a figure of a saint stands at most of the corners of the streets: at one Gabriel killing the Devil, at another St George killing the dragon. Often one sees a native on his knees before the image, generally an old woman. We strolled through the market. Fruit in great abundance – cartloads of pumpkins, melons, grapes, peaches, green figs, &c., all very cheap. The howling in the market was deafening. The Maltese poor live on very little, pumpkins, beans and onions, a little fish and bread with oil and garlic, quite luxurious living. Twopence a day is ample to feed a native. The population is very great for the size of the island, but so many emigrate, and all the coasts of the Mediterranean are stocked with Maltese, who appear to thrive.

Sun. 20th Campbell called on me and took me to his lodgings to dinner – therm. 90°. In the evening we took a stroll through some of the streets and past some of the fine old Auberges, or palaces of the Knights of Malta. The costume of the native ladies has a sombre appearance with the black silk hood and skirt, although one sees occasionally a pretty face under the hood or faldetta, and a pretty foot and ankle under the skirt. The fronts of the houses are sometimes profusely ornamented with carved stonework, especially the balconies.

This morning I was awoken by a thundering salute just over my head. My cabin in the *Ceylon* is pretty roomy. Lieutenant Bridge is in command, and there are only four other officers besides myself waiting for ships. Dr Livesay, Assistant Surgeon of H.M.S. *Asia*, also left here for cholera duty.

Thur. 24th I was ordered to do duty at the Naval Hospital as H.M.S. *Bellerophon* had a number of cholera cases on board, which they had sent to Hospital; also the *Hind* cutter. I went up to the Hospital and saw Dr Liddell the Surgeon, and commenced duty at once. The sight on entering the cholera ward was dismal: eight cases in the beds, two fine young sailors in *articulo mortis*, blue features and sunken eyes and gasping breath; three others tormented with cramp, groaning and tossing in their beds. Soon afterwards a fine tall sailor was brought in, prostrated, and in another hour he was dead. One case rallied after injection of salt and water in his veins, but it afterwards failed, as did most other treatments, till the disease appeared to wear out, and the cases were less virulent.[5] I had to sit up all night.

[5] See p. 172 n. 14.

Thur. 31st No more cholera cases, the *Bellerophon* and *Hind* having gone to sea. Of those cases left, most of them have consecutive fevers. The man whose veins were injected is dying of fever.

Le Grand, Assistant Surgeon of the Hospital, goes on leave to Sicily in the *Hind* and I remain to do duty in his absence. Mrs Le Grand is a very pretty little woman, daughter of the Chaplain of the Embassy at Constantinople. Le Grand was Assistant Surgeon of the *Thalia* and married her there. Whitmarsh, Apothecary and Medical Storekeeper, is a Weymouth man whose wife is a pleasant little woman and her sister, Miss Silver, a pretty girl engaged to be married to Bulkeley Jones, Assistant Surgeon of *Hind*. Mrs Whitmarsh has two sons, sixteen and eighteen, by a former husband. They all form a pleasant society at the Hospital. As the Hospital is immediately over the sea, we get plenty of bathing from the rocks below, where the water is clear and deep, every morning and sometimes three times a day. Our Chaplain, Le Mesurier, is not much of a preacher, but a pleasant old man. We often have a little music and dancing of an evening in Le Grand's or Whitmarsh's rooms, which overlook the harbour, and sit out on the balconies in the quiet warm evenings listening to the songs and music in the Maltese boats, or the military bands from the opposite side, and watch the lights in Valetta reflected in the dark, still water, with the boats leaving lines of phosphorescent light in their trail. We are sometimes joined by Mrs Kay, wife of the Surgeon of the flagship, a lively little woman. Therm. 83° at the Hospital, but it is about the coolest place on the island. It is 94° on board the ships in Dockyard Creek.

SEPTEMBER

Mon. 4th The days pass away pleasantly enough; evening songs by Mrs Le Grand, who has a pretty Grecian face, accompanied on the guitar by Miss Silver.

Wed. 6th No more cholera and Le Grand has returned to duty and I to my little hot cabin on board the *Ceylon*. At night we had a grand thunderstorm and in a sudden squall our awning was split into ribbons and carried away with part of the hammock netting and other damage.

Thur. 7th The Turkish squadron came into harbour, consisting of a frigate of fifty guns, brass, a corvette and a brig, and also an Austrian frigate anchored near the *Bellerophon*, a pretty sight. In the evening went over to the Naval Hospital to take tea and bathe with the young Gulivers, Mrs Whitmarsh's sons, and afterwards went on to Isola to witness the *festa* of Sta Vittoria. The streets were illuminated – a priestly procession with banners and images of saints, &c.; crowds of fat old padres and friars, and lots of black-eyed and black-hooded Maltese girls, generally attended by their duennas who were not always too watchful. The whole accompanied by a deafening clanging of church bells, fireworks and a great crowd, but orderly, and the band of the Maltese Fencibles finished with "God Save the Queen" and bonfires on the quay.

Fri. 8th Went over to the Bormla [?] at Valetta to see Fort St Angelo salute with twenty-one guns an Austrian Prince who landed from the frigate, which returned the salute. Afterwards returned on board the *Ceylon* to dinner and in evening Bridge, Livesay and I took the dinghy and rowed about the harbour. Bridge took his guitar and serenaded the ladies living in the dockyard and round the creek, some of whom came out on their balconies, but darkness prevented our being recognised. We then pulled round the Turkish ships – another frigate came in today. A storm of thunder and lightning sent us back to the *Ceylon* and to bed.

Sun. 10th I was awoke by a great bustle overhead. Signalling. The *Princess Charlotte* and the *Rodney*, line-of-battle ships, and the *Rapid*, 10-gun brig, coming into harbour. Livesay and I went over to Valetta to see. The Admiral, Sir Robert Stopford,[B] was saluted by the Turkish Admiral and the Austrian frigate and H.M.S. *Bellerophon*, which salutes were returned by the *Princess Charlotte*, so there was a great deal of smoke and noise. It was a fine sight to watch the great ships coming in through the narrow entrance of the harbour in full sail and firing a salute, three shortening sail all at once and swinging round to their anchors. We afterwards took a walk to Pietà. The weather is cooler after the thunderstorms. We saw a great number of the green lizards, but there was no catching them.

Mon. 11th Went on board the *Princess Charlotte* to see Easton and McDougall. Found them in the gunroom and stayed to dinner at 12 o'clock – a large mess, thirty-six officers, many young lordlings amongst them. Met

Lord Edward Clinton. After dinner we went up to the sick-bay and I was introduced to Kay, the Surgeon. Afterwards Easton returned with me to the *Ceylon*, where we had another dinner at 4 o'clock. Then we went to the Hospital and bathed, and then back to the *Princess Charlotte* where the officers had got up some theatricals. The quarterdeck was fitted up as a stage, and *She Stoops to Conquer* was performed capitally by the gunroom officers, the female parts taken by midshipmen. Afterwards some songs were sung and the ship's band played some good music.

OCTOBER

Tue. 3rd Had the satisfaction of receiving my first paybill, £37 14. 0., on the 30th ult. Went over to Valetta to cash it at one of the merchants. Weather getting much cooler. Took a boat and went outside the harbour to have a swim in the sea. There was a great swell on, bad weather coming on.

Sun. 8th Thunder, lightning and rain came down in torrents. A sad occurrence happened. Newman, a supernumerary lieutenant, lately promoted, had appeared out of health for a few days, and melancholy. This morning he appeared depressed and after breakfast went to his cabin, which was next to mine. I heard him groaning and Livesay and I went to him. He said he had a headache and seemed impatient at being questioned. His pulse was hardly perceptible, eyes suffused and bloodshot, extremities cold. We got him to take a little brandy and Livesay remained with him and I went to walk on deck, but soon his boy came running to me and said Lieutenant Newman was in a fit. I went down and found the poor fellow dying. We suspected poison. After his death I looked in his desk and found a letter addressed to Bridge and another to Newman's brother, who is Assistant Surgeon of H.M.S. *Hermes*. He writes: "My dear Bridge and Messmates, I can resist the temptation of happiness in another world no longer, therefore hasten to quit this." He thanked us for our kindness to him. He stated he had swallowed arsenic and ended by saying, "My time is short. I feel it is working." Newman was the son of a warrant officer, a carpenter in the Navy. Had been sixteen years a mate, great part of this time in a Revenue cutter. He bequeathed his watch to some lady.

Mon. 9th An inquest was held on the body of poor Newman, which had been removed to the Naval Hospital. We were summoned to give evidence at 2 p.m. The Coroner and jury are Maltese and took a long time, although only Bridge, Livesay and Newman's servant were examined. There was a post-mortem by two Maltese doctors, at which I was present; nearly half an ounce of arsenic, in substance, was found in his stomach. The verdict was "temporary insanity". We afterwards carried him to his last resting-place in the cemetery of the Hospital. Bridge was chief mourner, all officers and a party of seamen from the *Rapid* attended. Smith and I were pallbearers – a union jack for a pall, his cocked hat and sword on the top.

"Poor Newman's funeral"

Sat. 14th H.M. Steamer *Firefly* arrived from Gibraltar without a medical officer, Taylor, Assistant Surgeon, having poisoned himself in his cabin. This makes the third naval officer who has committed suicide on this station within the last week. The other was a mate who shot himself.

I received my appointment to the *Firefly* from the Admiral this afternoon.

H.M. STEAM VESSEL FIREFLY

Mon. 16th Joined the *Firefly*. Campbell and Livesay came on board to hold a survey on the medical stores on board. The *Firefly* is a paddle-steamer of 600 or 700 tons[6] employed at present in carrying the mails in the Mediterranean, commanded by Lieutenant Joseph Pearse. W.H. Smith, an old mate, second in command;[7] Mugford 2nd Master; Richard Reep, Clerk; S——, an old Scotchman, Chief Engineer.

[6] See note on tonnage in Appendix 1 (p. 268).

[7] W.H. Smith, "a good-natured old mate, disgusted with the service, as he is of twelve years' standing and unable to get promotion".

In early December Cree receives an order from the Admiralty directing him to *Childers*, 16-gun sloop under the command of Commander the Hon. Henry Keppel and bound for service on the west coast of Africa. However, since he has already joined *Firefly* to fill a death vacancy, he is allowed to remain on. Later that month, Cree, with two companions, takes a trip from Alexandria to Cairo – by way of the Alexandria Canal and the Nile. In January 1838 he visits Beirut and Sidon.

1838

Firefly at sea

Alexandria

JANUARY

Sun. 28th ... We had received an invitation to a ball at the Swedish Consul's in honour of the Swedish squadron here. We landed at 8.30 p.m. and found a crowd with torches outside the house and a guard of Swedish Marines from their ships. The squadron consists of a Swedish frigate and a corvette and a Norwegian corvette.

We ascended a handsome flight of steps to some fine large rooms brilliantly lighted and decorated, presenting a splendid appearance and crowded with company. Ladies of all sorts, sizes and complexion in all sorts of costumes, and the gentlemen in uniforms of various countries. The Swedish naval officers were all in full dress, so were we, and their uniform is much like ours. Most of them speak English and some of them have been in our service, and Smith found an old messmate amongst them. The rooms were elegantly furnished from Trieste and the ballroom had fine statues in the corners. About 700 people were present – Swedes, Norwegians, French, Russians, Dutch, Spanish, Italians, Greeks and Turks, in their various costumes. Not many English, as it was Sunday. There were lots of pretty girls, especially the daughter of the Spanish Consul, with whom I had the pleasure of waltzing, although we could not understand each other's speech. There was also a lovely Greek girl in the costume of her country. Many Turkish and Egyptian officers in gaudy uniforms of scarlet and gold. The Admiral of the Fleet [Stopford] was there, but he sat looking on stroking his long white beard.

There were plenty of partners, though none of them that I met could speak

English. I was introduced to a pretty Italian girl, whose name I forget, but we were so well pleased with each other that we danced together for the remainder of the evening. Sweetmeats were plentiful: 300 pounds, I hear, were ordered from one confectioner alone in Alexandria; and there was plenty of negus and lemonade, and claret and water. The supper was at a buffet in another room and there was plenty of cold chicken and cold meat, with jellies, creams and ices, which was done justice to, especially by the ladies who crowded up to the buffet and, after eating as much as they could, pocketed many of the good things. One stout middle-aged Frenchwoman was engaged in filling her pockets which were stuffed out with cold chicken and sweetcakes as she stood before me. I was eating a custard – the opportunity was tempting – so I emptied my glass into her open pocket, and a nice mixture she must have found when she got home.

We did not break up till 8 in the morning, but notwithstanding the broad daylight, I found my Italian partner stood the trying ordeal. We found our jolly-boat waiting at the jetty and we were glad to get on board to breakfast. My ankles were stiff enough with dancing so much on the stone floor.

Tue. 30th Abbott [English surgeon on the Egyptian flagship] came on board to breakfast, and afterwards Reep, [Midshipman T.E.L.] Moore and I went with him to his ship and then on shore to lunch on cold German sausage, oysters and preserved apricot pie. Met with a little Greek doctor with a wooden leg and met a French doctor who was carrying home a leg of mutton from the market. Dined on board on turtle soup and turtle pie.

Sailed at 4 p.m. with a fair wind and five passengers. The French Consul kissed his male friends at parting, on each cheek.

At Sea

FEBRUARY *Sat. 24th* Fine morning with breeze from south. Passed Zembra early and afterwards inside the Canes Rocks signalled the *Rhadamanthus* with mails for Gibraltar. In afternoon we were between Galite and the African coast going 7 knots. The wind hot and sultry and a lurid glare spread under a bank of inky clouds in the west. The barometer was falling rapidly. The clouds gradually formed an arch across the sky and suddenly the squall came on most furiously, taking us aback. Fortunately we had not many sails set and these were soon furled. The wind increased in violence and we made no headway by all our steaming. A heavy swell was getting up from the west. At night the storm raged most furiously and the wind screeched amongst the rigging, the vivid lightning flashed and thunder rolled and heavy driving rain. The sea ran very high and the poor little *Firefly* rolled as if she would have gone over. The night was very dark and we were not far from the black rocks of Galite. It was a night of trouble and anxiety.

Bizerta

Sun. 25th The gale still continuing and as we were making little or no progress we ran for shelter into Bizerta Bay and anchored off the little town about 1 p.m. in the territory of Tunis. It is surrounded by old Turkish fortifications. The country round is pretty and parklike, and rows of olives and dates adorn the gently sloping hills. A ridge of rocks, over which the sea was breaking, extended between us and the town. We spent a much pleasanter night than the last.

Mon. 26th The gale still continuing from NW. We remained at anchor. It thundered and lightened in evening.

Tue. 27th No change. In evening were visited by another thunderstorm.

Wed. 28th Every evening we have a thunderstorm before it comes on we are regaled by a delightful smell of flowers from the shore, coming from a kind of yellow broom.

Bône

MARCH

Fri. 2nd The storm not abating, the Commander determined to put into Bône if possible. Terrific squalls with lightning and deluges of rain succeeded each other in rapid succession. The foresail was split to ribbons. During the night it was discovered, during a break in the storm, that we were abreast of the Gulf of Bône, so we ran towards the shelter under trisails and anchored off the town about 4 p.m. It is a Moorish looking place but now French, built on a high rock and defended by an old Moorish castle, mountains at the back. This is the "Land of Dates". Bône was once a great resort of Barbary pirates.

Sat. 3rd About sunset, the wind having gone down, we proceeded on our voyage. A party of French officers came off in a boat to look at us.

At Sea

Mon. 5th Passed another unpleasant night. Blowing hard and ship rolling. Foresail split. Shipped a sea which rushed down the gunroom skylight in a very unpleasant manner. Stormy petrels following us all day; saw a couple of terns. In the evening the weather moderated a little.

Tue. 6th Wind still against us and to add to our chapter of accidents one of our wheels has gone wrong, and the rudder-head is shaky. A westerly swell. We are surrounded by turtles, some good sized ones. Moore went away in the jolly-boat and tried to turn one but did not succeed; then he tried to harpoon one and lost the harpoon, turtle and all. Then he tried to lay hold of one by the fin, but it was too wide awake and just vanished underwater. There were a dozen of them swimming round the ship.

Thur. 8th Fine and warm, nearly calm, wind changed to east. Going merrily along. Fourteen days since we left Malta. Passed Cape Ferrat.

Fri. 9th Fine and calm. About noon we passed close to the rocks of Cape Tres Forcas, a rocky headland of the most savage part of the north coast of Africa, inhabited by an intractable race of savages – pirates and robbers when they have a chance. We had a proof of this in passing a crowd of these fellows collected on top of a high rock. They were nearly naked but mostly armed with long muskets. Two of them presented their firearms and fired, and others were loading although we were out of range. It shows what sort of reception we should have had if we had attempted to land.

Gibraltar

Sat. 10th The Rock of Gibraltar in sight at daylight, when we arrived at 10 with only an hour's coal left. They kept us without pratique for some time. The packet for England was on the point of sailing when they allowed us to haul down the yellow flag. Our old messmate Reep, the Purser, was going home by her and bid us farewell. Many disasters at sea are reported from the late storm – fifty vessels on shore in Gibraltar Bay and many remain on the neutral ground, some complete wrecks. The *Bellerophon* grounded and will have to go to England for repairs. The *Orestes* was at sea and lost her rudder, and they did not discover it for sixteen hours afterwards. The *Volcano*, which left Malta some days before us, is at Cartagena repairing, having run down and sunk a merchant vessel at sea.

Malta

Wed. 21st . . . A welcome order has come out from the Admiralty which allows assistant surgeons in charge 1/-6 additional pay, so increasing my pay to 8/- instead of 6/-6.

1839

Malta – Trip to Gozo

Sat., March 30th We received orders early in the morning to receive the Queen [Dowager] and suite, to take her to Gozo.[1] So we hauled out of Dockyard Creek to the Valetta side. The Admiral Superintendent came on board and soon after Admiral Sir Robert Stopford and Lady. About noon we saw the royal barge coming from H.M.S. *Hastings* and Her Majesty came on board. We all mustered in full dress to receive her. As soon as her suite of about twenty were on board we started out of harbour with the royal standard at the main. The weather was fine but wind NW and we did not go very fast. I was introduced to Sir David Davies, the Queen's Physician, who asked me to give a dose of quinine to the Countess of Sheffield, one of the Queen's ladies – a beautiful woman.

[1] Queen Adelaide (1792–1849), the Queen Dowager, eldest daughter of George, Duke of Saxe-Meiningen, was the widow of William IV. Her visit to Malta was probably the first one made by a (former) crowned head to the island since that of Alfonso of Aragon in 1432. She had erected in Valletta, at her own expense, the Collegiate Church of S. Paul, the Cathedral of the Anglican Bishop of Gibraltar for the Maltese part of his diocese.

We got to Gozo about 2 p.m. and landed at Fort Chambray under a royal salute. All the conveyances on the island were only three calashes – one of which the Queen occupied. There were two or three horses and all the rest of the suite were mounted on donkeys, and off they set, a motley crowd. Smith, Moore and I soon followed on donkeys. We went to Rabbato and stopped at the Inn to see the old Maltese sergeant and his daughter Mary. After a little refreshment we had to return as fast as we could to get to the ship before the Queen and her party. At a turn of the road we fell in with the whole party, and old Smith's donkey, which was a long-legged, bony beast, took it into his head to stop in the middle of the road in front of the royal cortège and bray and commit other unpolite nuisances, which example was followed by the other donkeys. Old Smith whacked and whacked his beast, but it only made him bray the louder and make other unpleasant noises, which caused much

Queen Adelaide and the royal cortège in Gozo

confusion and laughter amongst the whole party. Maids of Honour and Ladies- and Lords-in-Waiting and officers of the Household the donkey did not care a curse for, but would just take his own time and complain loudly if they wanted to hurry him.

The Queen was expected to come to Rabbato and when we arrived at the entrance of the town we found the guard turned out and all the inhabitants dressed in their best, who cheered old Smith when he entered on his noble steed, to which he graciously took off his cap and bowed. All the party came helter-skelter down to the landing-place and were all on board by 6 p.m.

Cree leaves *Firefly* on May 30th. In June he visits his sister Percy at Ilminster, and then goes on to see friends at Bridport, Dorset. On July 10th he is appointed to the gunnery ship *Excellent*, based at Portsmouth. In early August, however, Assistant Surgeon Sinclair of the troop-ship *Rattlesnake* offers to exchange with Cree – "to which," Cree notes, "I am inclined, as I am tired of Portsmouth".

H.M. TROOP-SHIP RATTLESNAKE

Portsmouth

SEPTEMBER

Sun. 15th Went on board the *Rattlesnake* with Sinclair. The *Rattlesnake* is about 600 tons, stows 85 tons of water – with troops on board consumes $1\frac{1}{4}$ tons per diem; allowance for each man 3 quarts, and 1 pint for washing. She is an old 28-gun frigate fitted with a poop and intended for a troop-ship, Assistant Surgeon's cabin under the poop, and has the advantage of plenty of light from a window in the side. Commanded by Brodie, an old Master, a jolly old sailor on whom Sinclair and I called and had some punch with the old boy and were introduced to his wife. They are Scotch.

Fri. 20th Received my appointment to the *Rattlesnake* and joined her on 21st.

OCTOBER

Fri. 4th–Sat. 5th Busy paying mess bills and preparing to start, as we are ordered to Woolwich where we embark troops for Ceylon and expect to be away about a year.

Sun. 6th Went on board *Excellent* to bid my old messmates farewell. Got a warm reception from them.

Mon. 7th Disturbed early in the morning by the bustle of getting under weigh, and after breakfast all the new white sails were spread to the breezes and we glided steadily out of Portsmouth harbour with a party of ladies on board and anchored at Spithead to await a fair wind, as we have no steam like the old *Firefly*. I enjoy my snug little cabin where I can sit and look out of my window.

Tue. 8th Cloudy and cold. Get under weigh at 6 a.m. with a NE breeze. Passed the lights of Brighton in the evening and Beachy Head at 10 p.m.

Wed. 9th A beautiful day and fine westerly breeze. Passed Hythe, Folkestone and Dover and ran through the Downs, when it came on calm and anchored for the night off Margate.

Thur. 10th Blowing hard from east. Stood on with the tide. I was sitting reading in my cabin when there was a cry of "A man overboard". A great bustle in lowering a boat, which soon picked him up with no other damage than a ducking. He had got hold of the lifebuoy. One hardly knows one's messmates yet. The senior officer under Brodie the Master commanding is Cavell, a tall gentlemanly fellow; 2nd Harper, a jolly, good-natured fellow, pock-marked and I fancy given to rum and water; 3rd a strange red-whiskered fellow, – Waddingham, 2nd Master, who has been in the British Legion in the Queen of Spain's service as a lieutenant, and was tried by court martial for putting his captain under arrest. It was supposed that both of them were drunk. He seems to have an inordinate appetite – I found him devouring raw cabbage made up into a salad with chilies, vinegar and red herring. Arlington, a clerk, married and got his wife on board – a pretty looking girl of the dressmaker class.

Woolwich

Fri. 11th Made sail with the tide and had a pleasant run up the river with the tide and arrived at Woolwich at noon.

Sat. 19th Bid farewell to Woolwich. The *Lightning* steamer took us in tow, at 9 a.m., as far as Gravesend, where we anchored to take in troops for Ceylon. We have a detachment of the 90th [Perthshire Volunteers] Regiment and 100 Royal Artillery beside women and children, about 350 all told – 160 of the 90th Regiment.

Tue. 22nd Foggy. The *Lightning* steamer towed us from the river to the Downs, where we anchored for the night.

Wed. 23rd Remained in the Downs waiting a fair wind.

At Sea

Thur. 24th Got under weigh at daylight. Wind SE. After three or four tacks cleared the South Foreland and bore along with wind abeam, 8 knots. It turned out thick and wet weather. Sunset, Beachy Head in sight 12 miles off.

Fri. 25th When I awoke I knew by the steady roll of the ship that we were running before a steady fresh breeze and on looking out of my cabin window saw nothing but sky and sea.

Sat. 26th Steady easterly breeze. Rolling along at 6 knots before it, weather already getting milder. As I looked out on the northern horizon, thought of the many dear friends in old England I was leaving behind.

Sun. 27th Heavy swell but fair wind – lat. 47° 30′, long. 10° 5′ W.

Thur. 31st A gale and heavy sea and ship rolling much. Wind westerly and weather warmer. Thunder and lightning with heavy squalls last night. Lat. 46°, long. 15° W.

NOVEMBER

Sun. 3rd Nasty rough weather all the week, with heavy sea and no comfort for the rolling of the old ship. Today it has moderated but still a heavy swell over the broad Atlantic remains of the late gale. A shoal of dolphins following the ship, displaying their beautiful tints of blue and green in the bright sunshine. Mother Carey's chicken, the stormy petrel, are plentiful under the stern of the ship since we left the Channel, but they are all away today. A poor little chaffinch was caught on board about 400 miles from land. The weather is now delightful, therm. 69°; lat. 35° 38′, long. 14° 48′ W.

Tue. 5th Delightful calm weather. We have seventeen military officers on board – Royal Artillery and 90th Regiment – one of the former, Lieutenant Hamilton, has his wife and two children on board.* I dined with them. About sunset sighted Madeira, but it was blowing hard off the land, supposed to be 80 miles away. Guy Fawkes was not forgotten by the sailors, who in the evening dressed up a Guy and carried it round the ship and got an extra glass of grog from the officers.

* Military officers on board the *Rattlesnake* – Artillery: Major Gordon; Capts Stokes, Kaye; Lieut. 1st Hamilton, Wynne, 2nd Lawrence, Wilson, Dixon; Asst Surgeon Davis. 90th Regiment: Capt. Bowyer, Lieut. Woodgate; Ensigns Owen, Evatt.

Fri. 15th Running down the Trades – pleasant sailing, cloudy weather.

Tue. 19th Crossed the Tropic in long. 21° 35′ W. and entered the Torrid Zone – therm. 75° in my cabin, which is about the coolest part of the ship. Last night we had a heavy squall which took us aback, and deluges of rain.

Today there has been a disagreeable break in the quiet monotony on board. A military punishment of 100 lashes – an Artilleryman, for theft. I don't think it was more severe than a dozen from the naval cat. We also had a funeral of one of the soldier's children. We have rather much sickness from damp and overcrowding, rheumatism and erysipelas.

Sat. 23rd After a couple of days' calm we had a spanking easterly breeze which carried us past Cape Verde Islands and are now steering for the coast of Brazil. Therm. 78°.

Sat. 30th Father Neptune paid us a visit this evening, coming into the ship over the bows with his followers midst showers of water from the tops and flashes of gunpowder for lightning. He was attended by his wife, Amphitrite, in an old straw bonnet with red ribbons and a shawl, mermaids in caps, his barber and doctor. Neptune enquired of the Captain for his children and got a glass of grog and promised to be on board again on Monday morning at 10. He then wished us good night and departed over the bow and soon after a light was seen floating astern in a basket, which was supposed to be Neptune departing. . . .

DECEMBER

Sun. 1st We crossed the equator in long. 28°. We only got into the trade wind in 4° North four days ago – before that we had thick cloudy weather with a strong easterly breeze, very salty and oppressive. Today at noon 2° South lat.

Mon. 2nd Early in the morning preparations were making for the promised visit of Father Neptune, who made his appearance at 9.30, attended by his rabble with drums, fifes and horns, drawn in his car, made of a gun-carriage. His attendants were, beside Amphitrite, Tritons, Bears, Doctor and Butcher, Secretary, Barber's Clerk, Constables, &c., forming an outlandish crew. All the unshaven children were sent below, but I had tipped old Nep with half a gallon of rum, so I was allowed on the poop and saw the Major and other officers go through the operation, but they were treated gently as Nep and his crew expected a present of rum. I also took my turn with the rest. The lathering and shaving were dispensed with and I only got the ducking in the sail full of water, which formed a fine large bath all one side of the deck. There was great fun in ducking the fresh ones as they came tumbling in backwards. Some of the men got a lathering with pea soup and tar and scraped with a bit of iron hoop and a dab of tarbrush in the mouth if they opened it and afterwards half drowned by the bears. All the time the fire-engines played upon all of them and buckets of water were emptied down from the tops. By noon all was over, the decks cleared and sails stowed away and all got into dry

Crossing the line ceremony

clothes. The ship was put under easy sail and the sailors were allowed to get drunk on the rum which had been given by the officers – a regular saturnalia – but all was right again next day.

Tue. 10th ... Weather cool with easterly breeze, indeed the weather has been pleasant through the Torrid Zone, therm. seldom above 80°. Today it is only 75°, cloudy and squalls. Passed the small islands Trinidad and Martin Vass yesterday but not near enough to sight them.

Sun. 22nd Quite a calm, sea like glass. A couple of whales passed about a quarter of a mile off; they kept straight on, spouting at intervals. Some fishes, bonito and albacore, near the ship, and a few albatross and Cape hens. We are still 1,700 miles from the Cape.

Mon. 23rd A dead calm still continues, so we make little or no progress.

Wed. 25th Christmas Day. Blowing almost a gale from the westward so we bowled along at a good pace accompanied by a long ocean swell – a grand sight. All the officers of the ship dined with the Commander. Old Brodie gave us a good dinner, considering we have been so long at sea: turkey, duck, tinned roast beef, soup, plum pudding, and plenty of good port and sherry. The old Boatswain and Mrs Bull, who got leave to accompany her husband in the ship, were of the party. Mrs B. "did the Lady", Bull and the old Commander fought their battles over again – having both served in the French war, regular old sailor's yarns. Old Brodie was at the taking of the Cape of Good Hope in 1806 and Bull in the fleet blockading Toulon.

1840

Wed. 1st Weather cold and comfortless although midsummer here in South lat. 35° 14′, East long. 13° 24′. All on board quite tired of our long voyage, fresh provisions all gone, reduced to salt junk and biscuits and short allowance of water.

JANUARY

Fri. 3rd Strong SE breeze – Table Mountain, Cape of Good Hope, in sight, but no chance of getting in today. Stood off the land in the night.

Cape pigeon

Cape of Good Hope

Sat. 4th When I went on deck in the morning we were doubling Cape of Good Hope, which is a very insignificant port compared with the high mountains at the back. We beat into Simons Bay, the shores of which are bold and mountainous and barren looking. Put one in mind of the coast of Algeria. Took in a pilot and anchored off Simons Town at 4 p.m. The flagship *Melville*, Admiral Elliot,[B] here – also the *Brisk*. We met the *Curlew* going out.

Simons Town is a small place with about a hundred houses, whitewashed and surrounded by gardens situated at the bottom of a steep hill in a snug corner of the bay. At present everything is dear here. It used to be so cheap. In the evening I went on shore with some of our military officers. Liberated slaves and drunken sailors abound. Went to Miller's the Grocer's to order a fresh dinner for tomorrow. Strolled about the only street, if it can be so called, which has houses only on the side which faces the beach. We came off in the cutter manned by Artillerymen. The Major who was with us offered to take off a drunken sailor to his ship but he swore he would not go in the same boat with the blue Marines.[1]

Sun. 5th Went on shore after dinner and took a walk up the hill behind the town with Harper and Arlington. The wild flowers very beautiful amongst the rocks and birds of gay plumage – one that sings like a blackbird at home. The sand, which is blown about in the strong wind, is very annoying. The evening was cold. Went to Clarence's Hotel. Met some of our soldier officers there and all came off together in the cutter at 8.

[1] The Royal Marines consisted then of two branches – Artillery (Blue) and Infantry (Red). The R.M.A. were "Blue Marines", by which name they were generally called in the Navy.

Mon. 6th In afternoon went on shore with Waddingham. Met gangs of liberated slaves who look strong and healthy. They have some trouble with them when they are first landed from the coast of Africa, as their Portuguese captors have told them that the English will eat them. Unfortunately, when a lot were landed from the *Scorpion*, they were located over a butcher's shop. The slaves imagined they were only put there to be fattened before being devoured, so they refused all food.

Sun. 12th My twenty-sixth birthday. Caught a severe cold but went on shore for a walk in the afternoon. Met Tracey, Assistant Surgeon of *Melville*. I dined with him a few days ago on board the flagship. Met Webb, Assistant Surgeon, a Plymouth man. Grieved to hear of the deaths of two assistant surgeons who were with me at Plymouth Hospital – Browne, an Irishman, and McDougall, who also went out to Malta with me. Both died of the Coast fever as many other assistant surgeons sent there have done. There is a scarcity of medical officers on this station in consequence.

At Sea

Tue. 21st Sailed today delighted to leave the dull Simons Town. We were all day beating out of the bay against a light wind, for the old *Rattlesnake* is no clipper.

Wed. 22nd Running before a fine westerly breeze.

Tue. 28th Made a capital run since we left the Cape.

Wed. 29th Our wind increased to a gale.

Thur. 30th Light winds from south and cold. A long swell left by the gale of yesterday.

Sat., Feb. 22nd Crossed the Tropic of Capricorn in E. long. 84°. Our farthest south since leaving the Cape has been 39° 11′. Got into the SE trade wind two days ago.

MARCH *Sun. 1st* We have been getting on well till two days ago when we had a dead calm we lost our poor Corporal of Marines, Copperwhite, who died from acute rheumatism, which suddenly left his limbs and attacked his brain – delirium and coma ended in death. He was one of the best men in the ship, sober and obliging and hard-working. His body was committed to the deep this day.

H.M.S. ***Rattlesnake*** **at anchor, Colombo**

Mon. 2nd Today at noon the sun was vertical. The weather pleasantly hot, therm. 86°. A couple of sharks about 9 feet long were caught, to the great delight of the ship's company, who cut them up and cooked parts. I tasted a bit and thought it remarkably nice. The sailors liked it, but few of the soldiers and none of the women would touch it, as they thought of the poor Corporal of Marines.

Wed. 4th My Marine servant, Harris, died suddenly today from the bursting of an abscess in his spleen into the abdomen. I made a post-mortem next day. He was very emaciated, poor fellow. Crossed the equator in 85° East.

Wed. 11th We are now looking out for Ceylon, as we have been within 100 miles of it these last two days, but baffled with calm and slight, variable winds. We have been out seven weeks today.

Ceylon

Fri. 13th In the evening land was reported on the starboard bow, and soon all glasses were directed to the shores of the island of Ceylon. The sight of it gladdened all hearts on board.

Sat. 14th When I went on deck just before sunrise we were approaching the long low coast of Ceylon, about Colombo, lined with coconut trees and backed by a broken outline of lofty mountains in the interior, crowned by the remarkable Adam's Peak, distinct against the clear sky glowing with the rays of the rising sun; the sparkling sea dotted with light fishing canoes, with their large square calico sails and outriggers; the Governor's country house; the pretty bungalows scattered along the shore amongst the coco palms. We came to anchor about 2 miles off the town, at 9 a.m. We were soon visited by the health boat and the Harbour Master, Lieutenant Stewart. From him we heard of threatened hostilities with China, and the probability of our being sent on there after visiting Trincomalee to take on other troops. I anticipate great enjoyment from a visit to China. The Harbour Master is not a good specimen of the salubrity of Colombo, he being apparently destitute of bowels and liver, and a dirty parchment coloured face, which contrasted strongly with his beautifully white jacket and shirt. We were soon visited by Templeton, Assistant Surgeon of Artillery, and some other officers of the Garrison. They gave us all the news, as we had heard no English news since we left in November last.

Colombo from the anchorage has not a very promising appearance. The houses are low with red tiled roofs. The native town, or Pettah, which is

In the Pettah, Trincomalee

separated from the Fort by fortifications, is a collection of mud cottages extending along the shore, shaded by coco palms; the lighthouse on the point built like a round temple. As soon as we were at anchor a number of native traders came on board to "bargain" stones, jewellery, shells, woodwork, &c. – great rogues and vagabonds, who are accomplished cheats, and many of the youngsters were taken in with glass and brass. In the afternoon I and one or two others went on shore to have a look at the place. We landed at the Fort, which is a town of itself and has four or five good streets lined with trees. The houses are low with spreading roofs which form a veranda all round, quite open, with reed blinds to keep out the sun. When the weather is very hot the blinds are sprinkled with water. We walked to the Pettah, about quarter of a mile outside the Fort gate. In the market poultry, mutton, fish, fruit and rice in abundance. The Cingalese puzzle one at first, as the men are dressed so much like women with their petticoats and their long hair combed back off their foreheads and the comb stuck on the top of their heads. They have no beards and are altogether effeminate looking. The hair is tied in a knot at the top of the head and adorned with a large, flat tortoise-shell comb. I am told that some awkward mistakes have been made by strangers, especially by drunken sailors.

Mon. 16th Therm. remains about 87°. Went on shore for a stroll. Found an appoo or agent waiting on the jetty, so I engaged him to accompany me, but I soon found that the pride of these poor fellows won't allow them to carry the merest trifle, so I had to engage a coolie or porter to carry a few little purchases I made. Called on Stewart, an English merchant we met on Saturday. He recommended a native cabinet-maker, as I wanted some cabin furniture made after my own plan. I ordered a chest of drawers to be made of jackwood. We walked out by a good road bordered by coco palms and other trees. The appoo took me to a bath-house in a grove of coco palms, where I had a delicious cold bath and was rubbed down by coolies till the cuticle was nigh rubbed off. After drinking the contents of a green coconut I dressed and felt equal to a walk of a dozen miles. Returned to the "Rest House" and got something to eat and met a couple of messmates and returned to the ship with them.

Wed. 18th Our troops disembarked at daylight this morning. Every boatload as they left the ship gave three cheers – some of them to be stationed at Colombo and others leave tonight for Kandy. It was a pretty sight just before sunrise. The light clouds were tinged with rose colour behind Adam's Peak, which stood out in sharp outline, but after sunrise the mountains fade away. Last night was a great jollification with the soldiers and many a heavy head this morning.

Thur. 19th Harper and I dined at the Artillery mess, where we met our old shipmates and were introduced to Colonel Power, R.A. Slept on one of the sofas in the messroom and in the morning got a bath in Dixon's quarters, and returned to the ship after breakfast.

Tue. 24th The *Rattlesnake* officers dined at the Artillery mess and spent a very jolly evening. After we got back to the ship Waddingham, who had imbibed too much of strong liquors, fell so sound asleep on deck that he did not wake when we cropped one of his luxurious red whiskers. The next morning he did not know himself.

Wed. 25th In afternoon went for a drive with old Brodie and his son to the Cinnamon Gardens in a native carriage or buggy. We made the circuit of a pretty lake at the back of the Fort, scenery soft and tropical. Saw some of the natives washing clothes at the lake by dipping them in water and then dashing them against a big stone, by which European clothes suffer, making washing dear here at 6 rupees a hundred.

Sun. 29th Dined with Davis at Artillery mess. Met Templeton there. Slept at the Rest House and next morning after a bath and coffee met James Brodie and Waddingham and we all drove out into the country in the beef contractor's buggy. We first went to his house in the Pettah, where he gave us native ginger wine. We then drove out to a bungalow on the banks of the river, where the contractor gave us breakfast of a capital curry and about a dozen other dishes. We crossed the river by a bridge of boats. It is here about 200 yards wide and said to abound in alligators.[2] The bridge was built some years ago by the Government on account of the frequent accidents to troops crossing by the ferry-boats. The river banks are well wooded and there are many pretty bungalows. On our way back we were taken to see a coconut-oil mill worked by steam – the engineer an Englishman. We also saw the native mode of making the oil by means of a beam worked in a socket like a pestle and mortar by a bullock. We got back to the Fort just in time to save us from a drenching, as it came on to thunder and lighten and rain with a vengeance. Went to the Garrison library and saw the English papers up to Feb. 4th. Met with Brodie and went off to the ship with him.

[2] Alligators: Cree means crocodiles, as he does in two subsequent references in his Journals.

Tue. 31st Embarked part of the 90th Regiment for Trincomalee, but the wind being unfavourable we did not sail till next morning.

APRIL *Wed. 1st* At daylight the land breeze taking us well out to sea. Some of the officers who came out from England with us are still on board, destined for Trincomalee – Kaye, Woodgate and Davis. We have also Colonel Macpherson, Ceylon Rifles, Captains Marin and Pugh of 90th and Heyland of 95th [Derbyshire] Regiment, and Kelly, Assistant Surgeon, staff, who has his wife and two children on board. Mrs K. is a stout, jolly little woman, somewhat affected; her husband a smart little man, but dying of consumption. He is great on epidemics and fumigation. We had a great deal of sickness amongst the troops – choleric diarrhoea. Old Macpherson is great fun, a

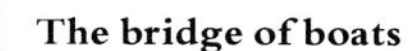
The bridge of boats

regular fire-eater in his cups, of which he takes a great deal, but he has seen much service in the Peninsula.

Sat. 11th Trincomalee in sight. It fell calm about 8 o'clock and the sea breeze did not set in till noon. Meanwhile we were sweltering under a vertical sun. We took advantage of the first puff and anchored in Back Bay about 5 p.m. The country round is very pretty, hilly and covered with trees and jungle and the coast rocky. Captain Higgs, the Harbour Master, came off and piloted us into the harbour. We were scarcely at anchor before five or six of the military officers of the Garrison came on board and we got an invitation from the officers of the 18th Royal Irish to dinner for tomorrow.

Sun. 12th At daylight our troops began to disembark in large pontoons, and by breakfast-time we had a clear ship, the first time for the last six months. At 7 p.m. Harper and I went on shore with old Brodie to dine at the mess of the 18th Royal Irish, where we met nearly all our late shipmates. Introduced to Colonel Burrell.

Mon. 13th Harbour Master Higgs came on board as soon as the sea breeze sprang up and took us round into the harbour, very picturesque amongst rocks and islands covered with tropical vegetation. The harbour then opens out into a fine lake-like expansion of water surrounded by jungle covered hills. We moored near the dockyard.

Sun. 26th The south-west monsoon commenced with squalls and rain, the first rain for five months. There is a cooler feel in the air although the therm. is still 96° in the shade.

Mon. 27th Cholera has broken out amongst the 18th Regiment, Headquarters of which we are to take on to China. So we are being hurried away and made an attempt to get out of harbour, but having carried away our jib boom had to anchor again for the night. A couple of transports have arrived from Madras to take the rest of the regiment to Singapore.

Tue. 28th Went out of harbour and anchored in Back Bay.

Wed. 29th Embarked the Headquarters of the 18th Royal Irish Regiment. Young Call, an ensign, remained on board in charge of the men. He is a nephew of Sir William Call, an old friend of my uncle, Captain Giles.[3] Young Call's father is Paymaster of the 18th Regiment.

MAY

Sat. 2nd Colonel Burrell and the remainder of the officers of 18th came on board, namely Dr McKinlay, Surgeon, Majors Adams and Dillon, Captain Collinson, Lieutenant Wilson, brother of 1st Lieutenant of *Excellent*, Sir William Macgregor, G.F. Call, Hon. C.H. Stratford, Captain Call, Paymaster. One of the men was taken with cholera last night and had to be landed and died today. The old ship is once more filled with troops, this time without the women and children but with a supply of ducks, fowls and sheep for a six weeks' voyage to Singapore.

[3] Stephen Giles had married Cree's aunt, Elizabeth Cree, in 1810. He became a 2nd lieutenant in the Marines in 1804, and saw service in the Napoleonic War and American War of 1812. In 1828 he served with the R.M. in Portugal, assisting in the restoration of Don Pedro, and consequently was created a Knight of the Tower and Sword, an ancient Portuguese order. In 1851 he was appointed Colonel Second-Commandant of the R.M. Headquarters at Plymouth, dying in the year of his retirement in 1854.

At Sea

Sun. 3rd Got under weigh at daylight with the last of the land breeze which soon carried us out of sight of land with its coco palms and jungle.

Mon. 4th Very light breeze so did not make much progress.

Tue. 5th Got the benefit of a strong SW monsoon.

Fri. 8th All sail set. Running for the Straits of Malacca. In the afternoon the band of the 18th gave us a little music on the quarterdeck, much to the dismay of old Brodie who has no soul for music.

Thur. 14th Running along in sight of the low coast covered with high jungle backed by high land and anchored again at night off Malacca.

Fri. 15th No wind, so we did not lose sight of Malacca till the afternoon and remained broiling in glowing sunshine. H.M.S. *Larne* (16 guns) passed us and made her number. She is standing towards Penang. A couple of Malacca boats came alongside laden with fruit and poultry, so we replenished our stock of ducks and fowls and bought a quantity of pineapples, bananas and mangosteens. This part of the Straits is very pretty, the sea being studded with small islands well covered with trees and the hills inshore clothed to their summits with trees.

Mangosteen

Singapore

Sun. 17th Cooler today. We got under weigh about 10 a.m., a good many ships in sight. We buried at sea one of the soldiers who died from consecutive fever after cholera. About noon got sight of the shipping at Singapore, amongst them H.M.S. *Wellesley* with the flag of Sir Gordon Bremer,[B] Commodore.[4]

[4] Bremer, Admiral Elliot's second in command, had taken temporary charge of the expeditionary fleet pending the arrival of the Admiral from the Cape (where the Admiral had been aboard *Melville* on *Rattlesnake's* arrival in January).

Mon. 18th Went on shore with Call to have a look at the place, which is quite novel to me and very amusing – a sort of mixture of Indian and Chinese. There are good quays and warehouses on each side of a small river, which does not smell very sweet from the amount of drainage running into it. The houses are mostly of two storeys, with the upper one projecting beyond the lower. The windows are closed with wooden shutters. Some of the houses are Chinese looking, turning up at the corners and altogether put me in mind of the pictures on an old china plate of the willow-pattern. The people are as ugly as they are made with their flat yellow faces, small piggy eyes and long pigtails.

Tue. 19th Call and I went on shore and took a stroll about the place. Visited a new josshouse or Chinese temple, not of great size but gaudily painted and ornamented with fantastic porcelain dragons, &c., some beautiful carving on the pillars and screens with birds, flowers, &c. Two lions at the gateway carved in hard stone. In the mouth of each is a round stone, movable, but not to be taken out of the mouth. A Chinese artist was painting the outside with a little camel-hair brush. The doors being shut, we could not see the inside except through the carved windows.

On our way back we visited the stores of a well-known Chinese merchant, Whampoa, whose son, who now manages the business, was educated in Edinburgh, at the University, and is a very intelligent man and well read in English literature. Major Dillon joined us and we went to the French hotel[5] and ordered dinner of M. Dutronquoy, which was good and consisted of pork chops, curried fowl, roast duck, ham, cheese and potatoes for a dollar each and gave us good beer, madeira and claret.

[5] It was called, somewhat incongruously, the London Hotel.

We remained at Singapore till May 30th. I went on shore frequently, strolling about, the shops affording lots of amusement. Chinese articles for sale tempt one to spend money. Most of the things are reasonable in price, notwithstanding the number of officers now about the place. Chinese silks of all sorts, very beautiful birds, pictures, &c. Dutronquoy's hotel is comfortable, the landlord is a civil, amusing fellow, once an actor but who lately had a situation in Borneo. He sings French songs; has a couple of good billiard tables. His is a place of general resort for officers. I met many old friends and

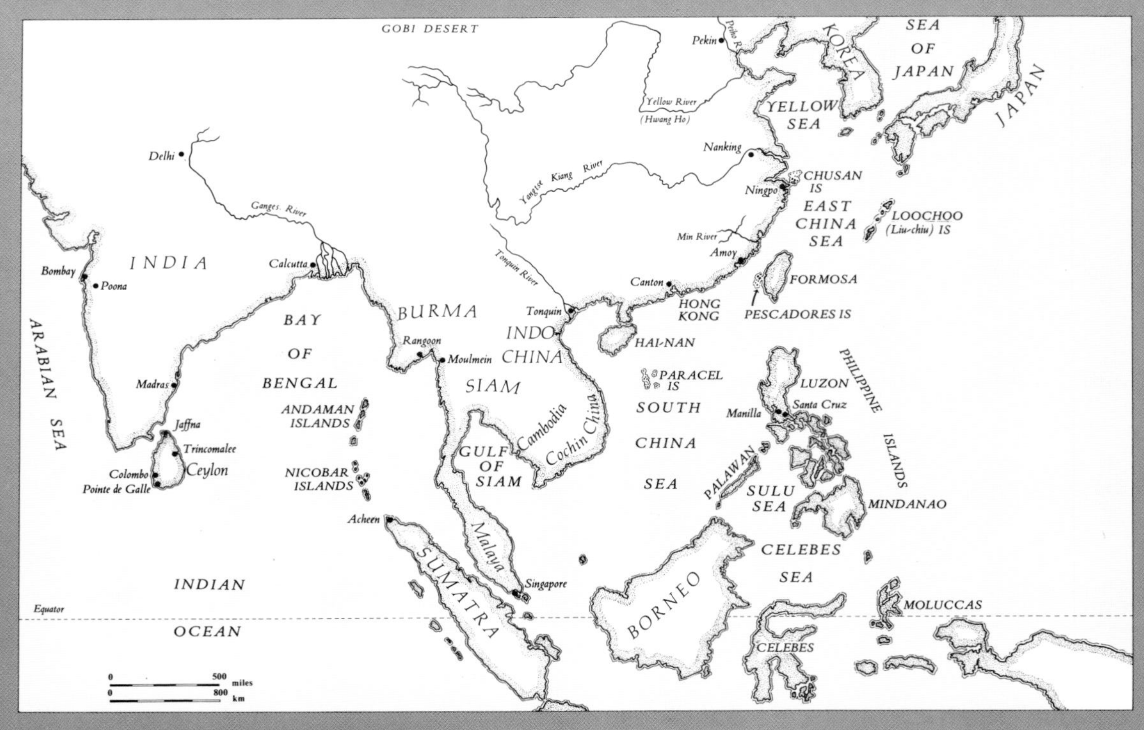

India and the Far East

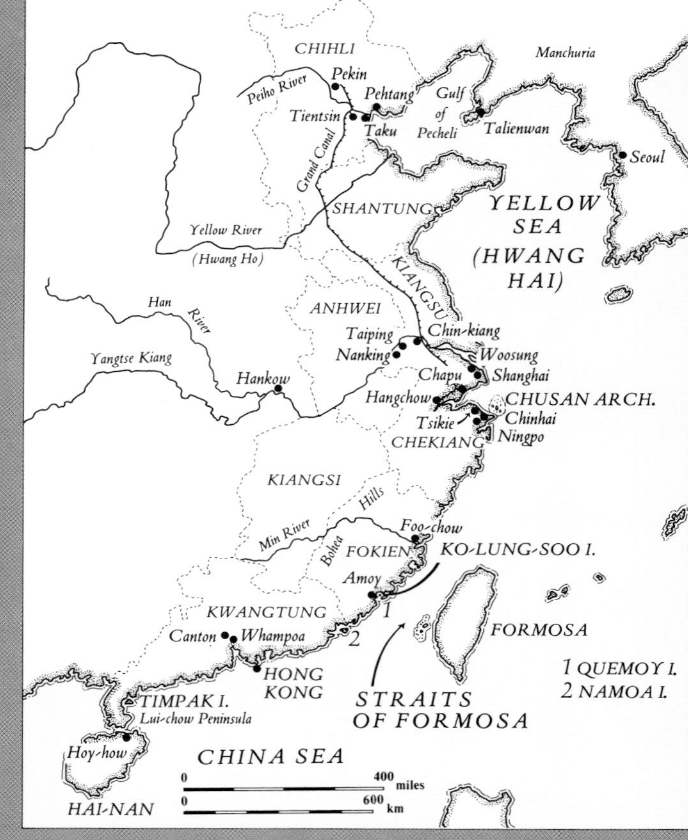

The coast of China

acquaintances there. The seamen and Marines are frequently on shore for exercise and have sham fights, to the astonishment of the inhabitants. A band played every evening on the parade where all the beauty, not much, and the fashion of the place assembled. Very few English ladies, but Dutch and Portuguese half-castes, some going about in smart equipages, buggies and palanquin carriages. The country round is hilly and pleasant and pretty well cleared and planted for a mile or two. Beyond is all jungle, where tigers and other wild beasts abound. Good roads are cut through the jungle in various directions. The Governor's House on a hill above the town is a pretty bungalow and has a pleasant view. There are many spice plantations, principally nutmegs and cloves. The tigers frequently carry off a coolie or two at work at the edge of the jungle. A reward is given by the Government for every tiger's head brought in, as they are so destructive to cattle as well as men. There are no elephants, so the tigers are not hunted here.

The harbour presents a busy scene, filled with ships of all sorts: six men-of-war, four steam vessels, thirty or forty transport and store-ships, twenty or thirty Chinese junks, the oddest looking craft I have seen. The latter will soon be leaving for China, as they only make one voyage a year, with the monsoon each way.

Straits of Singapore

Sat. 30th At 10 a.m. the Commodore fired a gun, loosed sails and weighed anchor, which was a signal for all the fleet to do the same and we were soon dropping out of Singapore harbour on our way to China. It was a pretty sight, so many transports and men-of-war headed by the old *Wellesley*, all with their white sails spread to the breeze. Some of the Chinese junks also got under weigh and kept with us for some way, but we lost sight of them before dark. We were on the weather quarter of the Commodore. The afternoon was squally, which added to the interest, some ships in the sunshine going before a fine breeze, others under a black cloud, all aback or shortening sail to a squall, thunder and lightning all round. The coast and islands are very pretty, being indented by creeks and rivers, with hills worked to their summits.

China Sea

JUNE

Wed. 10th Making but slow progress towards China. Weather intolerably hot – calm, rain and squalls. The fleet keep very well together, sometimes manage to get foul of one another. We keep just astern of the Commodore. The time passes pleasantly enough on board. We are all on good terms with the military officers, one or other of us always dining at their mess. I pass the time reading, drawing, walking on deck, eating, drinking and sleeping. Not much trouble with the sick, although we have had a few cases of fever.

Thur. 11th Hot and sultry morning – lat. 7° 5′ N., long. 107° 10′ E. At noon a breeze sprang up with a black cloudy sky. I was sitting reading in my cabin when I heard the dismal cry of a man overboard. I rushed up on the poop and saw about 20 yards astern poor Messenger, a young Marine, striking out for his life towards the lifebuoy which was within 5 yards of him. He was tugging away towards it but did not get nearer, although he was a good swimmer. The cutter with Harper and a crew had almost reached him when he disappeared to rise no more. They tried to reach him with the boat-hook; as the water was clear, they saw an enormous shark had got hold of his white jumper in the middle, gradually going down deeper and deeper till they disappeared. The men in the cutter tried to reach them with the oars, but no use, and the fellows had to return melancholy to the ship. This cast a gloom over the ship, for Messenger was a favourite with all hands. He was somewhat superior to the private Marine in general and had received a pretty good education. I hear he leaves a widowed mother near Portsmouth. He had jumped from the poop into the mizen-chains to clear the lead line when his foot slipped and overboard he went. I had been speaking to him only an hour before, enquiring about a small ulcer he had on his foot. This makes the third Marine we have lost out of six with which we left England.

The breeze freshened and the ship was put before it and we soon lost sight of the melancholy spot.

Fri. 12th Cloudy and squally, fair wind, all our ships about us, the Commodore ahead. A couple of very large sharks followed the ship for a couple of hours this morning but refused to take a bait of a 4-pound piece of pork.

Wed. 24th Squally weather. Yesterday we were all in conjecture when we saw the *Alligator* frigate standing out of the Canton River with a signal flying for the *Conway* to form the fleet into three lines, the *Conway* leading the centre line.[6] We were to follow the *Conway* and stood along the coast to the eastward. Colonel Oglander of 26th [Cameronian] Regiment died on board one of the transports after an illness of some days.

[6] The Commodore had gone ahead, leaving the frigate *Conway* to lead the convoy.

Fri. 26th The *Algerine* came alongside this morning and told us our destination was Chusan in 30° N., where there was formerly an English factory. We have been under reduced sail all day waiting for the Admiral. Lots of Chinese junks about. They appear to have a great coasting trade, junks of all sizes from a small sampan to vessels of 250 tons. One crossed our bows last night not bigger than one of our cutters, and we were at least 50 miles

"Interesting Intelligence" – China Sea, June 24th 1840

from the coast. We are out of the Tropic and the coast of China visible on the larboard side about 30 miles off. In the Straits of Formosa.

Sun. 28th From a fresh gale the wind suddenly shifted and came ahead, with a fog. We anchored for the night.

Mon. 29th Got under weigh but were soon obliged to anchor again from the coming on of a thick fog. We could hear the guns of the *Conway* booming through the fog and we kept drums beating and the bell going to warn other ships, as some of them being transports were not far from us. The thermometer fell 10° yesterday and we have some cases of dysentery.

Coast of China

Tue. 30th The fog having cleared, up anchor and stood along the coast and rendezvous at Buffaloes Nose, a small island south of Chusan. The *Conway* led the way and we maintained three lines in going into the bay. We were accompanied by hundreds of junks and fishing-boats. Here we anchored. The country round is mountainous and cultivated in the lower levels in patches and appears populous.

The Chusan Islands from the top of Trumball Island

Chusan harbour from Trumball Island

Wed. 1st The *Wellesley* (74), two steamers and four transports hove in sight and were soon at anchor with the rest of the fleet. They had left the port of Canton blockaded by the *Volage* (28), *Hyacinth* (16), *Druid* (36) and *Larne* (16), and brought the English mail of April with them. We could not purchase anything of the Chinese except some fish. The steamers astonished them and they would not venture near them.

JULY

Chusan

Thur. 2nd At daylight we weighed and proceeded towards Chusan, but the wind fell light. The steamers took the big ships in tow. A lot of junks followed us at a distance. The scenery is pretty amongst the islands which are very numerous and hilly, dotted about all round and well cultivated. In the afternoon the wind fell light and we anchored in the Chusan channel. The tides are very strong and the eddies sometimes turned us round. The population seem large and industrious.

Fri. 3rd Weather very hot. We were visited by some boats filled with natives, who came on board. They were poor fishermen. We brought them into the gunroom while we were at dinner and gave them some ale and rum and water, which they seemed to like, and also the pea soup. I was taking the likeness of one of the fellows, who immediately dropped his soup and ran out as fast as he could. The rum made them very talkative. A pinch of strong snuff setting them sneezing, they all set up a laugh. They brought us a present of some common looking tea grown on some of the islands, but we did not like it; it was so smoky in flavour.

Sat. 4th All the ships up anchor, but it fell nearly calm. The *Wellesley* took the lead, towed by the *Queen* steamer, Indian Navy, and proceeded to Chusan City [Tinghai]. We all followed as best we could and anchored off the town in the evening. Completely landlocked harbour surrounded by lovely little green islands. Numbers of boats filled with natives passed and repassed without fear. Chusan is hilly and picturesque with the low ground planted with rice. The hills, which are perhaps 700 or 800 feet high, are much terraced for irrigation and grow tea, sweet potatoes, &c. Bamboo and the talipot palms also grow in the valleys. It seems a shame to carry war into such a peaceful country, but one must leave that consideration to the Home authorities.

The city is about a mile from the beach, along which a suburb of mean looking houses is built and a lot of war junks moored with flags flying and gongs beating and great wicker shields, on which are painted tigers' faces. In the muzzles of the guns are tampions representing guns of enormous calibre. To the right is a hill, on which is a gaily painted josshouse. The city is surrounded by a thick wall about 20 feet high. It is in a well-cultivated plain at the foot of a range of high hills. We anchored in front of the suburb and abreast of one of the war junks. The other men-of-war and flagship took up their positions along the shore. The transports were left outside. Crowds of natives were to be seen along the beach and on Josshouse Hill, some with banners, and there was great excitement among them. Our Commodore sent to summon the Governor, who returned a contemptuous answer to say the outer Barbarians must go away immediately and not dare to insult the Celestial Empire. The Commodore also sent to the Chinese Admiral of the war junks, but he declined to answer till they were preparing to tow his vessel out to the flagship, when he made his appearance with some of his followers. The Commodore explained to him, through Mr Gutzlaff, the interpreter, what he should do if there was any resistance to our occupation of the place. The poor old Chinese Admiral replied that although he was not prepared for our reception, he must fight if he had one man beside himself or he should lose his head by the laws of his country. So he returned to his junk to make preparation.

All that night there was great noise of gongs and excitement on shore. Thousands of lights appeared, moving about, and the Chinese were evidently preparing to give us as warm a reception as they could.

Sun. 5th The day broke cloudy and lowering, with every prospect of rain. The Chinese appeared to have made the best use of their time during the night. Josshouse Hill was covered with armed men with flags and banners, the junks were placed in a line before the beach, each having one or two guns in the gangway and small swivels and wall pieces or gingalls about the bulwark. Two or three batteries had been constructed on the hill and mounted with old guns. We could see through our glasses that the arms of the Chinese soldiers were of a motley description, and consisted of bows and arrows, spears and swords, matchlocks and gingalls on tripods. A big red flag was mounted on one of the batteries and large boards with ugly black faces painted on them were suspended on the sides of the junks between the shields to frighten us away. The flagship hoisted a signal "Prepare to land troops". The boats with their complement of soldiers assembled under the lee of the flagship and a final message was dispatched to the Chinese Admiral, who was given till 1 p.m. for his answer, and our men went to dinner.

At 1 p.m. no answer, so a shot was fired from the *Wellesley* – which curiously hit the staff of the big red flag and brought it down and threw up a cloud of dust behind it. The plucky old Chinese Admiral promptly answered with a shot from his junk, up went the blue flag in the *Wellesley* with a broadside and all the ships opened fire and the fight became general, and all noise and smoke. A signal was hoisted "Cease firing", which had only lasted about five minutes.

The attack on Chusan, July 5th 1840

On the smoke clearing the Chinese army were to be seen running in all directions and disappearing over the hill as fast as their legs would carry them. However, they had not all gone, for in about five minutes after we had ceased firing, bang, bang, came shots again from the junks and we recommenced sending our shots through and through the old junks abreast of us. Away hissed a shell from the *Queen* steamer and burst in the city beyond.

Again firing ceased and when the smoke cleared not a living Celestial was to be seen except in the distance running away. The junks and houses along the beach presented a woeful sight, with shot-holes pretty thick. The former soon became waterlogged and settled in the mud. Three cheers were given from all the ships and the soldiers in the boats were landed under the josshouse which, with the hill, was soon occupied by them.

The boats were soon decorated with trophies, in the shape of Chinese flags and banners, and laden with the arms the Chinese had thrown away in their flight. Bows and arrows, spears and swords were plentiful. A good many killed and some wounded Chinamen lay about the beach; the latter were taken on board the flagship to be attended to. There were some shocking sights: one poor fellow with both legs carried away and another with half his head and still living. I hear that the Chinese had eighty-four pieces of ordnance, such as they are, mounted and pointed at the ships, not half of which had gone off. The Chinese still held out in the city and we could see the walls covered with flags and they kept up a fire from the walls, but our artillery soon got a couple of field pieces and threw a few shells amongst them and they were quiet enough before dark, except one or two guns during the night, but in the morning all was quiet again. A few of our Sappers crept up to the place to blow open the gates, but found the place deserted. The natives, taking what they could, had fled. A quantity of plunder was found in the suburb and many of our men got drunk on samshoo, a spirit distilled from rice, which they found in the houses.

Mon. 6th At 3 o'clock this morning a fire broke out in some of the houses near the beach and spread with great rapidity. A fine sight in the surrounding darkness. The engineers put it out after pulling down the surrounding houses. A number of dead were found during the day in the paddy-fields and in the canals between the suburb and the city. I was not able to land today, having an attack of dysentery, which is very prevalent in the ship at this time. An old Buddhist priest was found in the josshouse on the hill, and refused to leave and said he would trust in the Barbarians. In the night guns were heard outside the harbour. The *Wellesley* threw up a rocket.

Tue. 7th The guns proceeded from H.M.S. *Melville*, which had arrived from the Cape of Good Hope with Admiral Elliot. He came into harbour in the *Queen* steamer as the *Melville* stuck on a rock while being towed in and is considerably damaged, as she is leaking a great deal.

The Admiral was saluted and while the firing was going on a lot of Chinese plunderers took to their heels and fled out of the suburb. Admiral Elliot hoisted his flag in the *Wellesley*, as the *Melville* has to be repaired.

The *Blonde* frigate arrived from England and on her way looked into Amoy, where they fired into her boat with a flag of truce and an interpreter in her, so she opened fire and destroyed their batteries and then came on here.

A large quantity of copper coin has been found in the city, with arms, matchlocks, &c. The Governor is said to have been wounded by a shell and has escaped to the mainland. The poor old Chinese Admiral was killed in his junk. The Chinese army has fled to Ningpo, which is said to be the next place of attack.

Thur. 9th Went on shore in the afternoon with Commander Brodie and landed on one of the islands, where we got fresh water and went to a farmhouse. Found the owner and his family who had not fled, as they had confidence in the Barbarians, and were very civil to us and sold us some ducks, for which we paid a dollar for six, with which they appeared well satisfied.

Chusan farmhouse "of the better sort"

We visited other farms; the houses seem well built and roomy, all on the ground floor, but not very sweet smelling. We saw plenty of pigs about, also bullocks, fowls and ducks and some goats. In one house we encountered three or four young women with thin, very little feet and broad flat faces. They were sitting down drinking tea, of which we took some, very hot and very weak, no milk or sugar, and of a very fishy flavour, for I find they dry their tea on the same mats on which they dry their fish. We got a few pumpkins and gourds. The gardens are well kept and fertile, but stink of sewage.

Fri. 10th We received orders to get ready for sea by tomorrow to cruise off Buffaloes Nose to look out for junks and English vessels coming here, so James Brodie and I took one of the boys with us to see if we could pick up

A street in Tinghai, Chusan

some fresh provisions. We first took a stroll round the suburb, where the shots and the fire had done such damage, and afterwards by Chinese plunderers. It was melancholy to see the smashed furniture, rice and other grain strewed about, roofs and walls pierced by shot and shell. Some of the unfortunate inhabitants who had returned were wandering about amongst the wrecks of their property. Sentries are stationed in every street to endeavour to stop plundering. Indian troops occupy the suburb and the 18th Royal Irish the Josshouse Hill. There is a canal at the back of the houses and branches across the paddy-fields to the city and round the outside walls it forms the ditch. A narrow paved road leads to the city, with a canal on each side. On entering the city gates we tried to cross the canal by a temporary wooden bridge, as the Chinese had destroyed the stone one. The paddy in the fields looks beautifully green, indeed the whole country round, even to the tops of the hills, is fresh and green. I saw plenty of brinjals, melons, and sweet potatoes growing. On entering the city I was struck with the thickness of the walls, which are double at the gates, where we found a guard of our soldiers. The streets are narrow but clean, the houses only one storey high. Some of the shops are again open, but most of the houses are shut up as the people left them. The doors decorated with quaint pictures and Chinese characters, some gilt.

... We strolled through great part of the city, which contains some good houses and a few small pagodas, one of three storeys; on a rising ground a curious monument near it on a pedestal. From this place we had a good view over the city and surrounding country, which is pretty, with scattered farmhouses peeping out from amongst clusters of trees.

After we had purchased as much poultry and eggs as we could carry, we returned to our boat and on board. Considering how poor the ducks and fowls are we did not get them particularly cheap. We bought them of different people standing in the streets. When we got on board we found our orders had been countermanded and we were not to go to sea.

Sat. 11th I remained on board skinning two birds I procured yesterday – a pied and a green woodpecker. The Chinese have it that a great mandarin is coming with an army to retake this place or lose his head. I think the latter the most likely to happen.

Tue. 14th I went with the Commander to call on Brigadier Burrell, who is made Governor of the city. We lost our way in the narrow streets and found ourselves in a great josshouse where the 26th Regiment are quartered, but the sight of it repaid our trouble as it was filled with the most grotesque figures, life-size and some bigger, standing in a row on each side of a large square courtyard, and beyond we found four gigantic figures in a hall by themselves, 12 or 14 feet high. In front of the door squatted a fat, laughing god of gilt bronze. A short walk brought us to the Chief Magistrate's house, where the Brigadier has taken up his abode. It consists of a low range of buildings round a square now overgrown with grass, the buildings on each side little better than sheds. There are the usual tall poles. We entered through a wooden gateway with large figures of warriors painted on the doors, then another square court with tanks of stagnant water on each side of the pathway, then another gateway, which was the guardhouse where there were twenty or thirty of our soldiers, the Governor's guard, then to another court and the private residence, a low, one-storeyed range of buildings with large figures of mandarins or suchlike dignitaries painted on the doors.

Josshouse figure

We found the Governor in a large hall with Colonel Adams and Captain Call of the 18th R.I., Sir H. Darell and another military man seated at wine. We joined them, each in a bamboo armchair, at a handsomely carved and varnished table. Some pictures of Chinese ladies and mandarins hung on the

Inside the Great Josshouse, Tinghai

walls. All the furniture was just as the Chief Mandarin had left it. While we were there Mr Gutzlaff, the interpreter, who is now Chief Magistrate of Chusan, came but did not stay long. He looks much like a Chinaman, although he is a Prussian missionary. He has been in China many years and has travelled where no other European could venture, he knows the language and the people so intimately. When he ventures into the country and with a false tail and dressed as a Chinaman, he could not be detected. He cuts an odd figure now with his rusty black coat and short nankeens.[7]

It was nearly dark when we got back to our boat. The number of frogs in the paddy-fields keep up a continual croaking.

Sun. 26th ... After dinner we made up a party with some of the sailors and a Marine, armed, as it is not safe to go far from the ships unarmed in foraging parties. We first landed on one of the islands and went to a farmhouse, but we found nothing but pumpkins. The natives are in great terror and fall on their knees and kowtow. We then crossed over to another island and landed on a muddy beach and walked a couple of miles inland to a small village. On our approach the natives came out to meet us in a crowd and made signs that they had got no pigs, goats or poultry and wished to direct us to a village farther on. We tried to make friends with them and went into some of their houses and

[7] The Pomeranian-born Reverend Charles (Karl Friedrich August) Gutzlaff must certainly have cut an eccentric figure, though one to be reckoned with, for he did remarkable work – fulfilling various official roles for the British Government, running a class for Chinese children with his niece, Miss Parkes, and writing numerous books and articles in five languages. He had advocated punitive action against the Celestials, by means of a naval expedition to the Chusan Islands, "to give a death-blow to Chinese arrogance", a proposal that had been conveyed in March 1835 to Lord Palmerston, Foreign Secretary in the Melbourne administration.

took tea. We picked up a couple of pigs, a goat and some fowls, for which we paid them a fair price, but they evidently did not wish to have any dealings with us. But hungry men were not to be driven away from food.

All the low ground is irrigated and kept very clean, in which the rice is growing. I also saw cotton and Indian corn. A number of tombs are scattered about; some are handsome, stonework inscribed in large Chinese characters. The houses in the village are one storey and consisted of three or four rooms on the ground floor, which in the better houses is paved with flagstones. We visited many of the farms and collected a few fowls and pigs. A few of the natives followed us. On our way back we visited an old deserted war junk which had drifted away from her anchorage.

Sat., Aug. 15th Last night slept at Wilson's quarters but much plagued by mosquitoes. This morning at 4 Wilson called me and brought coffee and afterwards started on our excursion. We mustered twelve altogether – seven officers and five servants, taking refreshments and fowling pieces and pistols, as we did not know what force of Chinese we might meet as some of our people have been kidnapped and murdered in the country. After skirting the city wall we went along the valley to the eastward, then struck through the hills into another valley, which we also traversed, visiting several of the farmhouses. We met with plenty of fresh stock in the shape of goats, pigs and poultry, which we collected as we went, paying a fair price for everything, but the natives are so threatened by their government that they are afraid to supply us with anything. The roads are paved pathways, raised in the paddy-fields and broad enough for two people walking abreast and do for horses. We crossed two or three canals by substantial stone bridges. The country is pretty, particularly amongst the hills, well cultivated, very little waste ground, and that is generally occupied by the coffins which take up a deal of ground. The sides of the hills are terraced and irrigated by various machines. I saw a kind of chain pump mostly at work by one man with two handles which drew up a large stream of water from the lower level. All the machines used in husbandry are ingenious and well contrived. They have winnowing and threshing machines and mills worked by oxen. We saw a funeral, the coffin, surrounded by matting carried on the shoulders of four men with bamboo poles, preceded by a man carrying a lighted candle in a sort of flat candlestick. The coffin was followed by some well-dressed Chinese and a woman in white frock and trousers and a white veil. She toddled along very clumsily with her little crippled feet. They laid the coffin in a field on the side of a hill and there they left it for the time.

We met several of the natives, both male and female; they were all very civil. Some of the women are not bad looking but very shy. Their little feet make them get along very clumsily. We stopped at a nice spot near a farm on the side of a hill, in front of an old tomb, and refreshed with cold meat,

Foraging party (*top*)

Peasants of Chusan (*above left*)

Dibbling, husking and sifting paddy (*above right*)

Chinese funeral party (*below right*)

Irrigating rice fields, Chusan

The country expedition of August 15th

bologna sausage, hard-boiled eggs and biscuits with brandy and water, under some trees. From the farmhouse they brought some goats and eggs for sale and were very civil. We walked a few miles farther, but I felt very seedy and could not keep up. I had pain in the stomach and a burning thirst. We got to a farmhouse and I laid down on some clean straw. I had a great shivering fit and thought I was in for fever. They made me some tea at the farmhouse, which refreshed me, and I was able to walk slowly back, for the rest of the party went to visit some farmhouses farther on. I was supplied with a brace of pistols and I had my heavy walking-stick as a protection against any attack from the enemy who might be inclined to molest a single man. However, none did so and I had not gone many miles before I heard our party coming up behind – and they assisted me along. The thirst was intolerable and pain in stomach bad. I had high fever and tongue dry as a chip. However, I managed to get back about 5 o'clock and got some tea at Wilson's quarters. I got on board in one of the *Blenheim*'s boats and went to bed.

On August 3rd *Blenheim* (74) came into harbour, followed on August 20th by the gun vessel *Nimrod* (20). Now *Melville* has to be heaved down for repairs following the damage she sustained in early July, *Rattlesnake* being warped on one side of her and *Blenheim* on the other. These repairs are completed, not without difficulty, on September 28th. On August 21st the Chinese Government issues a proclamation offering "100 dollars for every white devil's son's head and 50 dollars for every black devil's son's head", and a much higher price for every officer's head. All this time the temperature is stiflingly hot, being 90 °F in the coolest place, and by the end of August, as a result of "bad water and bad provisions and a damp climate", almost 900 British servicemen are laid up with dysentery and coughs. Cree himself has suffered attacks of dysentery.

Heaving down H.M.S. *Melville*

SEPTEMBER *Fri. 18th* The Chinese have made off with Captain Anstruther of the Madras Artillery. While he was out surveying or sketching yesterday a party of Chinese soldiers came upon him unperceived and carried him off slung to a bamboo – a very unpleasant and undignified mode of conveyance for the gallant captain. As he was missing last night a party of soldiers was sent out to look for him, but by that time they had carried him off to Ningpo. The Chinese Government have offered great rewards for the Barbarians, dead or alive. The troops sent out met with some resistance in one of the villages, but they were ordered not to fire on the Chinese.

Captain Anstruther of the Madras Artillery being carried to Ningpo

Fri. 25th Poor Tracey, Assistant Surgeon of *Melville*, a great friend of mine, died this morning after an illness of four days of dysentery. He was a general favourite. He died in the temporary hospital ship *Victoria*. Death is making great havoc in the force, which is very sickly. I don't wonder at it considering the water we are drinking, stagnant from the paddy-fields, all well mixed with liquid manure. It stinks and is white and flatulent, but there is no other to be got in the neighbourhood.

Sat. 26th ... The Admiral has come back from his expedition to the north and is now at the Quesan Islands. A steamer has been sent in, but we have not heard much news except that they were received with politeness and the Emperor's court were rather astonished at the arrival of a steamer in the Peiho, and this roused the Celestials to the fact that the outer Barbarians had some complaint to make and threatened to visit the Son of Heaven himself. Mr Morrison,[8] the interpreter, who went in the steamer, was informed that Keeshen [Ch'i-shan], a member of the Imperial Cabinet and Governor of Pechelee [Pecheli], had arrived and would listen to the complaints of the foreigners and would forward them to Pekin. The steamer then recrossed the bar and rejoined the fleet, which anchored 10 miles off as the water is so shallow. On the 10th a mandarin came on board the *Wellesley*, attended by several boats with bullocks, sheep and poultry. Soon afterwards another

[8] John Robert Morrison was the son of the late Reverend Robert Morrison (d. 1834) – an eminent scholar and the first British missionary to enter China – and had succeeded his father as interpreter. *See also* p. 115 n.

mandarin called Showpei Pih, an intelligent sort of fellow, came out to the *Wellesley* – Pih being Chinese for white he was called "Captain White". The ships in company of the *Wellesley*, the *Blonde* and *Modeste* had some nice trips to the coasts of Manchuria and Tartary, &c. It is reported that the Emperor sent a present to the Admiral of sycee silver, 15 pounds weight, beside valuable silks, &c. The ships had to wait ten days for the Emperor's answer.[9]

Two mandarins have arrived from Ningpo with a chop desiring peace, but there does not seem much probability of it, for I hear that the *Kite*, a hired surveying vessel, has been wrecked on the coast. The captain of her was Mr Noble, who had on board his wife and child. Lieutenant Douglas of the *Melville* was in command and she had some seamen and Marines on board and a few guns. Noble and his infant child were drowned. Mrs Noble escaped on shore but was taken prisoner by the Chinese, who treated her with great brutality, dragging her by the hair from village to village and then putting her into a wooden cage, so small that she could only sit in it doubled up with knees and nose together. The others who escaped from the wreck were seized similarly and then taken to Ningpo, where they were imprisoned in irons after being carried round for exhibition. Captain Anstruther is a fine specimen of a red-headed Barbarian and Mrs Noble is a raw-boned, red-headed Scotchwoman, poor thing. This has caused great indignation in the force against the Chinese, who won't get much mercy when a chance comes of retaliation. I met Noble and his wife when we were at Trincomalee.

[9] On July 28th Rear-Admiral George Elliot, the Commander-in-Chief, had sailed with a squadron of ships for the mouth of the Peiho. His sole purpose was to effect delivery to the Emperor of a letter from Lord Palmerston asking for a trade settlement, arising from the Canton imbroglio. Copies of the letter had been rudely rejected at Amoy and Chinhai, but it was hoped that the British presence so near to Peking would help elicit a response. Much to Palmerston's consternation, however, Elliot – a sick man and blind to the ways of the Chinese – contented himself with personal assurances from the High Commissioner, Ch'i-shan, a person of forceful character and considerable charm, with influence at court. Elliot resigned for health reasons at the end of November.

Mrs Noble on her way to Ningpo

I hear of a number of other prisoners the Chinese have kidnapped and sent to Ningpo and some of our black dhobies or washermen from Madras.

Thur. Oct. 1st Arlington and I called on Mr Gutzlaff. He showed us a curious collection of translations of Chinese State papers, principally concerning the opium question – very quaint and formal. Mr G. says the Chinese Government are making dupes of us.

The chop from Ningpo

Interior of a Siamese junk, Chusan – forepart

Afterpart of the Siamese junk

1841

Chusan

JANUARY

Fri. 1st [Therm. 56°] Celebrated the new year by heaving down H.M.S. *Nimrod* and finished her repairs. I walked up to the city and purchased some curious china. Spent the evening at the club.

Sat. 2nd [Therm. 57°] While on shore I was amused by watching a Chinese puppet show, very cleverly managed although very similar to the English translated into Chinese.

Sun. 3rd [Therm. 43°] The changes in the temperature are occasionally very sudden and very unpleasant, and occasion violent chills and cause much sickness. The natives manage very well, piling on overclothes of padded cotton, so that in winter-time, or in cold weather, a Chinaman looks double the size he does in warm.

Sat. 9th In the afternoon I took my sketch-book and went for a walk beyond the city 2 or 3 miles up a pretty valley with a clear stream bubbling along the bottom. I met no one. I sat down on the ground and was busy sketching when some bird near made me look behind me. I saw about a dozen Chinamen coming over the hill at a quick pace. I did not like the look of them, so I shut up my sketch and walked off towards the city. I saw that they quickened their pace and were gaining on me, so I quickened mine to a run,

"Chased by Chinamen"

for I did not care to be carried off on a pole like a pig to Ningpo like Captain Anstruther, and put in a cage. All the Chinamen chased me and it was a question of wind and legs. I found that I had soon distanced all but three and when we got in sight of the sentry at the city gate they stopped and beat a hasty retreat. On getting to the gates I reported the circumstance to the officer of the guard and a picket was sent out, but of course the fellows were far enough away. The Chinamen were all armed with bamboos. I never had such a run and was glad to catch sight of the sentry.

Sun. 10th Glad to rest after my run of yesterday.

Mon. 11th Walked into the city and saw two Chinamen flogged by order of the Chief Magistrate for theft and their [pig]tails cut off.

Tue. 12th My twenty-seventh birthday. Mrs and Mr Bull gave an entertainment in their cabin to myself and messmates.

Wed. 20th Left our anchorage for the eastern passage to look out for fire-rafts which the Chinese are said to be preparing to send against us.

Thur. 21st Keep our guns shotted to give the Chinamen a warm reception if they venture with their fire-ships.

Fri. 22nd The Chinese great festival has commenced with the beating of gongs and letting off crackers.

Mon. 25th Went 4 or 5 miles over the hills shooting with James Brodie. Saw many wild geese but could not get near them. Wild ducks occasionally pitch in the harbour near the ships, but they are getting more wary than they were at first.

Fri. 29th [Therm. 29°] Snowing.

Sat. 30th Snowing.

Sun. 31st Snow.

FEBRUARY *Mon. 1st* All the surrounding hills covered with snow.

Fri. 5th Chinese feast of lanterns. At night all round the islands hundreds of lanterns and plenty of crackers.

Sun. 7th Great excitement last night in the middle watch. Hundreds of

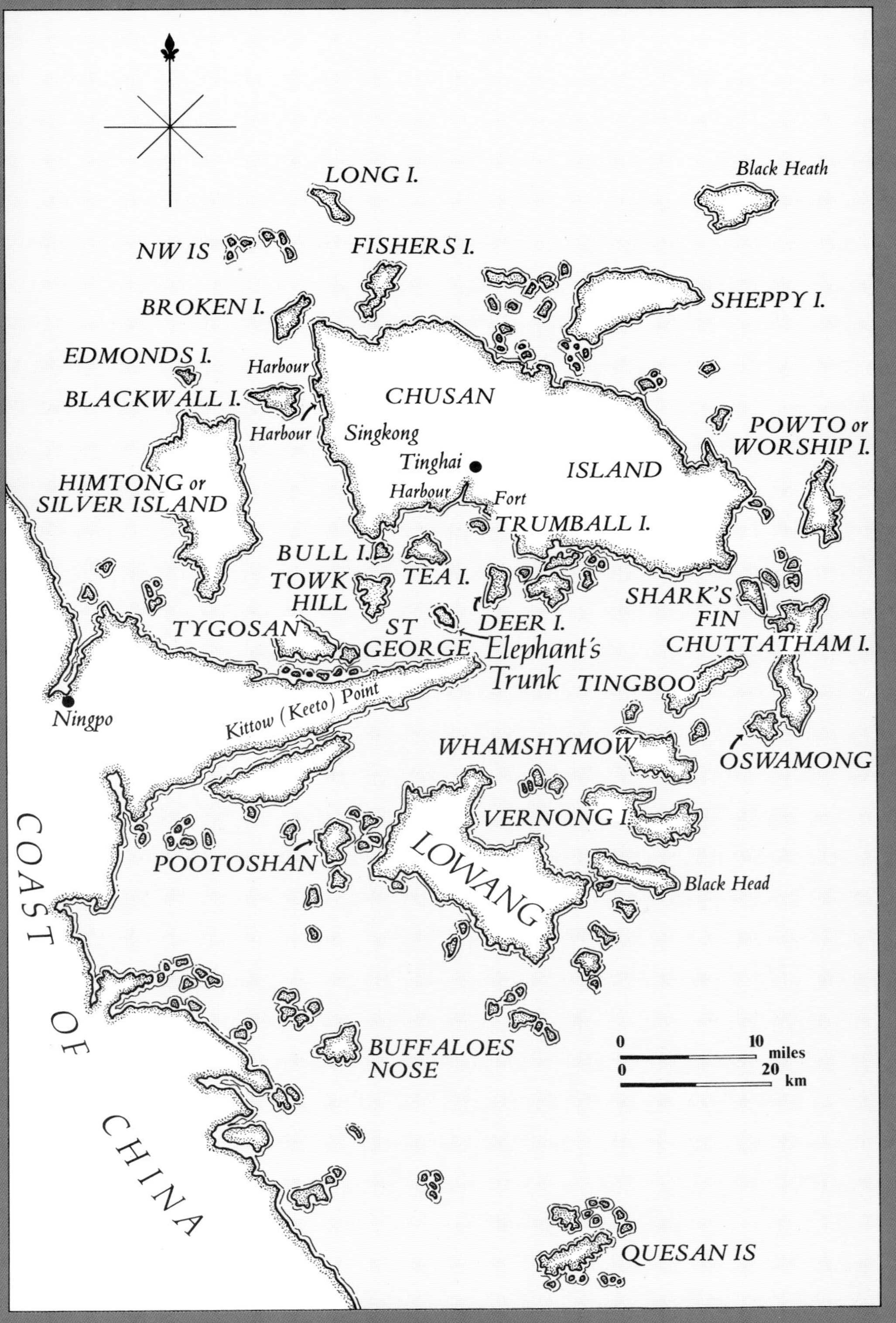

The Chusan Archipelago

Chinese junks were reported as coming down upon us. The guns were loaded and men at their quarters and the troops we had on board were mustered on the poop, when the junks turned out to be merchant junks on their way to the south.

Mon. 8th H.M. Brig. [Steam Sloop] *Columbine* arrived, having beaten up the China Sea against the monsoon. News from Canton and letters from home. A signal from the Commodore sent our Commander to the *Blonde*, where he received orders to come into harbour and embark part of the 18th Regiment for the Canton River. Two mandarins were with the Commodore, having brought chops from Ningpo with dispatches from Sir Gordon Bremer at Hong Kong, ordering the force here to evacuate the islands as a treaty of peace was said to be concluded with China, after the children of the Flowery Empire had got a severe drubbing and about 600 of them killed, and the forts in the Canton River knocked about their ears. Admiral Elliot has gone down ill, probably sick of the work out here, so that Sir Gordon Bremer is again Commander-in-Chief. When the *Columbine* came in she confirmed the news and brought me the first letter from home that I had received since I left, and it was thirteen months old and had postmarks on it Colombo, Trincomalee, Calcutta, Singapore, &c., and smudged all over.

Wed. 10th Left our anchorage and came into the inner harbour to embark the 18th Regiment and in doing so got foul of an opium clipper.

Sat. 13th Last night of our meeting at the Chusan United Services Club.

Sun.14th The Chinese authorities of Ningpo sent an insolent message to the Commodore, directed to the English Barbarians, the most inferior natives, and refuse to deliver up the prisoners. The letter was sent back.

Tue. 16th Laid up with a severe cold, which is just now a very prevalent complaint. Embarked the luggage of the 18th Regiment.

Wed. 17th Embarked part of the 18th Regiment. A steamer was sent to Ningpo demanding the prisoners.

Tue. 23rd Went over Tea Island shooting with Jimmy Brodie and some of the 18th. Got some wild duck and a few snipe.

Wed. 24th Great excitement: two junks arrived with the prisoners from Ningpo – Captain Anstruther, Lieutenant Douglas and poor Mrs Noble[1] – dressed in Chinese clothes, some sailors, soldiers and Indians. The ships manned rigging and cheered them as they passed. Latterly they were pretty

[1] About a year later Mrs Noble's cage was shipped to England for display at the United Service Institution in London. The R.U.S.I. museum was disbanded in 1962, its exhibits being sold off and dispersed, and it is not known what became of the cage.

well treated by their jailers. Captain Anstruther was kept employed in drawing the Queen of England, the Prime Minister, the Admiral and General – of course striking likenesses. We afterwards weighed and dropped down to Kittow [Keeto] Point where we anchored for the night.

Canton River

MARCH

Tue. 2nd Ran into the river and anchored off the NW end of the island of Hong Kong, a mountainous, desolate looking place with only a few fishermen's huts to be seen. We were astonished at not finding the fleet here but soon heard they were all up the river, that another battle had been fought, great numbers of Chinese killed, amongst them their great Admiral Kwan. In running in we passed with a fair wind a number of high mountainous islands. We anchored and spoke one of the fishing-boats, which gave us the news. We heard that the fleet had gone on towards Canton. The Bogue forts were taken on the 26th.[2]

Wed. 3rd H.M.S. *Nimrod* arrived last evening and sailed up the river this morning.

Thur. 4th In the afternoon some transports came in from Chusan and the *Queen* steamer from the Commodore with orders for us to proceed up the river immediately. The night was light but very foggy, blue lights and rockets were burnt as signals to our boats away. All excitement at the prospect of an attack on Canton. The Governor has only sixty hours to answer an ultimatum.

Fri. 5th When the fog cleared we weighed and proceeded with three transports, but had to anchor in the afternoon off the south end of Water Island, or Chun Tang, as the wind failed us in the evening. Some more transports coming up. We fired guns as signals to them.

Sat. 6th At daylight proceeded with a stormy breeze and passed Lantao and Lintin Islands. A fleet of merchant ships at anchor in Tong Koo Bay. The breeze fell light but we got up past the fishing stations with their nets and boats. Pretty scenery with multitudes of islands, a few pagodas and villages scattered about. Passed many dead bodies floating down the river naked and blown out, some of them mutilated by our shot from the ships' broadsides in taking the Bogue forts. Here and there were masts of sunken junks appearing above water in the shallow parts. In the evening we passed the dismasted and ruined forts, Tycocktow and Chuenpi. The river here is about a mile and a half wide. When we got abreast of Anunghoy Fort there was a great flash and a tremendous explosion, a great volume of smoke, dust and rubbish with big

[2] The Chinese had not provided the guarantees requested of them, of fair trading and compensation for opium losses. Therefore Captain Charles Elliot (cousin of the Admiral, George Elliot, whom he had accompanied on the abortive Peiho expedition), Chief Superintendent of Trade, put into effect his threat to destroy the forts guarding the Bogue, or Bocca Tigris, the eastern channel leading to the Canton or Pearl River. The task was accomplished by Commodore Bremer on January 7th, and when the Convention of Chuenpi (under which an indemnity was to be paid and the island of Hong Kong ceded to Great Britain) was not ratified, on February 26th the guns of the repaired Bogue forts were again silenced by British ships.

Destruction of Anunghoy Fort, Bocca Tigris, March 6th 1841

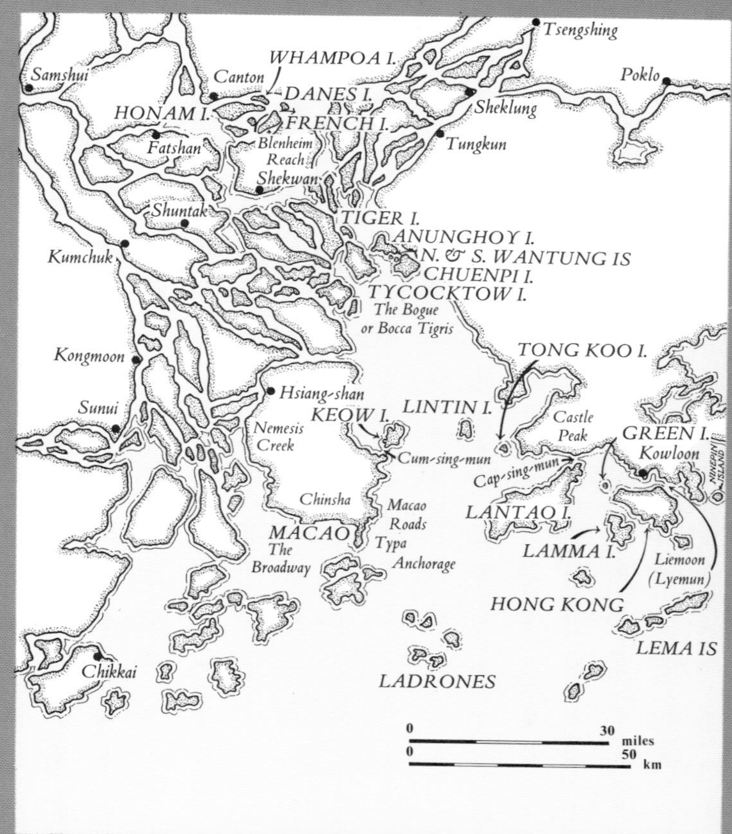

The Canton Delta

stones flying about, showing that the work of destruction of the Chinese defences was still going on. Some of our Engineers were on shore doing the work. At the Bogue we found the three line-of-battle ships with many others at anchor. The *Blonde* frigate and *Columbine* brig overtook us during the afternoon, and here we anchored for the night.

"John Chinaman in his bad weather dress"

Sun. 7th At daylight weighed and stood up the river with a very light breeze. The *Blenheim* fired a shot at some Chinese plunderers. Passed Tiger Island, a bold, strange looking basaltic rock. The river widens out to 3 or 4 miles, but there are so many large islands that one cannot judge to a mile or two. The banks are low and muddy, intersected by streams and canals, planted with paddy, mountains in the distance. On two hills a pagoda. Numbers of fishing-boats and junks in the sluggish streams, the navigation impeded by numerous sandbanks, and the water very muddy. Many of the ships had got ashore. One of the transports, the *Romany*, was hard and fast and we had to take some of her troops out of her; others were distributed among the other ships. Chinese boats voluntarily assisted, so much for their patriotism. Afterwards a fellow came on board and offered to pilot us up to Whampoa for 150 dollars. When we were within a few miles of Whampoa we found the *Blonde* frigate hard and fast and we were ordered to anchor and assist her off, much to our annoyance, and soon afterwards Captain Elliot,[B] the British Minister or Plenipotentiary, came alongside in the *Nemesis,*[3] a new light draught steamer commanded by William Hall,[B] a Master in the Navy. Captain Elliot told us that it was all settled. Nothing more was to be done at Canton, for some of the forts had been taken within a couple of miles of the city and the Hong merchants had come to the Plenipo and begged them not to proceed farther, as they knew that Canton was at our mercy, but they could not come to terms without the Emperor's permission. The Chinese were fitting out a large East Indiaman as a man-of-war, but one of our steamers threw a shell into her and blew up her magazine and a number of unfortunate Chinese who were in her. A lovely moonlight night, so I spent most of it on deck, enjoying the scene – numbers of native boats came alongside to sell fruit, eggs, &c., mostly managed by women, some not too modestly clad.

Mon. 8th [Therm. 72°] Detained by the *Blonde* in assisting her off the mud, and afterwards in picking up her anchors. Many of the ships passed us on their return to the Bocca Tigris. In the afternoon the *Queen* steamer came down with the Commodore on board and towing H.M.S. *Druid*. The *Blonde* saluted with thirteen guns Sir Gordon Bremer.

Wed. 10th At daylight we weighed and returned to the Bogue, anchoring north of Wantung Island. A newly found cousin of mine, Collins of Bristol, Surgeon of the *Sophia* transport, came to look me up. I found him a pleasant

[3] *Nemesis* – the first iron steamer to double the Cape of Good Hope – had survived a hazardous voyage of almost eight months to the China station, reaching Macao on November 25th 1840. Built at Birkenhead in 1839, of experimental construction, she was 184 feet long, 29 feet in breadth, with a burden of about 700 tons, and could attain 120 horsepower. She drew not much more than 5 feet and her two false keels could be raised, which proved to be great assets in negotiating shallow waters. A unique safety factor was provided by the seven watertight compartments into which her hull was divided. She played a vital part in various naval operations, from the time of the first attack directed against the Bogue forts, and continued serving in Borneo and Chinese waters until 1852.

Cantonese boat-girl

man. I dined with the 18th officers and after dinner took an oar with them to Wantung Island to see the fortifications, which were very strong and extensive. Our shot had made sad havoc in some of them, but not much impression on their admirable sandbag batteries. They wanted better guns, which were great unwieldly affairs, and better gunners. We came across some half-buried killed, but the sight and smell were anything but agreeable. They were in a trench. I picked up a curious chain-shot of Chinese make.

Tue. 16th J.H. Collins called. I dined with him on board *Sophia*. The *Nemesis* steamer has made a successful raid on the forts and junks in the Broadway, a back passage to Macao, on the 12th and 13th. She destroyed a lot of forts and junks and guns, 105 pieces of cannon, nine junks burnt – to the astonishment of the Celestials. The boats of the *Samarang* went with *Nemesis*.

Sun. 21st Major-General Sir Hugh Gough,[B] K.C.B., came on board to inspect our troops. He has been appointed military Commander-in-Chief. He is an old Peninsula man.

Mon. 22nd Went with W. Brodie to have a look at Tiger Island and visit the ruins of the forts there. There are some curious tombs and a cove where some of the natives have stowed away their household goods during the troublous times. The cliff at the back of the island is very smooth and precipitous, a palm and shrubs growing at the foot of the cliff.

Mon. 29th Two officers of H.M.S. *Blenheim* are missing, supposed to be kidnapped.

Tue. 30th – Wed. 31st After we left Chusan three store-ships arrived there. The Captain of one landed at Kittow Point to pick up information, when he was immediately seized by some Chinese soldiers and murdered. They also attacked the ship but were beaten off. The ship has arrived at Macao and reported it. A second ship was seen going in, but has not since been heard of. It is also reported that the *Golconda* transport with native infantry on board has been wrecked on the coast and the crew all murdered by the Chinese. Many merchant ships have gone up to Whampoa for cargo,[4] but an edict has arrived from the Emperor to exterminate all the Barbarians.

[4] Whampoa, 12 miles downriver from Canton, afforded a convenient harbour for merchantmen, from which their lighters conveyed cargoes to and from the European factories.

APRIL

Thur. 1st With a party of officers went to a village at the back of Anunghoy Island, where we saw a Buddhist priest with his fingernails of enormous length – one on his left hand was 14 inches long, like a big quill – enclosed in bamboo cases which fitted on the ends of his fingers. He was supposed to be peculiarly holy.

Sat. 3rd The bodies of the two officers of the *Blenheim*, supposed to have

Village near Anunghoy, Canton River

been kidnapped, have been picked up on the shore murdered – Toole and Bligh, and a mate of the schooner [cutter] *Snipe* who was with them, Field. He had had his ears cut off – a large wound of his head and a spear wound through his body. They had been thrown into the river and washed up on the beach.

The *Atalanta* steamer arrived with orders for us to go to Hong Kong.

Sun. 4th Hot and calm morning. As soon as we had any wind we weighed and dropped down the river. Received a visit from Colonel Adams and some of the officers of 18th Royal Irish. Twelve sail of transports accompanied us. Some of the force remain to garrison Wantung Island. We passed several merchant vessels on their way up to Canton. The tea trade is said to be going on briskly at Canton where the people are displaying the Emperor's mandate and have driven some of his "exterminators" away. His Celestial Majesty says there can be but one nation in the world and that China. One of our soldiers died of consumption, the third from that disease since we left Chusan. We anchored for the night on Lontin Sands. All night the mountains round were alight from burning the grass and had the appearance of thousands of moving lamps. Assam, our comprador, says they burn the dry grass to give fresh pasture to their goats. We asked Assam for the news from Canton. He says Keeshen the Commissioner "He go to Pekin. I think Emperor squeeze him. You go burn Canton, very proper. You catch Emperor, hang him, all very proper". Received a letter from my sister dated Oct. 1st.

"Long nails"

Hong Kong

Tue. 6th Weighed with the tide and proceeded through the Threat Gates, at some places so near you could pitch a biscuit on the rocks. The tide runs strong and soon swept us through the narrows. We passed the entrance of Pirate Harbour and saw a large junk that had been attacked the night before by Ladrones, but they were driven off. These fellows have become very daring since the war.

Wed. 7th Anchored yesterday in afternoon in Hong Kong harbour. Went on shore in the cutter with some of the 18th. Landed in a pretty, secluded bay and walked up to a village, but the natives are shy. The women all ran away and shut their doors. We passed a herd of buffaloes, not pleasant looking animals. Went into the village school where we saw a lot of moon-faced urchins were acquiring the rudiments of the Celestial learning, and put one in mind of some of our village schools. They seem pretty much the same all over the world. On our way we came across some funeral urns in niches in the bank by the pathway. They contain the bones taken from the coffins. On our way back through a valley, through which ran a stream of sparkling water, we met Sir Fleming Senhouse[5] and Sir Hugh Gough and A.D.C. with a guard of Marines. They stopped to have a talk about the place. In the evening two boats with about thirty Chinese girls came alongside the ship, but Commodore Brodie very properly would not allow them to remain.

[5] Captain Sir Humphrey Le Fleming Senhouse, as senior naval officer, had taken over command of the China squadron in Commodore Bremer's absence. Bremer had sailed for Calcutta on April 1st for the purpose of securing more steamers for river-work as well as troop reinforcements.

Mon. 19th Dined with the 18th officers. Afterwards went over to Hong Kong, where the people all living under canvas. A great influx of natives – all the ruffians from Canton – have erected huts and shanties, where are drinking booths and gambling booths and every kind of debauchery.

Tue. 20th We hear of pirates in the neighbourhood getting very bold attacking small vessels between this and Macao.

Wed. 21st We hear shocking accounts of the cruelty of the Chinese Government which appears mad with rage at their defeat, five mandarin officers who commanded at the Bogue forts being burnt alive in boats, and poor Keeshen and all his family executed.

Tue. 27th Dine with the 18th and after went over to Kowloon to see a cricket match between the officers of Navy and Army. The Chinese looking on appeared to be greatly interested.

Wed. 28th Captain Chilcott of *Prince George* [transport] sent his gig in which we went on board, then went with him in his longboat to a village on

Victoria, Hong Kong, in April 1841, before the town was built

the mainland and walked a few miles. We were well armed and the natives were very civil. We brought some lunch – ham sandwiches, sausages and ale, which we enjoyed under a banian tree surrounded by a gaping crowd of natives.

Fri. 30th On shore with Bull and his wife to see the new village which is springing up rapidly on Hong Kong and roads are being constructed. Thousands of Chinese labourers are being employed.

MAY

Sat. 1st H.M.S. *Nimrod* arrived from Macao. Went on board her, but my friend Davidson has been sent to the *Sulphur*. We are ordered to be ready for sea by the 10th. Amoy is said to be our destination.

Tue. 4th The gunboats are gone up to Canton to protect the merchant ships there as the mandarins are getting saucy again.

Thur. 6th The trade is stopped again at Canton. More gunboats are sent up there as the mandarins are threatening the ships.

Tue. 11th H.M. Brig *Columbine* has returned from Chusan with very unsatisfactory news. The people and authorities would receive no "chop", and the only account they could get of the captain of the transport was that he was seized at Kittow Point by Chinese soldiers and murdered. At Chusan they were very busy building new forts.

Thur. 13th Signal "Prepare for sea".

Canton River

Tue. 18th We are to go up the Canton River again.

Wed. 19th Weighed at 7 a.m. with *Blenheim, Blonde, Nimrod* and *Hyacinth* and transports. It fell calm at noon and we anchored south of Lantao Island. Went on again in afternoon but not far and anchored for the night west of Lantao.

Sat. 22nd Weighed at 6 a.m. and proceed up the river with the tide. Passed two of the transports on a mud bank. Some pleasant scenery on the river banks. Anchor at the south end of Danes Island. Last night the Chinese sent down fire-rafts with the hope of burning H.M.S. *Alligator* (26), but they were on the alert in the ship and towed the blazing raft to the river bank, where it harmlessly burnt out. We came up by a lately discovered branch of the river, which has been called French River. Chinese jealousy prevented its being used by Europeans. It is found to be a better passage to Canton than the old one.

Sun. 23rd Weighed at 7 a.m. The *Atalanta* steamer took us in tow. Pass many large villages in a pretty and rich looking country, picturesque creeks, a pagoda and houses of wealthy Chinamen. Pass the *Blonde* and *Blenheim* at anchor. We anchored near the Macao branch of the river, about 4 miles from Canton. I went to the mast-head to have a look at the city through a telescope. Saw an extensive fire in the suburbs at night. At midnight a detachment of the 18th came on board from the *Futty Salaam*, one of the transports we saw on the mud bank. She has had a narrow escape from fire-rafts which the Chinese sent down against her.

Mon. 24th Ordered to disembark troops at noon. Plenty of excitement and bustle. A number of tea boats have been seized for the use of the troops, all the big boats of men-of-war and transports employed to carry guns and soldiers and their crews, the steamers to tow them up to Lantao. We had a great tea cargo boat alongside to take some of our soldiers. These boats are very light with a great roof over them. About twenty men had got on the roof when over it went, throwing the men into the water. Fortunately the boats were close to and the soldiers were soon picked up, and only some of the muskets and ammunition lost. Each man had two days' provisions in his haversack and sixty rounds of ball cartridges, so it is a wonder some of them were not drowned. The tea boat was soon righted and the men were not allowed on the roof again. The force moving up the river was a fine sight, such a crowd of boats, the steamers towing as many as they could. They all went off with three cheers. I spent the afternoon at the mast-head, from where I could see the firing and plenty of smoke. I could see the flashes of the guns and some

"Hurrah! for Canton"

heavy explosions and two large fires which broke out in different parts of the city.

This being the Queen's birthday the firing commenced with a royal salute of twenty-one guns from each ship at noon, soon followed by a deadlier one. Nearly all our men are away, very few left on board and no boats but the dinghy, so for safety and to prevent any attempts at boarding by gangs of Chinese robbers we had all our guns loaded with grapeshot. The night was illuminated by the flames of the city and shells and rockets flying. Our force consists of about 4,000 soldiers and sailors and the Chinese have about 30,000. I stayed up most of the night watching the fires.

Tue. 25th Firing continues and clouds of smoke rise thick and heavy from the devoted city and shells are seen bursting through the roofs of some of the larger buildings. I spent most of the forenoon on my perch at the mast-head. The suburbs on both sides of the city are in flames. Shells and rockets are flying into enemy's encampments outside the walls. One of our ships was firing briskly into a fort about 2 miles above the city. We had an alarm in the night from the guard-boat and ship ahead of us firing muskets and burning blue lights, and as we are senior here we sent the dinghy to ascertain the cause. We found some Chinese boats lashed together had drifted across the bows of the leading transport, but finding so good a look-out, the boats had pulled to the shore. At 3.30 a.m. there was a second alarm from the same cause. The night

The English factory, Canton, May 24th 1841 (*black and white*)

Canton River: fire-rafts coming down

was very dark. We were quite prepared for fire-rafts coming down on us. We have a kedge anchor hanging from our jib boom and connected with our cable, so that it could be dropped into a fire-raft and we could slip and drop down out of the way.

Off Canton

Wed. 26th A further attempt has been made to burn H.M.S. *Wellesley*, no less than thirteen fire-rafts were sent down on her at one time. She was surrounded by them, but their boats managed to tow them all away to the river bank, where they all burnt out.

Reports of many killed and wounded and heaps of slain amongst the enemy. Poor Fox, 1st Lieutenant of the *Nimrod*, has died of his wounds, his leg shattered. The 18th Regiment have fired away all their ammunition and sent down for more. They also have a good bit of killed and wounded. Some of the latter are on their way down to me.

Thur. 27th Our troops have possession of all the heights round the city which now is at our mercy. The Chinese mandarins have been brought to their knees. The city is to be ransomed for 6 millions of dollars. Amongst the 18th Captain Sargent has a ball in his arm; Lieutenant Edwards shot through the arm; Kendall of *Nimrod* has lost a leg; Vaughan, Assistant Surgeon of *Algerine*, wounded slightly; Lieutenant Hilliard of 18th, slightly.

Fri. 28th As a good many of our men are away at Canton I went up in the dinghy with Arlington and a couple of boys to look after them. We took muskets, pistols and swords in case we fell in with any of the plundering Chinese on the river, for we had a pull of 4 miles as our landing-place was about 2 miles above the city. We left the ship about 1 p.m. and got alongside the *Nimrod* just as a heavy squall came on. Went on board to see poor Kendall, who has had his leg amputated just below the knee. We had to pull up the river about 7 miles farther to where the *Sulphur* is lying above all the transport junks. We passed some of the better sort of Chinese houses near the river. All appeared deserted. Plenty of fruit trees along the river banks, lichees, shaddocks, oranges, plums and bananas, &c. We met boats laden with furniture and families escaping to quieter parts. We passed many blackened ruins, still smouldering, of houses, temples and forts. It was getting dark when we left the *Nimrod*. We pulled up in the centre of the river, as there was danger of being picked off by matchlock men on the bank. There are still roaming bands of Tartar soldiers about. The wind fell but it still rained hard and thundered and lightened and we were wet through, but the forked lightning was grand. We had the tide with us and we were soon swept up the creek to where the *Sulphur* and *Starling* were at anchor. We found some of our men in a large junk where we took up our quarters and got some "omnium gatherum" soup made from the proceeds of their foraging and some good tea taken from one of the deserted villas. We had to pick out the softest planks to lie upon – hard enough – and slept as well as the myriads of mosquitoes would allow. There has been some hard fighting from this to the heights and many of the stragglers and camp followers have been kidnapped and their heads taken by the Chinese, for which they get a reward from the mandarins.

Heights of Canton

Sat. 29th Glad to get up from the boards at daylight. Landed at a deserted villa, where a detachment of the 18th and 26th Regiments are stationed. We got breakfast with them of fowl pie and claret. Here I met Collins, who is doing duty with the 26th. He took me to see the garden at the back of the house, a fanciful place in Chinese taste, with paved walks, lakes and bridges in miniature, a little pagoda and distorted trees. We waited for the escort to march up to Headquarters on the heights, 4 miles off. A party of the 18th was the escort. In the garden were tanks with the sacred lotus growing, grottoes and fantastic rocks. Hundreds of pots with plants in them ranged along low walls. The paths are paved with variegated tiles. There is a swimming-bath with a pretty little house on piles in the centre. Deer and sheep-pens and conservatories. The verandas are adorned with plenty of carved work with gilding over roof and doors, cool stone and bamboo seats scattered about and easy chairs. There are plenty of fine trees. Collins took me to see a poor Chinaman whose arm he had just amputated. We marched along a narrow paved road with cultivated fields on each side, first through a deserted village. In a pond near a mandarin's house we saw three dead bodies floating, one a woman, probably committed suicide in their fright. The Chinese had removed nearly all their killed and wounded.

We had a good pull up to the fort in the heights where the 18th are in occupation, and for which they had a good fight, as the road was flanked by the city wall. However, they got some guns and howitzers within 300 or 400 yards and silenced the guns of the fort; they were carried at the point of the bayonet, which the Chinese won't stand. The whole chain of forts were taken, but not without considerable loss of officers and men. On our way we passed through some large cemeteries filled with tombs, which much impeded the dragging up [of] the large guns. Some of the tombs are handsome and surrounded by life-sized stone figures of horses, elephants and men. The other troops and sailors occupied the other forts they had taken and a large village at the foot. The accommodations were miserable enough. The court of the fort was ankle deep in mud this wet weather, even in the huts left by the Chinese. In the centre of the fort is a square tower or keep, from which we had an

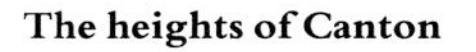

The heights of Canton

extensive view over the city to the river, to the ships and surrounding country. Opposite this fort is a square five-storeyed building, just inside the city wall, said to be one of the oldest pagodas in the country. It is painted red and behind it is a considerable hill on which is a josshouse and entirely commands the city of Canton. It was to have been assaulted yesterday, but the Chinese authorities have offered peace – all along the walls white flags are planted and a truce is granted on the following terms: all the Imperial troops and the three Commissioners are to quit the city and retire 60 miles away within six days; 6 million dollars to be paid within a week, 1 million to be paid immediately – our positions to be retained till it is all paid, the amount to be

Canton from the heights

increased if not within twenty days. They are also to pay for the destruction of the factories and a Spanish ship they destroyed. Our troops are not satisfied with this armistice, as they think Canton ought to be entered as they have been so insolent and treacherous, but we have only 2,260 men and a good many sick and wounded and the Chinese have 20,000 soldiers in the city.

The red five-storeyed temple opposite is much venerated by the Chinese and the authorities have begged us not to injure it. However, a couple of shells had gone through the roof. The city appears very extensive and densely inhabited but there are some fields and trees inside the walls. Most of the houses are only one storey high. We managed to get some refreshment with the officers of the 18th. I made a few sketches and started on our return to our fort without any escort. It was raining hard and we soon got wet through. The wet probably kept away any Chinese prowlers. We saw some fellows peeping from behind one of the tombs and, fearing an ambuscade, I pointed my fowling piece at them and shouted, at which they took to their heels. We soon afterwards met the Plenipo with an escort on their way up to the fort. He stopped and gave us a reprimand for venturing down without an escort. It was quite dark when we got back to the boat.

While I was engaged sketching an ancient Mohammedan tomb outside the walls of Canton I heard the sharp "whip" of a shot near my head and saw the smoke issuing from one of the embrasures, so I shifted my quarters pretty quickly. I afterwards found a shot-hole through the brim of my hat, a straw one, too close to be pleasant.

When we got down to our boat we found it too dark and squally to go

Ancient Mohammedan tombs near the walls of Canton, Cree sketching in foreground. It was here that a musket-ball pierced the brim of his hat.

down the river to the ship, so we went to the large junk where we now were stationed and laid down on the deck of the cabin. It was raining and blowing hard, but I was so tired that I soon fell asleep. I was awoke about midnight by the rain coming through the roof over me, but I managed to find a large Chinese umbrella and finished the uncomfortable night under that, cold and damp.

Canton River

Sun. 30th At daylight, the weather having cleared, we left our uncomfortable quarters in the junk and started down the river with the tide. Got on board the *Rattlesnake* in time for breakfast. We soon heard that our troops had been attacked by a large force of Chinese militia and braves who had nearly cut off a party of the 27th [Madras] Native Infantry who had lost their way and got their powder wet, as they had only the old flint muskets. They were rescued by the Royal Marines who had gone out to look for them. In these affairs we lost many officers and men. This affair happened against the orders of the Chinese authorities who apologised and said it was quite a mistake of the country people. They had paid 5 million dollars of the ransom and satisfactory security for the other million and we shall soon drop down the river again.

Mon. 31st In afternoon our party of the 18th came back from the camp. They had sad accounts of killed and wounded. The latter were put on board one of the hired transports, the *Allalivia*,[6] which is converted into a hospital. I went on board her to see the wounded. Amongst them a case of tetanus from a trifling wound of the foot. Captain Sargent shot through the arm – I extracted a large gingall-ball from under the shoulder-blade of a soldier. There have been many deaths from sunstroke.

[6] *Allalivia*: Cree's handwriting here is hard to decipher, an alternative spelling – *Allalivie* – occurring later. No trace of this vessel has been found in shipping indexes of the period, nor in various other sources consulted.

JUNE

Tue. 1st Visited the hospital ship again. The case of tetanus terminated fatally and the man from whom I extracted the ball is showing symptoms of tetanus and died this day and we have a lot of men sick with fever and diarrhoea.

Thur. 3rd Weighed at 6 to proceed down the river – thank God! – as sickness is on the increase and the wounded are not doing well.

9 a.m. got aground on a mudflat at low water, but floated again when the tide rose. Went to the *Allalivia* to see the wounded and sick. Weighed in afternoon and in evening anchored near the *Blenheim*.

Fri. 4th Weighed at 6 a.m. but were not able to get far down the river. Anchored abreast of a large village.

Macao

Sat. 5th Weighed at 5 a.m. and got ashore on the second bar. By 9 p.m. we were almost on our broadside. We righted again and got off at midnight. The *Nimrod* is going to Calcutta with dispatches – Captain Grattan going in her with the military dispatches and Captain Barlow to England with the naval. No one expects the ransoming of Canton to bring the Chinese Government to terms, but we expect to get some prize-money out of it.

Sun. 6th Passed through the Bocca Tigris in afternoon.

Wed. 9th Anchored in Macao Roads, but a long way out so that it will take a long time to go on shore – 8 miles.

Fri. 11th . . . I went to see poor Lord Edward Clinton who is staying at this hotel [Smith's, Macao] having been wounded in the knee at Canton. He is a lieutenant of the *Modeste*. I had known him before, in the Mediterranean. The ball had lodged in the knee joint, but had been extracted. There was great inflammation. I saw him with Allen, the Surgeon of Macao Hospital who is attending him and wished to consult him with me about him. There is no doubt amputation ought to have been performed, but I believe he would not consent to it. He has much fever and is labouring under great nervous shock. The poor fellow died two days after I saw him. I also went to see Kendall of the *Nimrod* who is here and recovering from his amputated leg.

Hong Kong

Mon. 14th Weighed and sailed for Hong Kong, where we arrived about noon. Half the ship's company on the sick list with fever (intermittent). Poor old Brodie very ill, but he would get up to work the ship, and even went aboard the flagship to report himself to the senior officer. On his return took to his bed, from which he never rose. I was just able to crawl into his cabin to see him and give him some medicine.[7] All the ships at Hong Kong had their flags half-mast as Sir Fleming Senhouse, Captain of H.M.S. *Blenheim*, had just died of fever. He was senior officer at Hong Kong; I had met him a few days before at Canton looking quite well.

[7] For two days Cree had been suffering from fever.

Tue. 15th Had a severe attack of ague. The Commander no better. The Boatswain very bad with fever, unable to do duty.

Thur. 17th Soon after daylight James Brodie came to tell me that his father was delirious, so I crawled out of bed and into his cabin, and found the poor old Commander shouting violently and apparently shortening sail in the midst of a storm. I was too ill to do anything for him and sent for Robertson [Assistant Surgeon of *Hyacinth*]. Soon afterwards he became comatose and the fine old sailor and good-hearted man breathed his last.

Fri. 18th Poor old Brodie was buried in the afternoon in the new cemetery in "Happy Valley", Hong Kong. He was much respected by both Navy and Army and large numbers followed him to his grave.

Sir Gordon Bremer arrived from Calcutta in the *Queen* steamer as Commodore.

Sat. 19th Another friend of mine, Wilson, Adjutant of 18th Regiment, has just died of remittent fever soon after arriving from Canton, on board *Futty Salaam* transport. Many men of the 18th Regiment have also died; many of the wounded from tetanus. Many a gallant fellow who escaped in the field has succumbed to disease. I was able to return to duty.

Sun. 20th Poor Wilson was buried in "Happy Valley" near Commander Brodie.

Mon. 21st Half our ship's company laid up with fever.

Tue. 22nd Mr Sprent, Master of H.M.S. *Wellesley*, was appointed in command of H.M.S. *Rattlesnake* and came on board and joined.

On July 21st a typhoon of exceptional force strikes Hong Kong, inflicting much damage upon the ships anchored there – the transport *Prince George* and others are made total wrecks, and *Rattlesnake* is badly mauled. A less severe typhoon follows on July 26th.

"Happy Valley", Hong Kong

The typhoon of July 21st 1841, Hong Kong

AUGUST

Mon. 2nd Captain Elliot the Plenipotentiary has gone to Canton to confer with the new Chinese Commissioner, who would not receive the Plenipo. They are staking the river again.

Tue. 10th Sir William Parker[B] has arrived as Commander-in-Chief in the Indian steamer *Sesostris* and hoisted his flag in the *Blenheim* and was saluted by the *Wellesley* at daylight.

Colonel Pottinger[B] has arrived from India as Plenipotentiary.[8]

Sat. 14th The General in command of the troops came on board and told me I was to have medical charge of the soldiers sent on board and was to receive the Indian allowance for them. Afterwards I received a visit from Dr Grant of the Madras Artillery, who said I should receive 250 rupees a month allowance in addition to my naval pay.

Admiral Sir William Parker came on board and informed us we were to go to the north with the expedition.

[8] Sir Henry Pottinger had been appointed in place of Charles Elliot, whose pacific, and somewhat parochial, attitude towards the Chinese, had set him increasingly at odds with British Government policy. Elliot had become obsessed with Canton and its attendant problems, which he saw as a microcosm of China, a viewpoint that was not shared, it seems, either by the all-powerful, and Peking-orientated, Emperor, or by Whitehall.

On August 21st the fleet sets sail for Amoy, upon which an attack is launched on the 26th with broadsides from *Wellesley* and *Blenheim*. It takes two to three hours to silence the Chinese batteries. Forty guns are taken and 2,000 Chinese are killed, the general commanding the batteries and all his suite dying at their posts. The batteries are then blown up with their own gunpowder and the dockyard destroyed. The fleet departs for the Chusan Islands on September 6th, arriving there on September 25th.

Chusan

OCTOBER

Fri. 1st A signal from the Admiral last night "Troops to hold themselves in readiness to land at 8 a.m.". Accordingly the *Phlegethon* steamer came alongside at 8 and our troops marched on board and our boats took part of the 55th [Westmoreland] Regiment. All the other boats of the fleet took the troops from the transports. In the meantime the ships kept up a brisk fire with shot and shell and rockets amongst the Chinese troops crowding the hills and batteries, which returned our fire in very gallant style. It was near 11 a.m. before we landed the 55th Regiment on the point under a heavy fire from the matchlocks and gingalls of the Tartar troops as well as round shot from the battery there. The 55th soon formed on the beach and poured in their steady volleys, but the enemy stood the fire well and only retreated slowly up the hill as our fellows advanced on them with the bayonet. All the troops were landed at this point while the howitzer battery kept up a fire from Trumball Island on to Josshouse Hill, which had been strongly fortified.

The second taking of Chusan, October 1st 1841

The Tartar soldiers crowded the top of the hill and fired briskly from amongst the little fir plantation, but our men gradually forced them back in spite of a couple of Tartar officers' waving red-and-blue flags. One of them was soon knocked over and a shot struck the earth in front of the other and covered him with dust, but he only shook himself and waved his flag again when a shell from the *Phlegethon* struck him right in the middle and burst amongst his fated followers, who were blown in all directions. Our soldiers drove the enemy along the top of the hill to the signal towers where they made another stand and a few sallies from each of the three towers, till the steady advance of our men dislodged them, then they took to their heels down the hill towards the town as hard as they could under a withering fire, leaving many dead and wounded on the field.

In the meantime the 18th Royal Irish advanced round the bottom of the hill and took the long beach battery in flank which at first was hotly defended by the Tartars [who] made many rushes at our men till they saw their countrymen running down the hill, driven by the 55th. They then took to their heels and the 18th rushed on to the fort on Josshouse Hill, which they found deserted as they had been shelled at by the artillery on Trumball Island and the ships. The Chinese had kept firing nearly all last night on the men working at the howitzer battery, none of whom were hit.

As we were landing the troops, the round shot and grape from the battery and from matchlocks and gingalls fell thick about us and a few of the men were wounded and poor Ensign Duell was shot dead while carrying one of the colours of the 55th Regiment soon after landing – and many of the men were badly wounded in the advances up the hill. Three of the 18th soon fell in the advance along the battery and I brought them off to the ship which was lying close to and attended to them, and afterwards a number of other wounded were brought off. I had all the cots I could muster slung on the main deck, quite a large hospital.

The 18th then advanced to the south gate of the town which the Chinese were barricading, but the Royal Irish were too quick for the Celestials. The 55th took the north gate, where there was another fight which did not last long and the Chinese fled in all directions leaving some number of dead and wounded, principally on the hill and long battery.

Sat. 2nd Amongst the wounded under my care: Private Gorman, gunshot in left eye, which was knocked out and the ball had passed downwards behind the lower jaw – insensible; Sergeant Murphy, gunshot through calf of leg, a large gingall-ball; Privates, stabs in left side, wounding lung, from one of the short swords – two dreadfully burnt from an explosion. Captain Wigston had

The fight at the signal towers

The vale and city of Chusan (Tinghai) from 49th Hill, scene of the principal battle on October 1st

a narrow escape but he pistoled a fellow who was making a lunge at him with a spear. Sir Hugh Gough was struck in the shoulder by a spent ball. The 55th Regiment have seventeen wounded and one officer killed. All the 18th wounded are under my care on board, as both their medical officers, McKinlay and Maclean, are gone on to Singkong with the regiment.

On October 10th Chinhai, a strongly fortified town at the entrance to the Ningpo River, is captured – 130 brass guns and a large number of unfinished ones being taken, as well as considerable quantities of brass and copper in the foundry. After the onslaught, 1,500 Chinese lie dead in the field in addition to those drowned in the river and killed in explosions. Cree learns that Ningpo itself surrendered on October 15th without a shot fired, £5,000 in sycee silver and £10,000 in brass coins being taken. On October 18th cholera breaks out among the troops at Chusan.

DECEMBER

Sun. 12th An opium clipper arrived from Hong Kong with accounts of the loss of the *Madagascar*, E.I.Co. [East India Company] steamer, which was burnt at sea between Hong Kong and Amoy, the crew saved but taken prisoner by the Chinese. As she was bringing up the mail I fear I have lost my letters and I have not received any since May last.

Mon. 13th–Thur. 16th Our men were snowballing on deck. The poor Indians in the expedition with their light clothing feel this weather and are quite afraid to touch the snow as it "bites" them, but their prejudices prevent them from putting on warm clothes and they persist in going about half naked, wrapped up in a white sheet, which shows off their black faces and limbs, now looking green and blue.[9]

Fri. 17th The hills are all covered with snow.

Thur. 23rd J.B. [Brodie] and I landed to shoot swans, which we found on a mudflat in a shallow lake about 6 miles inland, near Sinkong. I managed to shoot one wild swan with ball and three wild ducks. We passed through some pretty country and went into a butcher's shop where we got some pork chops and some sweet potatoes which the butcher's wife cooked for us and attracted a crowd of natives to see us eat. We hired a Chinaman to carry our game.

Sat. 25th Xmas Day. No roast beef or plum pudding, but we managed to get some roast pork and plain pudding and were as merry as possible under the circumstances. H.M. Brig *Algerine* arrived from Amoy after thirty days' beating up the coast, battened down most of the time.

[9] Cold weather was not the only thing that afflicted the Indian troops. The majority of them were high-caste Hindus and forbidden by their faith from eating the food aboard ship, and their basic diet of peas and rice proved to be no safeguard against dysentery. By contrast, sickness among Muslims serving in China was minimal.

Swan shooting on Chusan, natives shrimping

Sun. 26th At Amoy they expect to be attacked by the Chinese, who have sent down fire-rafts. One of the 18th there deserted to the Chinese and took some muskets and rockets with him, but the Chinese flogged him and brought him back under an escort of matchlock men with a message to say they did not want deserters as we did, seeing we had Chinamen serving in the *Wellesley*.

In Chusan on January 18th 1842 Cree learns that General Gough has recommended him to the notice of Admiral Parker for promotion for his services to the sick and wounded soldiers. In the succeeding months *Rattlesnake* visits Hong Kong, Singapore and Trincomalee. On arriving at Hong Kong in May, Cree hears of surprise attacks made on March 9th by the Chinese on Ningpo and Chinhai, and of counter-attacks on the Chinese army, a force of 8,000 Chinese being defeated at Tsikie, some 15 miles NW of Ningpo. On May 18th the garrison of Chapu, NW of Chinhai, is taken by the British. *Rattlesnake* now proceeds via the Chusan Islands to the Yangtse. On June 16th Woosung is captured, Shanghai being evacuated by the Chinese shortly afterwards.

1842

Golden Island

Yangtse Kiang River/Chin-kiang-foo

JULY

Wed. 20th Weighed at daylight and proceeded. The river begins to narrow and is divided into numerous channels by beautiful islands. The banks are more hilly and still rich in cultivation. Such a large fleet of ships crowding up the river makes a fine and imposing sight – something new for "the heathen Chinee" – but many of the ships get aground in the numerous windings of the stream. At a sudden bend of the river to the west we came in sight of the line-of-battle ships and steamers at anchorage near a large walled city – Chin-kiang-foo. At this point is a beautiful wooded island, covered with pagodas – Silver Island [Seung-shan] – a steep rock with deep passage for ships on each side, 14 or 15 fathoms, and two picturesque rocks beyond – and beyond again the fairy-like Golden Island [Kinshan] in the centre of the river with its tall pagoda on the top and its sides covered with temples, gardens and trees, the walled city of Chin-kiang on the left hand and high blue mountains beyond. Farther up the river is the entrance of the Grand Canal. The whole makes a beautiful picture – the noble river, beautiful islands and pagodas.

We anchored astern of the flagship near Golden Island and abreast of the city, about 11 a.m. I went with Sprent in his boat to the flagship and was introduced to the Surgeon, Dr King, and dined with him, and after dinner we three went to explore Golden Island. . . .

Thur. 21st Our force assembled here in the Yangtse Kiang consists of about 12,000 fighting men – 9,000 soldiers including Marines; the Naval Brigade in the men-of-war, about 3,000 sailors.

A reconnaissance was made by the General, Sir Hugh Gough, from some hills which overlooked the city which appeared as if deserted, as perfect stillness prevailed throughout the town – no guards on the ramparts, no troops collecting in the open spaces, but on some low hills to the south two considerable entrenched camps were seen, and also a few white tents on a part of the city walls. All appeared silent and it was thought there would be no opposition. No Chinese were to be seen at the landing-places.

Major-General Schoedde's[B] brigade was to land under cover of some steep hills to the left of the town and take post within gunshot of the walls. Major-General Bartley's[B] column was to land on the right, and Lord Saltoun's[B] brigade was also to land on the right, opposite Golden Island – and intended to attack the entrenched camps. The landing, however, was very irregular, and orders appear to have been misunderstood, but it was effected without accident and the Chinese did not take the advantage they might. Sir Hugh Gough with his staff ascended the heights overlooking the city on the right. The brigades commenced their movements about 8 a.m. The morning sun shone down upon the long and glittering columns, their colours unfurled all looking very bright and gay.

General Schoedde established a rocket battery on the hill to the left and the *Auckland* steamer threw shells into the NE corner of the city. Lt-Colonel Knowles, R.A., advanced with his field pieces within 300 yards of the wall and the rifle company kept up a fire at the loopholes and embrasures while the scaling-ladders were brought and placed against the walls.

The troops began to land at daylight in five divisions. It was noon before ours were on shore. They were taken on shore by the steamers. No enemy opposed their landing and we began to think there would be no fighting. It was a frightfully hot and sultry day, therm. 97° and no wind. The different divisions marched on different parts of the city. The firing commenced about 8 o'clock by the advanced skirmishers of Lord Saltoun's brigade marching against the entrenched camp, which opened fire with round shot and grape, which was effectively returned by Major Anstruther's field pieces.

The steady advance of the 98th Regiment, the Sappers and 41st Madras N.I. [Native Infantry] was too terrible for the Imperial troops, who soon wavered and fled, although many of the mandarins on horseback tried to rally them. But the sun was more formidable than the Chinese troops, for thirteen men of the 98th Regiment dropped in the ranks from sunstroke and expired before night. Others had to fall out, but recovered.

The enemy now opened with round and grapeshot against General Schoedde's post, but they were so occupied that they did not appear to notice the scaling-ladders which the men were now climbing up as fast as they could. The storming party consisted of the grenadiers of the 55th Regiment under

Chin-kiang-foo: Lord Saltoun's brigade landing opposite Golden Island

The taking of Chin-kiang-foo, July 21st 1842

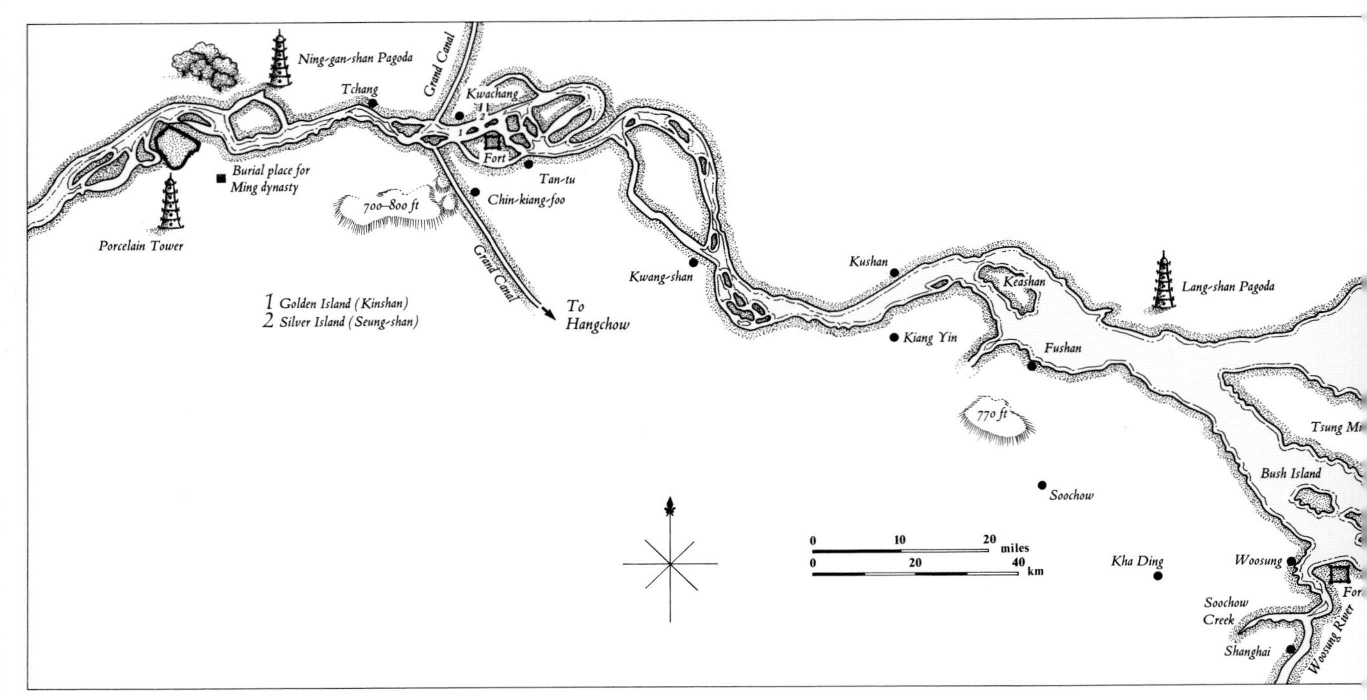

The Yangtse Kiang from the sea to Nanking

Captain Maclean. —— Murphy [?] dropped down from sunstroke after he had ascended the wall. There were only three ladders but a considerable number of the 55th Regiment and 6th N.I. had got up before the Tartars saw them, so effectively had the covering party occupied their attention. When they were seen there was a desperate fight as the Tartars rushed against them with great fury and from the gardens below a galling fire. Many of our men dropped, but at last they forced the Tartars back to one of the guardhouses, which had to be cleared at the point of the bayonet. General Schoedde had managed to get the gateway open, through which the 2nd Regiment N.I. rushed – but the Tartars still fought desperately and were only forced back inch by inch, a number of men falling on both sides. At last, after the 2nd N.I. was admitted – the gates had been opened by one man after a desperate resistance – the Tartars defending it being nearly all bayoneted.

After our men were joined by the 2nd N.I. they forced their way along to the west gate, when the 18th and 49th [Princess Charlotte of Wales's or the Hertfordshire] Regiments were engaged with the enemy and preparing to blow it open from the outside. Lieutenants Heriot and Johnston and a party of the 55th Regiment had got down to the inner gate which they found barricaded with sandbags, which they removed after great exertion. But in attempting to remove the sandbags from the outer gate they found they could not, and not hearing any firing on the outside thought the 18th and 49th Regiments had gone to some other point. Fortunately they did so, for directly they had retired from the gate a tremendous flash and explosion took place,

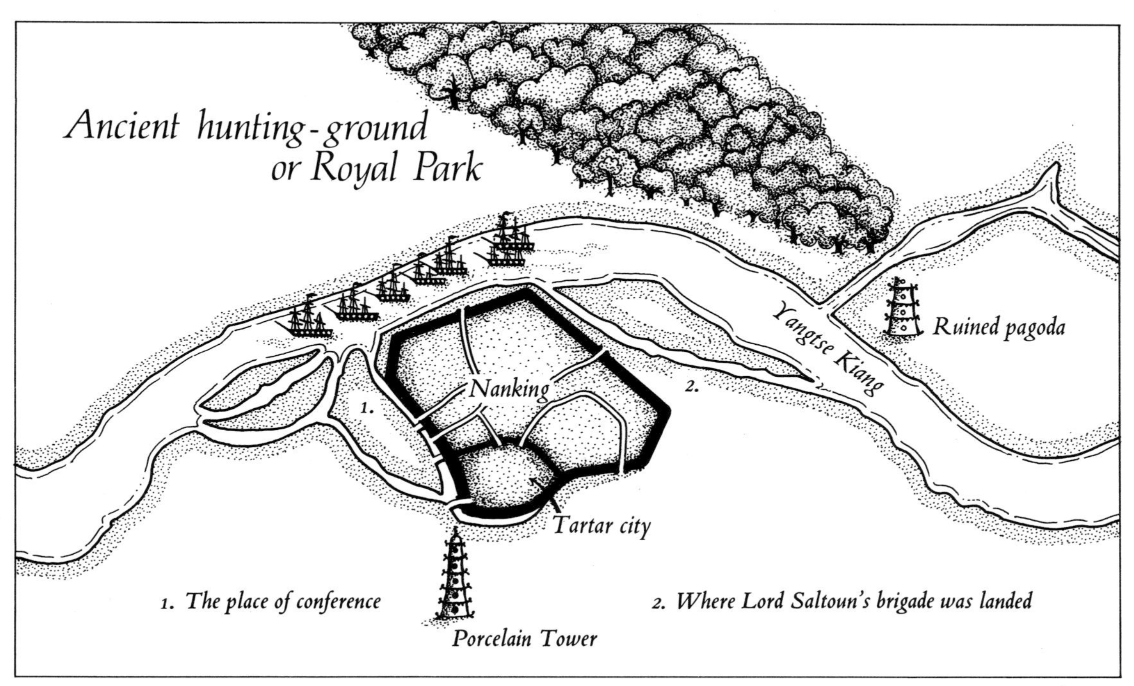

Plan of Nanking (*after a sketch by E. H. Cree*)

blowing up the gateway and guardhouse over it, and the 18th and 49th rushed in to meet their friends. The enemy defending it had nearly all been killed.

The 3rd Brigade, under General Bartley, had landed on the west side of the city, near where Lord Saltoun's brigade landed. They were joined by Sir Hugh Gough and directed their course towards the west gate of the city which they reached through a suburb outside the walls and crossed the south canal by a bridge [and] were able to clear the parapets on each side of the gateway.

In the meantime four field pieces with a detachment of Artillery had come up the canal in two of the boats of the *Blonde* with Major Blundell, a strong

Blowing open the west gate

current sweeping them up to near the bridge when they were exposed to the fire from the walls, where every embrasure and loophole sent forth a shower of balls which soon disabled many of the men, and obliged the others to seek safety. One boat got under the bridge while the other ran on shore not a pistol-shot from the walls. After getting the wounded out of the boats they took their shelter amongst the houses on the bank. The Admiral, hearing of the disaster, dispatched armed boats with Marines from the flagship *Cornwallis*.

It was noon when Captain Pears, the Chief Engineer, heading a party of Sappers, carried the powder-bags containing 160 pounds of powder across the stone bridge under cover of a rapid discharge of musketry from the 18th and 49th Regiments, and placed the powder-bags against the gates, leaving the fuse burning. The explosion was most successful, blowing the gates in, off their hinges, for several feet. The 18th and 49th marched in through the blinding smoke and dust, met friends instead of expected enemies on the inside.

In the meantime the boats from the *Cornwallis* had brought a scaling-ladder, which they put up against the right flank of the gateway bastion. The first man, a Marine, who ascended was shot through the head and others who followed were wounded. They made a lodgement in the ramparts. The gallant remnant of the enemy, refusing to surrender or accept quarter, perished by ball or bayonet.

The 2nd and 3rd Brigades were directed to take post at the city gates and occupy such quarters as were available. The heat was terrible and now that the excitement was over many of the veteran soldiers were unable to bear it any longer. Even Sir Hugh Gough was compelled to seek shelter and lie down.

All the work inside the city seemed over for the day, when a heavy volley, followed by considerable popping of musketry, was heard, which turned out to be the last volley of the unfortunate Garrison of Chin-kiang-foo, who meant to die in defence of their houses and country. It seems they had been driven from the walls and gates, had assembled in the public buildings and barracks in the centre of the city, where their general had harangued them, and exhorted them to die for their country rather than submit to the hated Barbarians. They had first rushed into their homes and slaughtered their wives and children, then joined their general to fight to the last man. It seems that the 18th and 49th Regiments had been directed to make a circuit of the walls, and were going past some garden ground, when, after some shots from the neighbouring houses, the unlooked-for foe suddenly emerged from one of the streets and poured a volley into the exposed flanks of the regiments, killing and wounding two officers and many of the men. After the exchange of a few more volleys our men charged down the slope of the rampart and engaged in a close and savage contest. The grenadiers of the 18th were furious at the loss of a favourite officer, Captain Collinson, who was shot dead on the rampart

"The last stand of the Tartars"

"A chamber of horrors"

just before, made great havoc amongst the Tartars, who fled into the intricate streets, but only to commit suicide, as was found afterwards.

Everything was soon quiet and guards placed at most of the gates.

Fri. 22nd There were many alarms during the night, from many of the survivors escaping over the walls, and from plundering Chinese about amongst the houses, and some desperate rushes made upon sentries and guards by Tartar soldiers, who had secured themselves in the houses and were killed by our enraged soldiers. Some encounters took place inside the houses, where our men had been quartered, at discovering a Tartar soldier or two hidden away.

There were shocking sights in the city, which was now almost a ruin, its ramparts and streets encumbered by the bodies of the slain, the wounded and dying, its finest buildings destroyed, as there had been many fires in the night – beautiful shops and houses gutted by the Chinese marauders, who flocked into the city notwithstanding numbers were shot down by our soldiers. The south-eastern gate had no guard during the night and many marauders and fugitives passed in and out through it. I have no doubt much of plunder went out of the city that way, as the Chinese are most expert and desperate plunderers.

Armed parties were sent out at daybreak to patrol the Tartar quarter and search for concealed soldiers and destroy the arsenals and military stores and fatigue parties to bury the dead, which already from the heat were beginning

Street scene, Chin-kiang-foo, after the battle

to give out an unpleasant smell. Frightful scenes were witnessed among the houses; whole families were slaughtered in their own homes by their own people in the streets occupied by the Tartar troops and mandarins – little children, some still breathing and writhing in agony with a broken spine or a stab. In one house seven dead or dying persons were found in one room. In another house an old man, probably an old retainer endeavouring to tend two dying children, both with their spines broken. The poor old fellow was weeping bitterly but would not say who committed the shocking barbarity. On a bed near lay the body of a beautiful young woman, quite cold and dead, her neck covered by a silk scarf to hide a terrible gash in her throat, and near her the body of an older woman stretched on a silk coverlet, with her features distorted as if she had died by strangulation. A dead child, stabbed through the neck, lay near her, and in the veranda were the corpses of two more women suspended from the rafters by twisted clothes, both young, one quite a girl who was said to be quite lovely notwithstanding her distorted features. These were only a sample of the horrors to be witnessed in the devoted city.

I was unable to leave the ship today as I had many sick and wounded to attend to. Captain Collinson, who only left us yesterday morning in high spirits, is amongst the killed from a shot through the heart. Lieutenant Bernard was brought on board with thirteen of the 18th men wounded. The 98th lost many from sunstroke and shot, and many of the sailors. Major Uniacke, R.M., H.M.S. *Cornwallis*, dropped dead from sunstroke. Colonel Stevens, killed – and many others I have not yet heard of.

I fancy we might [have] shelled the enemy out of Chin-kiang from the ships, without such a sacrifice of our own men. Besides, the men in one regiment were kept standing in the sun buttoned up to their throats with stiff leather stocks and heavy shakos, three days' provisions and sixty rounds of ammunition, till a dozen of them dropped in the ranks from sunstroke. Major Colin Campbell[B] is considered a good old soldier, but I think he did not consider the risk he ran in exposing his men when shelter might have been had for them.

Sat. 23rd I went up with the Commander to view the scene of our victory at Chin-kiang. We rowed up the canal as far as the west gate, the scene of the grand explosion, a terrible scene of ruin, all the houses round smashed and the city gate and guardhouse above, which the Tartars so hotly defended, a smoking ruin. We met a party of women coming out in terrible fright – the unfortunate wives and daughters who had escaped slaughter. They fell down on their knees to us as they passed and knocked their foreheads against the ground. The walls were higher and thicker than in any Chinese city I have visited, but I did not see any large guns, but plenty of the man-destructive gingalls. We went up to where Captain Wigston and the grenadiers of the 18th were stationed, in a barrack on a rising ground near the wall. We saw

Nanking from the Porcelain Tower

some shocking sights around, whole families lying drowned in the ponds and wells near; others murdered and lying in the ditches and pools of water. It is reported that in the more remote parts of the city murder and suicide are still being perpetrated, but our men are not allowed to roam about the streets.

The number of dead still lying about are already creating a great stench, but our people are burying them as fast as they can. Many of the Tartar soldiers are supposed to be still lurking in the city and they and Chinese plunderers render it unsafe to go about without an escort. I missed my escort and had to go a mile to the next guard alone, which I did not relish although I carried loaded pistols and my sword. I was glad enough to hear the challenge of the next sentry. It was now dark and some of the houses were still on fire and threw a lurid kind of light over the place. The city is very extensive and the plundering has been considerable. Silk dresses and furs are lying about the streets – sycee silver in lumps, watches and other valuables have found their way into the possession of the soldiers. A good many timepieces and other things of Dutch and French manufacture were found. The women are better looking and fairer than those at Chusan and many have natural sized feet, not crippled as at Chusan, "the lily feet". The dresses found were all very handsome, embroidered silk cloaks, &c. At the gates we found a number of Chinese selling fruit and vegetables, showing the confidence they have in the English.

Our loss in killed is estimated at 200, but I never knew of so many deaths from sunstroke in one day. The enemy's loss is reckoned at 2,000 out of 5,000 said to have been engaged. The *Blonde* frigate had a good many of her men wounded in the boats in the canal.

We had an escort down to our boat, of a corporal and three men, and got off to the ship about 8 p.m.

Sun. 24th The city still in flames in three or four places. Empty junks and rafts continue to float down the river as well as numbers of bloated dead bodies – such are some of the horrors of war.

Fri. 29th We embarked our troops again this morning, preparing to sail for Nanking. The April mail arrived. I received welcome letters from Father and Sister and wrote back, as the mail will be made up today.

Sat. 30th H.M. Troop-ship *Sapphire* arrived from Amoy – Cole, Master-Commanding, died on the passage.

AUGUST *Fri. 5th* Got under weigh, but the wind failing were soon obliged to anchor again near the opening of the northern portion of the Grand Canal – the southern entrance is close by Chin-kiang-foo. There seems to be a large town at the northern entrance. The country flat and well cultivated, with villages in plenty. The river is about a mile and a half wide. Of course we have

The outer wall of Nanking from the mast-head of *Rattlesnake*

blockaded the canal and stopped the supplies going through to Pekin. Depth of water here 20 fathoms – stream 4 knots.

Sun. 7th . . . The country gets more hilly on both sides of the river and a very pretty country in the distance rising into mountains. We passed some large villages and Tchang, a large town on the north bank with the usual ornament, a tall pagoda. Many of the hills are surmounted by a pagoda, a josshouse, or a fort. The river winds much, is a wide and noble stream. Pass many low islands covered with tall reeds which grow out into quite deep water, the whole way along a sight of high civilisation and wealth, but with such bigoted rulers and fossilised customs they have neglected to provide effectively for their own defence. Most of the people appear to have deserted their houses near the river. We only see an occasional boat; most of the junks are deserted; all silent and sad where there must have been once the bustle of an extensive commerce.

We anchored for the night where, from the mast-head, I could just see the top of the Porcelain Tower and part of the walls of Nanking.

Off Nanking

Wed. 10th Nanking is about 250 miles from the sea. The river here is wide, like a lake, but still deep and swift. On the northern shore is the Royal Hunting Ground of the emperors of the Ming dynasty, a fine large park walled round, said to be filled with game. It is hilly and well wooded.

Thur. 11th The outer wall of Nanking appears in this part only about 30 yards from the river bank, and on it are displayed some white flags, which looks as if peace was sought for. We can see tents and soldiers within the wall and sandbag batteries, but no other hostile demonstrations.

Fri. 12th That fellow "Corporal White", who has now mounted a white button on his hat, attempted a visit to the Plenipo on board the *Queen* steamer but he was refused admittance. Then he tried the Admiral on board *Cornwallis*, but they sent him off. The ships hauled into station to commence firing to breach the outer wall abreast of them but a blue button mandarin, said to be the Tartar general commanding at Nanking, came off escorted by the everlasting Corporal White, so the Plenipo refused to receive him.

Sat. 13th The report is that the Imperial Commissioners have arrived at Nanking empowered to offer terms to the "Intelligent Nation", no longer Barbarians, as the Emperor has said after his continued defeats that he must "bow gracefully to the storm", so we have some hope that this wretched war will soon be brought to a conclusion.

On Wednesday last the flagship *Cornwallis, Blonde* and steam vessels ranged themselves close inshore, ready to breach the wall with their broadsides, the *Blonde* up a branch of the river close to the wall on the north side, very narrow but deep – the frigate looks as if she was planted in the field. Near this the 98th Regiment, flank companies of the 55th and two Indian regiments and some Artillery and Riflemen were landed. The 26th were landed lower down. The 18th and 49th were to have landed in the breach intended to be made today by the ships.

All warlike proceedings are stopped for the present and negotiations have commenced and the talk is of peace. Davidson, Assistant Surgeon of the *Starling*, came to see me and I went to dine with him on board the little schooner [cutter]. She lies so near the shore that one could almost step from her side into the field, yet one lies in 10 fathoms of water. The country people about say that there is no Chinese army outside the walls of Nanking but all the Tartar troops with some cavalry are stationed inside the city. Lord Saltoun has established his headquarters at a large village outside the northern wall, Makin Keow, where they found some extensive farm buildings and rich mandarins' houses and stabling for the ponies of the Madras Artillery. These ponies were captured at Chin-kiang and have proved very useful. Some of the men came upon a warehouse full of raw silk and, not knowing what it was, used it for swabs to clean out their quarters and even for litter in the stables till they found the ponies got into such a tangle that they could not extricate their legs and it was found they had destroyed hundreds of pounds' worth of raw silk.

Nanking

Sun. 14th A formidable park of artillery was landed yesterday, of various calibre and description, in the event of the Chinese Commissioners' not agreeing to our terms. A troop of Horse Artillery from Madras has also been landed from one of the transports, which is quite near to the Celestials. Plenty of fodder has been found for the horses at Makin Keow and the horses are in capital condition considering they have been so long on board ship.

All these warlike preparations have quietened the movements of the Chinese. A mandarin came at night to the bank of the river abreast of the *Queen* steamer and was heard to hail in accents of distress. A boat was sent, which took him on board, when it was found he came to beg the High Officers to delay any attack on Nanking as the Emperor's Commissioners were on their way to offer terms of peace.

Mon. 15th Negotiations still going on between Sir Henry Pottinger and the Chinese Commissioners, Eleepoo [I-li-pu, Viceroy of Chekiang] and

Keying [Ch'i-ying]. They have met in a building outside the walls of Nanking. Another Commissioner, New, said to be a near relative of the Emperor, whose name in English is bullock, and looks a heavy sort of fellow resembling that animal.

Thur. 18th Great distress is said to prevail in all the northern districts of China from our stopping the supplies on the Grand Canal and there is great exasperation against the mandarins.

Fri. 19th The Chinese Secretary is Yang, an intelligent Chinaman. An order has gone out from the Plenipotentiary with respect to kind treatment of the Chinese now negotiations for peace are going on.

Sat. 20th Great day on board the flagship, where there was a meeting of the Plenipo, Admiral and General with the Chinese Imperial Commissioners and their suite. First Sir Henry Pottinger was received under a salute of fifteen guns. Soon after, a string of barges came down the canal from the city gate, one flying the Imperial Ensign, a yellow flag with black characters on it and a red border. The other boats had white flags of truce, except the military. The *Medusa* steamer was waiting to embark them. They were received on board the flagship under a salute of three guns, which is the usual Chinese one for a great man. Eleepoo, who appears to be an infirm old man, had to be helped up the accommodation ladder. They were met on the quarterdeck by the Admiral and General and principal officers in full uniform. A guard of Marines presented arms as Eleepoo stepped on the deck. The Plenipo was in his official uniform of blue embroidered in gold and met the High Commissioners half-way on the quarterdeck. There was a large retinue of mandarins and also a crowd of naval and military officers in full uniform on the poop. Eleepoo had on a blue dress, a red sash and coral button in his conical straw hat. The Emperor's relative wore a blue crape dress, a yellow sash and red coral button. The General of the Tartar army wore a yellow crape coat, a peacock's feather. The "bullock" had a two-eyed peacock's feather. The everlasting "Corporal White" was in the suite. Then came mandarins of all classes of buttons, red, blue and white.

The Chief went into the Admiral's cabin to talk and refresh, Mr Morrison being the interpreter. The other mandarins, some in the wardroom and some in the gunroom, were regaled with cherry brandy, wine, and rum with brown sugar, till some of them were not over-steady. They were taken round the main and lower decks and were surprised at the number and size of the guns. Eleepoo wished to examine one of the officer's swords, so Lieutenant Fitzjames handed his, which Eleepoo in bending to test the steel, it broke, so he would not think much of the English swords.

After staying a couple of hours they again embarked in the Admiral's barge and the other boats and were rowed back to the entrance of the canal, where they again went into their own barges and junks and we lost sight of them. I have no doubt they were glad it was over, for on first coming on board they appeared a little nervous. All the time they were on board the ship the city wall was crowded with natives. It was their own proposition to visit the Plenipo on board the ship.

Mon. 22nd Eleepoo and the other mandarins were to have received the Plenipo and British officers on shore, but the day has turned out so bad that the visit has been put off. I had to go to the flagship in answer to a signal about returns of sick since we have been in the Yangtse Kiang, which has been something terrible. I found Dr King in the sick-bay up to his eyes in business as Stanley his assistant is ill and the other is lent to another ship.

Wed. 24th About 8 a.m. we sent a guard of honour, consisting of the grenadier company of the 18th Regiment and officers, under the command of Captain Wigston, to the meeting-place of the Imperial and British officers – a return visit of ceremony. I went with the 18th officers first to the *Blonde* frigate where we all assembled, from there to the creek leading to the city gate. No small difficulty in getting the boats over a number of sunken junks, over which the stream was rushing in fury, although the seamen had been making a passage during the last week. We landed at a wharf under a sort of wooden ornamental gateway and marched up a dirty street in a suburb, following our leaders into a large josshouse on the opposite side of the canal to the city. Here we were met by a number of the inferior mandarins and showed into a large courtyard, where was a guard of Tartar soldiers, unarmed and drawn up in two diagonal lines. They were fine, dark, weather-beaten men with foxes' or squirrels' tails in their caps and every fifth man an officer with a banner. We then passed through another gateway, in which were colossal figures of Chinese gods, into a second court where our British grenadiers of the 18th Regiment were drawn up on each side of the pathway, their clean arms and bayonets glittering in the sun, looking very fit for army service, their band in white playing "St Patrick's Day". The Chinese had two or three bands, not musical but something like asthmatical bagpipes. At the end of this second court we ascended two or three steps and entered a large hall, at the end of which was the presence chamber which was crowded with officers both naval and military in full dress. In the centre was a table covered with fruits, preserves, wines, tea, &c., which were constantly handed round by the inferior mandarins. At the head of the room, in an armchair, sat the Plenipo, Sir Henry Pottinger, on his right the General Sir Hugh Gough, and on his left Admiral Sir William Parker. On the General's right sat Eleepoo, the Chief Commissioner, and on the Admiral's left Ki Quang [Ch'i Kwang], the Emperor's uncle, and next to him New King [Niew-kien], the Governor of

Landing-place at Nanking

The Chinese Commissioners receiving the British officers

Reception of the Chinese Commissioners for the British Plenipotentiary, Sir Henry Pottinger

1. *Imperial Commissioner Keying (Ch'i-ying)*
2. *Imperial Commissioner Eleepoo (I-li-pu)*
3. *Major-General Sir Hugh Gough*
4. *The Plenipotentiary, Sir Henry Pottinger*
5. *Vice-Admiral Parker*
6. *Ki Quang (Ch'i Kwang)*
7. *New King (Niew-kien)*
8. *Major Anstruther – the "red-headed Barbarian"*
9. *J. R. Morrison, interpreter*
10. *The Reverend Charles Gutzlaff, interpreter*

the Province. Chairs covered with cloth were placed round the room. The floor was covered with red cloth. It formed a glittering scene. Our party shone in scarlet, blue and gold, even eclipsing the mandarins who had on their light summer dresses. A banquet was served in the outer room and refreshment given to the guard in a separate building, while a couple of sentries guarded their piled arms, which the Tartars eyed curiously. The place was crowded with mandarins of all ranks and buttons, who were very civil. We had four interpreters there, Morrison, Gutzlaff, Thorn and Davis.[1] In this hall they have a large model of the Porcelain Tower and some curious josses. Cakes and

[1] On many occasions "these gentlemen [specifically John Morrison and Robert Thom] were personally exposed to the fire of the enemy little less than either soldiers or sailors. They showed the utmost coolness and personal courage. . . . Their knowledge of the language and their good judgement frequently enlisted in our favour the people of the country, who might have offered great annoyance, and they were often able to mitigate the hardships even of war itself". – *The Nemesis in China*, etc., from the notes of Captain W.H. Hall, R.N. and the personal observations of W.D. Bernard, Esq., M.A. Oxon. (London, 1841), p. 139 n.

The grenadier company of the 18th Regiment marching from the conference.

sweetmeats and dishes of unknown composition were handed round with wines and spirit of native composition, some of which tasted pleasant, and little cups of weak tea. There was a good deal of chin-chinning and after a couple of hours the visit ended. The band struck up "The British Grenadiers" and the guard marched down through a double line of Tartar soldiers and ended with "God Save the Queen". We followed, the mandarins accompanying us half-way down the court and then taking leave.

We got to our boats and went down the creek in procession to the river, and then to our respective ships. Junks crowded with natives lined the creek as we passed. Plenty of gay flags were displayed from the houses lining the creek. There are also some fine trees on each side, interspersed among the buildings. I only saw one female: she was looking from one of the large junks and was young and rather pretty.

Thur. 25th H.M.S. *Driver* arrived from England. I received a letter from my sister of March 17th and newspapers.

Fri. 26th The surgeon of H.M.S. *Siren* is dead. Assistant Surgeon Stanley has got his vacancy.

Sat. 27th Sir Henry Pottinger, with a party of Horse Artillery, went into the city by invitation of the Imperial Commissioners. Their Arab horses were greatly admired by the mandarins.

Mon. 29th The treaty of peace was formally signed by the Imperial

Commissioners on board H.M.S. *Cornwallis*. They went on board at 11 a.m. under a salute of three guns. A message from the Emperor saying he agreed to the conditions and would ratify it. A plain yellow flag was hoisted at the main and saluted with twenty-one guns.

The following are the articles of the treaty signed this day:

1. Lasting peace and friendship between the two nations.
2. China to pay twenty-one millions of dollars in the course of the present and three succeeding years.
3. The ports of Canton, Amoy, Foo-chow-foo, Ningpo and Shanghai to be thrown open to British merchants. Consular officers to be appointed to reside in them, and regular and just tariffs of imports and exports, as well as transit duties, to be established and published.
4. The Island of Hong Kong to be ceded in perpetuity to Her Britannic Majesty, her heirs and successors.
5. All subjects of Her Britannic Majesty, whether natives of Europe or India who may be in confinement in any part of the Chinese Empire, to be unconditionally released.
6. An act of full and entire amnesty to be published by the Emperor under his imperial sign-manual and seal, to all Chinese subjects, on account of their having held service or intercourse with or resided under the British Government or its officers.
7. Correspondence to be conducted on terms of perfect equality amongst the officers of both governments.
8. On the Emperor's assent being received to this treaty and the payment of the first six millions, Her Britannic Majesty's forces to retire from Nanking and the Grand Canal and the military post at Chinhai to be withdrawn, but the Islands of Ko-lung-soo and Chusan are to be held till the money payments and the arrangements for opening the ports are completed.

So ends the Chinese war. About the justice and policy of it I leave to more competent judges, but one thing I dislike in connection with it is the opium question. It has cost the lives of many thousands of human beings, and great destruction of property – and misery and sorrow to many.

SEPTEMBER

Sat. 3rd Tired from our exertions and the heat of yesterday.[2] Great sickness in the fleet. We are about the healthiest ship – only 4 sick out of 44. *Blonde* has 199 out of 280, *Bellisle* 110 out of 250, *Sapphire* 47 out of 50 and the others nearly in same proportion intermittent fever and dysentery.

Tue. 6th The ransom money continues to be paid on board the flagship.

Wed. 7th–Mon. 12th The mosquitoes are exceedingly troublesome and venomous and the troops are suffering greatly. The 98th Regiment, who came

[2] Cree had visited the famous Porcelain Tower with a party of officers of the 18th (Royal Irish) Regiment. He appends a note stating that it was destroyed in 1853 in the Taiping Rebellion – a quasi-Christian, agrarian revolt directed against Confucianism and the Manchu Emperor at Peking, which spanned the years 1851–64 and is estimated to have cost between 30 and 50 million Chinese lives.

The Porcelain Tower, Nanking

out in the *Bellisle* 720 strong, have lost 160 more by death and have 430 in hospital. She is the first ship to be sent down the river. All the troops are being re-embarked.

Wed. 14th Birthday of our new friend Tow Quang [Tao Kuang], Emperor of China and Brother of the Sun. All the ships hoisted the yellow flag at the main – the royal standard of China – and at noon fired a royal salute of twenty-one guns.

Thur. 15th A mandarin boat, gaily decked with flags and a great yellow banner with Chinese writing on it, came out of the creek and went alongside the *Queen* steamer with a party of great mandarins who brought the treaty of peace properly signed and sealed, with the great vermilion seal of the Emperor. It had been delayed on the road by the flooded state of the country about the Yellow River. The money is also being paid down as fast as it can be counted.

Fri. 16th The steamer *Auckland* left for Bombay and Suez with the treaty of peace which Major Malcolm, the Secretary to Sir H. Pottinger, takes home by the overland route.

On October 1st *Rattlesnake* leaves the Yangtse for Chusan, where by early January 1843 the health of Cree and that of his shipmates is restored. Cree remains there for several months, amusing himself in his spare time with shooting expeditions, dinner parties and games of whist. He visits various places – among them Ningpo, Sinkong, a village on the western side of the island, and the fishing town of Sing-ca-mun. On April 11th news is received of the death of the Imperial Commissioner Eleepoo (I-li-pu), "killed by the worry and disgrace of the late war".

Sing-ca-mun

MAY

Mon. 1st Our Commander Sprent and Arlington were up at Tinghai this morning and heard that I was promoted into the steam frigate [sloop] *Vixen* vice Naulty, Surgeon, invalided. I was at the 18th barracks doing duty for Cowan who was on leave at Tinghai and had about a third of the men sick and two officers, Wood and Armstrong. I was dining at the mess when Arlington came up to tell me the news. Of course there were plenty of congratulations and champagne, with speeches at the mess.

Tue. 2nd About 2 in the morning a Chinese boat came alongside with my appointment to the *Vixen* and order for survey on my medical stores, and a letter of congratulation from Schend, the Marine Magistrate, who had sent the boat. Of course I was busy enough getting ready and in the afternoon the surveying officers, Houghton, Surgeon of the *Driver*, Assistant Surgeon Whipple of the *Minden*, a brother of Whipple the surgeon in Plymouth, and Assistant Surgeon Nicolson of H.M.S. *Thalia* came on board. We all dined with old Sprent, the Commander, at the officers' quarters on shore, and kept it up till late.

H.M. Steam Sloop *Vixen*

H.M. STEAM SLOOP VIXEN

Wed. 3rd Bid farewell to all the "Rattlesnakes". I was sorry to leave the old ship, where I have spent some happy times during the last nearly four years. Succeeded by Assistant Surgeon D. Pritchard, also a Devonport man, who comes from the *Minden*. I left him in charge. The old ship's company gave me three hearty cheers as I went over the side into the cutter which was waiting for me and my baggage, to take us four medical officers into Chusan harbour, where we found the *Vixen* with her steam up ready to sail for Amoy and Hong Kong. Cowen and Burrell came on board to say goodbye. At 1 p.m. we started and rattled along through the SE passage at 9 knots, rather different to the old *Rattlesnake*'s going. Before dark clear of the Quesan Islands.

The *Vixen* is commanded, at present, by the 1st Lieutenant Downes, the late Commander Boyce having been invalided and gone to England. 2nd Lieutenant Moorsom;* 3rd Lieutenant Bailey, who goes by the nickname of "Butcher Bill", a thickset, bullet-headed, red-faced but good-hearted fellow. The Master, Robert Allen, I had known in the Mediterranean; the Purser, Harshaw, often called "Jack Hardjaw" from his habit of spinning yarns hard to be believed; Assistant Surgeon W. Webber, an Irishman but well educated and pleasant.

*Afterwards distinguished as the inventor of a shell. [In 1855/6 he aided Captain the Hon. Henry Keppel, of *St Jean d'Acre*, in command of the Naval Brigade before Sebastopol.]

Hong Kong

Sun. 7th Get down to the entrance of Canton River but too foggy to run in, so we hove to and the *Vixen* showed her powers of rolling and her spite in washing me out of bed and threatening to roll a chest of drawers on to my head.

Mon. 8th We entered Hong Kong by the eastern passage and anchored off the town about 8 a.m. I went to the flagship to call on the Admiral [Parker] and thanked him for the appointment to the *Vixen*. The great man gave me a gracious reception and said he had mentioned my name favourably to the Lords of the Admiralty and had no doubt I should be confirmed in the rank.[1] He asked me many questions about Sinkong and Sing-ca-mun and the *Rattlesnake* as a troop-ship.

[1] That is, of Surgeon. By the Navy reform of 1843 surgeons became non-executive commissioned officers, ranked with but subordinate to lieutenants.

Wed. 10th Dined with Captain Edwards and Sir William Macgregor of 18th, the latter going home on sick-leave in the *Algerine*. Chinese boats are not allowed to move about the harbour after 9 o'clock, as there have been so many daring robberies almost every night. A few nights ago they stole a brass 12-pounder gun from the dockyard, which took twelve men to lift.

Wed. 17th Another bit of gossip is that Lieutenant Rogers of the 18th has arrived from Trincomalee with the pretty little wife of a sergeant of the 90th Regiment, who came out with us in the *Rattlesnake*, and lots of similar accounts of the married ladies.

Thur. 18th A grand day on board the *Cornwallis*. Sir William Parker was invested with the insignia of the G.C.B. The Plenipo was deputed to perform the ceremony – officers in full dress, royal salutes fired by the ships and royal standard hoisted.

Sat. 20th The Admiral was deputed to return the compliment by investing Sir Henry Pottinger, the Plenipotentiary, with the G.C.B.: a procession of boats from the flagship to the shore, more royal salutes from the ships and battery. Some high-class mandarins have been on a visit to the Plenipo, consisting of Hwang, Judicial Secretary attached to the Imperial Commissioner Hwang Lung, the Tartar general who came to Canton, second in command to Eleepoo. There are five mandarins who came in an equal number of war junks. A house has been fitted up for them. The Plenipo gave an entertainment at Government House, to which all the English officers and their ladies were invited to meet the mandarins, who made themselves very agreeable. Hwang was quite the favourite with the English ladies.

JUNE

Wed. 7th The March mail arrived from England with letters from my sister. It is pleasant to have accounts from old friends at such a distance.

Sat. 10th A great deal of sickness: remittent and intermittent fevers and diarrhoea very prevalent. The line-of-battle ships have each 100 sick. The former disease is carrying off three men a day from the 55th Regiment at West Point Barracks. The sickness is attributed to turning up the new soil for building and road making and the quantity of disintegrating granite. There are no efficient drains made yet.

Sun. 11th At 2 a.m. Commander George Giffard[B] came on board to take command of the *Vixen*. He had just arrived by the mail from England. At Divisions he read his commission and afterwards read prayers. He dined with us in the gunroom and for the present will continue to mess with us. He is a nephew of Sir Edward Follett the judge, and belongs to a good Devonshire family.

Wed. 14th–Sat. 17th The nights are very hot and sultry, bad for the sick. Our 1st Lieutenant Downes, now he is superseded in his command, wants to leave the ship and go home. He is not well, so I spoke to the Inspector of Hospitals about him. He mentioned it to the Admiral and Dr Wilson came to see him as it looks like making a convenience of the service. I shan't be sorry if he goes as he is an ill-tempered man and too fond of flogging. Not many days pass but I have to attend a corporal punishment. The ship's company will rejoice when Downes goes.[2]

Sat. 24th The Admiral and Captains went to call on Keying, the Tartar general, and other mandarins. Plenty of chin-chin and drinking of tea.

[2] In these days there was a fair proportion of bad officers, heartily disliked and unable to exert proper discipline. It was not uncommon for an unpopular officer to be assaulted by his crew after paying off a ship. This happened to the captain of the flagship *Cornwallis* on return to Portsmouth from the East Indies in 1844.

Mandarins' boat at Hong Kong, June 1843

Sun. 25th Keying with his suite visit the Admiral on board the *Cornwallis*. Saluted with seventeen guns. All the war junks salute with three guns. The Captains of our ships go to meet Keying.

Mon. 26th Exchange of the ratified treaty of peace. Royal salute and ship dressed in flags.

Tue. 27th On shore with Lieutenant Bailey. We went to Government House. Called on Captain Collinson who is employed surveying.

Wed. 28th Keying returned to Canton in the *Ackbar*. Our gunner had entered in his "expenses book" under the expenditure of powder, &c., for a *feu de joie*, "Expended for a future joy". Sir Henry Pottinger's commission as Governor of Hong Kong was read, Keying and his colleagues being present. The troops of the Garrison were then reviewed and marched past in slow and quick time. Afterwards a dinner was given by the Governor. Fifty people were present and ended by most of the Celestials getting drunk, Keying amongst the number, who sung a Chinese love-ditty and afterwards called on Lord Saltoun for a song. Captain Quin of the *Minden* sang "Poll of Wapping". The Celestials were delighted with their entertainment. Keying said he should like to see Sir Henry Pottinger's legs under his table at Pekin. He took the gold bracelet off his wrist and presented it to the Governor and told him that if he was travelling in any part of China he would only have to show it and he would meet with many friends. Keying's name was engraved on many parts of it. They did not break up till 11 o'clock.

Sat. 1st Chosen caterer of our mess, a post the Doctor generally has to fill. JULY

Mon. 17th Just heard of the probable fate of poor McKinlay [medical officer of the 18th Regiment]. The lorcha which left Hong Kong on the 8th for Macao has not arrived there, and it is feared she has been taken by pirates, as she had a valuable cargo of cloves and other spice on board. I was one of the last persons to see him off, poor fellow – sad fate just as he was on his way home after twelve years' absence.

Wed. 19th H.M.S. *Dido* has been out to search for the missing lorcha. Found her wreck in the Cap-sing-mun passage, hardly a dozen miles from the harbour. It appears that the Chinese crew and some Chinese passengers, pirates, had risen and murdered the Portuguese captain and speared poor McKinlay while he was defending himself desperately with his sword, which was found broken. His body was picked up on the rocks near the wreck. After plundering the lorcha, they burnt her.

Tue. 1st Took a walk along the New Road with Captain Giffard. AUGUST

Wed. 2nd Nearly a hundred of the wives of the 55th soldiers arrived from Calcutta. I was on shore with Moorsom in the evening. We met many of the ladies in the road rather the worse for liquor. Amongst these, we met that

Naval vessels in the Cap-sing-mun passage

poor wretch Mrs Lloyd, who has been deserted by that blackguard Rogers, who has gone to England and left her to her fate. Jones, the Colonial Surgeon, told me he had been called to see her and found her suffering from delirium tremens. When we brought her out from England in the *Rattlesnake* she was a pretty, modest young woman. Now what a wreck she is, owing to that fellow Rogers.*

* Less than a year after this I was told she was found dead on the side of the road at Hong Kong after going through the greatest degradation.

Wed. 9th News from Sir Edward Belcher[B] of the *Samarang* surveying the coast of Borneo, that he had got ashore in the Sarawak River and feared he would not be able to save his ship, so we are ordered to get ready to go to his assistance.

Thur. 10th In getting up our main topmast the mast rope broke and down came the mast, the neck of it going through the deck. The rain has been coming down as it can do in the tropics.

Fri. 11th On shore paying mess bills before leaving for Borneo, but came off again early.

Sarawak

Sun. 20th Water smooth, sighted the high land of Santabong early. Ran into the Sarawak River – scenery pretty, rocks covered with tropical foliage, purple mountains in the distance. After running up the river about 15 miles found H.M.S. *Samarang* afloat again with H.M. Brig [Sloop] *Harlequin*. We took them both in tow and anchored at the mouth of the river. The *Samarang* is an old 26-gun frigate fitted as a surveying vessel. She got on a ridge of rocks in the centre of the river where the tide left her, and she fell over on her side and filled. She was eleven days with the water and mud half-way up her main deck, in a sad mess, instruments spoilt and broken. The officers have lost their kit. They got her up after great labour, taking guns and everything they could out of her, and pumping her out. I believe she is not materially damaged.

Mon. 21st We were visited by Mr James Brooke,[B] a gentleman formerly in the Indian Army, who left that service and came out here on his yacht, the *Royalist*, and assisting the Rajah of Sarawak, Muda Hassim, against some of his revolted subjects,[3] has remained here ever since. We went up the river about 25 miles and anchored 3 miles below the settlement, Kuching. The banks of the river are covered with jungle winding about amidst rich tropical scenery. About 10 miles farther up is a mountain, in which there are rich antimony mines which Brooke is working and exporting to Singapore on which he gains about 500 per cent on the cost of working.

[3] The people of the province of Sarawak were by August 1839, the time of James Brooke's providential arrival in the Sarawak River, in a state of open revolt following the exactions of the Brunei proconsul. Rajah Muda Hassim was therefore sent by his nephew, the Malay Sultan of Brunei (to whom he had ceded his right to the throne), to quell the insurrection; but it was Brooke who, with his force of twenty men (the crew of his schooner *Royalist*), brought this about.

Mr Brooke's bungalow by the Sarawak River

We found Mr Brooke a most agreeable man, well read and educated. He is a friend of the Templars of Bridport, a Somersetshire man himself. We found him very hospitable and keeps open house to all British officers in a bungalow he has built on the left bank of the river.

Tue. 22nd Allen and I breakfasted early and went up to Kuching in the gig. Kuching, the native town, the residence of the Rajah, Muda Hassim, is merely a collection of Malay houses built on piles at the edge of the river, which is here about 100 yards wide. The native houses, built of reed and bamboo thatched with palm leaves and matting, swarm with Malay women and naked children who paddle about in their canoes, hollowed out trees. The river abounds with alligators and is not safe to swim about in. The bungalow of Mr Brooke is on the opposite bank of the river, where we went and had a second breakfast. He seems to have a large establishment with Malay servants and retainers. After a good breakfast of eggs, curry, chicken and fruit with coffee and pipes, we went across the river with Mr Brooke to visit the Rajah, Muda Hassim, who is living in the largest house, a rambling place built on piles like the rest.

Kuching is prettily situated on a bend of the river. The jungle is cleared round the town. Mr Brooke's bungalow is built on piles like the other Malay houses, and has smaller houses near it for the servants and officers. He keeps great state. Has an English surgeon for his yacht, Mr Treacher, an agreeable young man, who lives with him, a captain of his yacht, an interpreter and a lot of Malay hangers-on. His large dining or sitting room is hung round with arms, muskets, swords, spears and creeses. He has a good library and many English comforts about him. The water from a well near is deliciously cool, which is a great boon in this hot climate.

The visit to Rajah Muda Hassim, August 22nd 1843

The Rajah's return call to *Vixen*

On our visit to Muda Hassim we were received with music from an old Dutch barrel-organ accompanied by drums and cymbals. We were ushered in to the presence of the Rajah by two of his brothers, who shook hands with each of us. The Rajah was in a large room seated in an armchair at the head of a highly polished dark wood table. He rose and shook hands as we entered and motioned us to chairs round. Tea was brought in and cheroots of mild native tobacco about a foot long and rolled round with a kind of grass. A tall wax candle stood in the centre to light them. The conversation was carried on by Mr Brooke and his interpreter. The Rajah enquired all our ranks and seemed pleased with our visit. Muda Hassim is an intelligent looking little man of about fifty, wore a dark coloured silk jacket with gold embroidered collar, loose dimity trousers, black leather pumps without stockings, a handsome jewel-hilted creese stuck in the shawl round his middle. A large diamond ring ornamented his finger and a gold chain his dark-coloured turban. His two brothers were similarly dressed. His bodyguard, some forty or fifty darkies, rather well dressed, squatted on one side of the room and separated from us by a low partition. They all carried spears with horses' tails attached to them or swords in red cloth scabbards, and small round shields. The Rajah's State sword bearer, the State spear bearer, the State umbrella bearer, tea bearer and pipe and betel-nut bearer squatted behind His Highness. This old fellow is moderate in his wants, having only thirteen wives, to whom we were not introduced as he is a Mohammedan. We saw many of the lower-class ladies, who are certainly not beautiful but of a fine mahogany complexion. The Rajah and his brothers are of a lighter shade. The ladies' dresses are not extensive or expensive. They are a small, slight race of people and not addicted to hard work. There are a great number of Chinese from Singapore, Canton and Amoy settled here, who do all the work, and also work at the antimony mines.

We started for the ship about 2 p.m. and got on board to dinner.

In the afternoon the Rajah came down to the ship to pay us a return visit, all his proas carrying his chiefs with red, blue, green and white umbrellas. His boat carried his standard, a yellow and red flag, in the stern. He came on board attended by his staff and bodyguard and inspected our ship throughout – the engines and the guns – but was evidently too proud to express any wonder or astonishment. One of our 10-inch guns was fired for his amusement, but he had no wish to see one of the large shot fired. After staying about an hour and taking refreshments he bid us farewell, shaking hands with all, and departed up the river with all his tagbag and bobtail.

Wed. 23rd When we arrived in the river on Monday we met the *Wolverine*, 16-gun brig, coming down with the Straits steamer *Diana*, which had all been assisting the *Samarang*. Treacher, the Surgeon, and some of Mr Brooke's people, came down the river with us and remained till this morning, when we got under weigh and towed the *Samarang* and the *Harlequin* out of the river, then disconnected our engines and made sail.

In the succeeding months *Vixen* calls at Manilla, Hong Kong, Amoy, Macao, Chusan, Singapore and Trincomalee. On January 11th 1844 Major-General G.C. d'Aguilar takes command of the Hong Kong garrison in place of Lord Saltoun; and on May 8th John Francis Davis arrives in Hong Kong to take over the governorship from Sir Henry Pottinger.

Dance on the quarterdeck of *Vixen* – Trincomalee, June 1844

1844

Singapore

SEPTEMBER

Sun. 15th A week in Singapore gets tedious, not much amusement – playing billiards at Dutronquoy's hotel, sketching a little, too hot to walk much. At the Singapore church only about a hundred people there, a sleepy sermon from Mr White, the Government Chaplain, whose daughter I was introduced to, a pretty black-eyed girl with a tinge of the black blood, but said to have a fortune of a lakh or two of rupees in nutmeg plantations, which would certainly make the black blood spicy. The fortune is said to come from the grandmother, who is not far removed from the jungle breed, but Miss Church is nevertheless the prettiest girl in Singapore, and accomplished. The church has a vinegar bottle spire. The perpetual swinging of the punkahs tends to make one close his eyes, during Mr Church's not over-lively sermons.

Wed. 18th In the evening walked along a good road through pretty country with plantations recently cleared of jungle. Saw many of the natives taking their evening bath in a little stream at the side of the road. Met a couple of drunken Englishmen driving in a gig, quarrelling and ending in a fight by the roadside, which terminated by their both tumbling into the ditch and the horse quietly going home with the empty gig. Old Quin is a patient of mine, whom I visit at the hotel every day.

Thur. 19th Lunched with Dr Little, who is in private practice here. He is an Edinburgh man and an old fellow-student of mine.

Sat. 21st Went out with Whampoa, the Chinese merchant, to his nutmeg estate a few miles in the country. There was a great dinner there to some of the other Singapore merchants, very good and very lively with good wine. In the evening we were entertained with a native dance by Malays in costume with the music of tom-toms, cymbals and native songs. Whampoa gave us a specimen of a Chinese song in a monotonous high pitch, anything but musical, like the cat on the tiles. But the scene, by lovely moonlight and torches, with the background of jungle, made a wild one. Well into midnight before we got back to the town. It is not a usual thing to hear a Chinaman quote passages from Shakespeare and Byron, but Whampoa recited long passages from both and put the proper emphasis on the words. He was educated at Edinburgh but is a thorough "heathen Chinee".

Street-sellers, Singapore

Singapore

"Mr Whampoa's entertainment"

Our object in remaining at Singapore so long is to repair our main shaft which has been cracked to a dangerous extent. Our engineers are welding an enormous iron collar to go round the shaft and so secure it. Ward, our Chief Engineer, is quite equal to the undertaking.

We continued to spend a pleasant time, and making the acquaintance of people of Singapore. A party of the ladies came on board to see the ship and amongst them the "Malay princess". I found some pleasant men amongst the officers of the native regiment stationed here and there were some good fellows in H.M.S. *Wolverine*.

Thur. 26th Went to a musical party at Dr José d'Almeida's, a Portuguese merchant who lives on the Campong Glam and has a large family of daughters – and sons too, I believe, but they are kept in the background. They are all very musical and get up delightful concerts in their house, twice a week, to which some of us have a general invitation. The ladies are not good looking – Portuguese seldom are – and they also have a palpable mixture of the Malay, which does not add to their beauty, but they sing and play various instruments divinely. There are ten daughters and four sons. We were received by an old priest, the father confessor of the family. Old José introduced us separately and individually to each member of the family, a formidable affair, and lastly to the Madam, a leaden coloured, fat old Malay woman who informed us "Me

Signor José d'Almeida's musical party

no speekee de Englezee". Some of her relations, Malay rajahs, were there and treated us to a hornpipe – one played on a fiddle some native airs, monotonous enough. It was a lovely moonlight night and the large room open to the veranda all round made it cool, so we were able to enjoy the quadrilles and waltzes – with a little flirtation.

Sun. 29th H.M.S. *Dido* arrived from Borneo, Captain Keppel.[B] She refits and then sails for England. I am sorry we lose Lieutenant Moorsom, who exchanges with Lieutenant Bonham[1] of the *Dido*. I am very sorry to lose Moorsom, who is a good fellow and a thorough gentleman.

[1] Lieutenant Charles W. Bonham was a cousin of Samuel George Bonham, Governor of Penang, Singapore and Malacca, who in 1848 succeeded Sir John Davis as Governor of Hong Kong.

Our main shaft being shipped and put in its place, we started in the evening for China. We still have some cases of remittent fever on board.

China Sea

Mon. 30th Passed Pulo Aor at 8 a.m. Wilkinson Dent, of the great mercantile house of Dent & Co. in China, goes up with us, as a friend of Captain Giffard, and Beale, one of the partners, going to establish a branch house at Shanghai.

OCTOBER

Tue. 1st Very hot weather – therm. 90° – no wind.

Fri. 4th Came on to blow from NE with a long heavy swell. Squally, with thunder and lightning. Sky very black and threatening. Making all secure for a typhoon.

Sat. 5th Wind and sea increasing and going round NW and W. 8 p.m. blowing a hurricane, a regular typhoon. Tremendous sea struck us on the quarter and stove in the deck lights, smashed the Captain's gig and the bulwarks, also the bulwarks forward, and part of the paddle-box. We shipped some heavy seas, and it was pitch-dark – deck leaking like a sieve, cabins swamped and altogether a miserable night. To add to the horrors we were somewhere near the Paracels shoals, but no observations having been made for a few days, all was uncertainty. If we had touched, no one would have lived to tell the tale. I tried to get a little sleep by spreading a mat under the table and getting an arm round one of the legs, but the rolling and pitching of the ship rendered rest impossible. Our three dogs huddled up to me for companionship, but we were all rolling about the deck with chairs and everything not made fast. The poor dogs were much distressed.

Typhoon in the China Sea, *Vixen* awash

Sun. 6th The typhoon moderated somewhat, but no breakfast to be had except some cold meat and a bottle of beer. Cook's galley, as well as the cooks, nearly washed away and the crockery smashed, but the weather is clearing, wind veering to SW to S. and to SE. There was a magnificent sea, tumbling about from two or three different quarters. At sunset the waves looked like mountains tipped with gold as the slanting sunbeams came horizontally from under the heavy purple clouds, but the wind was falling and we were able to rattle along again towards the coast of China.

Ningpo

DECEMBER

[2] Rear-Admiral Thomas Cochrane, who had succeeded Admiral Parker as Commander-in-Chief, East Indies station, in December the previous year.

Thur. 26th The Admiral[2] came on board at 9 a.m. and we started for Ningpo, which we reached at 1 p.m., but not without getting foul of the junks at anchor there, and a great noise and bustle cutting cables, &c., as the strong tide swept us round, crushing a dozen large junks together and doing a little damage to ourselves, smashing the Captain's gig and one of the cutters. The mast of one of the junks fell on our deck, injuring three of our men – one badly cut on the head, and the others cut and bruised. At last we got clear, after frightening poor John Chinaman considerably, and doing him not a little damage to his rigging, &c. I suppose John Bull will have to pay for it.

We anchored outside the junks. I landed and visited the shops in the main street, which are the best I have seen in any Chinese city, gay with gilded and scarlet signboards and carved work, and the silks and fans and chinaware, and the bustle of business, form an animated scene. The streets roofed over with screens of transparent oyster-shells form a pleasant arcade. A very different appearance from when I first visited Ningpo during the war, when our troops occupied the place. The public buildings then destroyed have not been restored. The beautiful Temple of Confucius, which was but slightly injured by our troops, is quite neglected, it is said from poverty, the result of the late war, which China will feel for a long time to come.

Fri. 27th Went to the top of the old pagoda. The atmosphere was clear, and the view very fine over the city and flat surrounding country to the foot of the mountains, with the fine rivers. This tower is said to be 700 years old. It has seven storeys, six sides, and is about 140 feet high. Afterwards walked out of the west gate, where the assault was made on Armstrong's guard during the war. I walked about 3 miles along the bank of the canal and passed some five archways and a curious bridge. Canal boats are constantly passing to and fro, some from the city laden with liquid manure, collected in the disgusting way usual in Chinese cities, obliged one to give the canal boats a wide berth. Met a wedding procession, I have seen five before, this morning. They seem to be in fashion now; I suppose the cold season has something to do with it. We saw them arrive at the husband's house, and dispose themselves in the front room, where the bride sat to be seen by the general public. She was rather pretty, but appeared bashful, as might be supposed when gazed upon and criticised by the outside Barbarians. Her outer robe was of red satin with gold embroidered dragons, and her train of gilt tinsel stuff. The quantity of artificial flowers did not add to her good looks, nor the quantity of chalk with which her face was powdered. The rest of the wedding party were tucking in the viands provided by the victim. They were all gaily dressed, the men had red caps with tassels, and their best clothes, like the johnnies at home.

On our return to the town we visited the debtors' prison, where a miserable

The collision with Chinese junks

A street in Ningpo

Ningpo from the river (*black and white*)

Tea Gardens, Shanghai

Near the north gate

set of wretches looked at us through the wooden bars of the door. We saw plenty of cages, such as the ones Mrs Noble and Major Anstruther were exhibited in – something like crates for crockery.

Sat. 28th Fine, clear and frosty. We got under weigh at 3 p.m. and started down the river with the Admiral and Thom, the Ningpo Consul, and his assistant, young Morrison, and accompanied by the *Medusa* steamer. We rattled along at a good pace, to the astonishment of the crowds of natives lining both banks of the river. We passed Chinhai and out of the river to the north for the Rugged Islands, where we anchored for the night.

Shanghai

Sun. 29th 8 a.m. got under weigh and on to the Yangtse Kiang – crowds of large junks entering the great river with the flood tide, opium clippers off the mouth of the Woosung River, but the great stream did not exhibit such an animated scene as when I last visited it with a fleet of above a hundred vessels. Proceeded up the Woosung River, which is a fine broad stream, a worthy tributary of the grand Yangtse Kiang. Country round flat and plenty of trees and junks going to and fro, some of the latter of large size. Anchor at dark below Shanghai.

Mon. 30th Fine frosty morning, like English winter. Land and call on Captain Balfour, the Consul, and on Mrs White and Miss le Foy, Mary Ann. Balfour lives in a large mandarin's house, a good Chinese specimen. The English merchants have houses outside the walls. I walked about the town, visited the shops, &c. Not such a good or large town as Ningpo and dirtier, more smelly, but there seems to be more trade and bustle in the narrow streets which are crowded and very slippery – shops with choice fans and curious china, for which they ask a high price. There is a great trade in silk and cotton. The people are civil, but crowds of beggars, cripples and disgusting objects, especially in the places of recreation. The public gardens are good specimens of the Chinese taste with lakes, temples, fanciful bridges and rockwork, plenty of tea-houses well frequented. . . . There were jugglers and puppet shows and singers, &c. Went into some of the picture shops where are curious caricatures of the English – curiosity shops with carved work, cups of rhinoceros horn, carved bamboo, &c., josshouses and idols but not equal to the Chusan ones, a large theatrical performance going on before the idols. The city wall about 20 feet high, with only a slight parapet and no guns mounted. On the wall we came upon a dead body of one of the beggars lying on his back, probably died in the night from cold and starvation, but these sights are common in Chinese cities. These beggars are a large class, regular professionals, and hereditary

"A walking pincushion and a mad beggar"

Tumblers (*top*)

"Early morning on the wall of Shanghai" (*below right*)

"Beggars' Hall", Shanghai (*below left*)

beggars, some of them said to be wealthy. Horrible smells in the streets from the sewers and the inconveniences in all the corners. From the river the town can hardly be seen for the crowd of junks moored up and down for a couple of miles in hundreds with a forest of masts, ranged in regular tiers before the town. Some of the junks are 400 or 500 tons – they are moored head and stern. Shantung cabbages are plentiful and good, 100 for a rupee. Fish and poultry plentiful and cheap – pheasants, hares, wild ducks and geese are snared in quantities. The pheasants are generally met with near the villages, dodging in and out amongst the graves. Dried prunes, large and fine, look like dates.

"Shanghai charmers" (*on silk*)

Tue. 31st We got under weigh early and proceeded farther up the river to above an ancient pagoda 5 or 6 miles above the town. The river winds about through a flat, well-cultivated country with frequent farms and villages and trees scattered about. We landed with our fowling pieces to try to shoot some of the pheasants which appeared plentiful, but I walked over to the ancient pagoda to make a sketch. It has seven storeys, has the gilt ball on the top, the upper part in good repair, but all the lower storeys are ruinous and the roofs and staircases gone, so there was no way of ascending it. The upper part is inhabited by a large colony of pigeons, daws and minas. There are some ruined josshouses round the base. Priests and bonzes are plentiful, and crowded round me while I was sketching, but were very civil. There is a good bridge near this place, over a creek, with immense flagstones for supports and cross-pieces of single stones 36 feet long which must have been brought from a long distance, as there is no stone for a hundred miles. The peasantry were very civil. They are robust and good looking. We saw some fine, big-limbed fellows. The young women were fresh coloured and buxom, and not very shy.

So ends the year 1844.

Amoy

JANUARY *Fri. 10th* Fine, clear weather, therm. under 50°.

Sat. 11th The Admiral returned from Foo-chow-foo last night and we are off with *Agincourt* and *Iris* to the south. Blowing hard from NE with heavy sea; passed Oxsoo in evening. Stood off and on during the night.

Sun. 12th My thirty-first birthday. Fresh breezes and fine weather. Noon, passed Dodds Island. 6 p.m. anchored at Amoy. They have no news from Hong Kong since we were here last. There is only one merchant vessel in port.

Mon. 13th On shore at Ko-lung-soo. Meet many friends, [Assistant Surgeon] Rawes and Captain Congdon of 2nd M.N.I., Lord Cochrane,[1] and with him call on Mrs Sulivan.[2] Met the Admiral and Captain Bruce[3] there. Mrs S. and all the family been ill with fever, so looks very ill now. Everybody on the island is sick, although the weather is clear and pleasant, tho' hot in the sun and chilly in the shade. Cultivation has been stopped on the island since the British have had possession, and the fields lying waste. The island looks pretty, but deserted and melancholy. The pretty western village is like a place of the dead, not even a dog or a child, both so plentiful in Chinese villages generally.

The detachment of the 4th M.N.I. left yesterday in the *Sapphire*. They have been dreadfully sickly: landed here a few months since, 240 men; yesterday only 104 left. Rawes and Congdon, like walking ghosts, have ague nearly every day. I lunched with them, and had some fine looking and well-tasted oysters. Oh how bad I was after! An attack of bilious cholera, and served the others in the same way. Lieutenant Collingwood dined with us and related how he had been robbed, by three Chinese, of all his kit. He is in the Royal Artillery. He chased the robbers with his fowling piece to their boat, and shot one of them, whom his companions immediately threw overboard, and made off with their booty. Robberies are so frequent here, that if the houses are not guarded the thieves will walk off with doors, windows and tiles.

[1] Lord Cochrane (1814–85), heir to the tenth Earl of Dundonald (the famous admiral, best known as Lord Cochrane), was a captain in the 18th Regiment. Cree had first met him in Chusan in October 1842.

[2] Mrs Sulivan was the pretty Jewish wife of the Vice-Consul of Amoy.

[3] Captain Henry W. Bruce was in command of the flagship *Agincourt*.

Hong Kong

Thur. 16th . . . We ran into Hong Kong through the Liemon [Lyemun] passage. Anchored at 10 a.m. No mail from England since we left.

Hong Kong builders at work

Tanka boat-girls

The first English residence built at Hong Kong – the Pagoda House, home of Dent the merchant, where Cree was often entertained.

Hong Kong from Kowloon

Fri. 17th The Admiral not having arrived, we went round Hong Kong to look for him, but saw nothing of him. Very wet.

Sat. 18th *Agincourt*, with the Admiral, and *Iris* arrived, having overrun the port.

Mon. 20th Beautiful weather. Called on the McKnights, late arrivals at Hong Kong, with three pretty stepdaughters, a pleasant addition to Hong Kong society. This is a good place for marriageable girls. McKnight is Agent Victualler and has a house at West Point.

Tue. 21st Walked through the town to see the new buildings, which are wonderful considering what Hong Kong was only two years ago. H.M.S. *Vestal* arrived from Canton with two millions and a half dollars on board, part of the ransom.

Thur. 30th Took *Agincourt* in tow round to Chek-pi-wan, where the small island of Little Hong Kong forms a narrow harbour. There is some idea of forming a dockyard here. Chek-pi-wan is a fishing village, the scenery is pretty, hills rocky, with one or two little waterfalls and a picturesque josshouse, which I went on shore to sketch. Government are busy making roads, and employ gangs of coolies, who live in the hundreds of Tanka boats congregated here, quite a floating town. Piracy has been rife in this neighbourhood.

FEBRUARY *Sat. 8th* My assistant, Webber, is sent away to the *Plover*, as her medical

officer [Assistant Surgeon G. St G. Bowen] has shot himself. The one before went mad. Webber is not likely to do either.

Fri. 14th The Navy got up a regatta. All the beauty and fashion of Hong Kong on board the *Agincourt*: about forty ladies and four times as many men. In the first race our second cutter pulled over the course, as none of the others would venture to compete with her. The race which excited most interest was one pulled by officers. After the racing the prizes, consisting of purses of dollars, silver cups, &c., which were distributed by the ladies on the poop of the *Agincourt*. At 6 dinner, but only half, about 140, could sit down at one time, although the table extended the whole length of the main deck. After dinner dancing commenced on the quarterdeck, which was prettily decorated with flags of all nations, chandeliers of bayonets, variegated lamps, transparencies and flowers. On the poop were card-tables, &c. About 11 supper was served; afterwards dancing was kept up till 2 in the morning. Altogether the affair gave great satisfaction and will serve to bring the Hong Kong people together. Everyone was asked, but one or two stuck-up ladies imagined themselves too good for the company, and stayed away, but they were not missed, as they are old and ugly. The belles of the party were Miss Hickson and Miss Bowra.

Sat. 15th Willcox and I went on shore to call on some of the ladies. Had a long chat with Miss Hickson, who is a pretty, fresh complexioned, Devonshire girl, jolly and good. We lunched with Pitcher and Dent,[4] and

[4] Pitcher was a tea-taster for the firm of Thomas Dent. The Dent referred to here is likely to have been John Dent of the same firm, not to be confused with Edward Dent, a mate in *Vixen* (next mentioned in Cree's entry for March 19th).

The naval regatta, February 14th 1845. From left to right, H.M. Ships *Agincourt*, *Iris*, *Vixen*.

then went to see an amateur Portuguese play, a vagabond place, but we were in mufti. We met there that donkey Paterson, Royal Artillery, with his wife, who is daughter of a sergeant. She is a pretty little girl and well behaved, but ignorant. The rest of the company were mostly Portuguese and policemen, and their "ladies".

Sun. 16th McKnight and his family, consisting of three stepdaughters and a son, came on board to see the ship, and the officers of course. Some friends of Bailey, our 2nd Lieutenant, also came on board: Mr and Mrs Pett, Ordnance Storekeeper, with two of their little girls, the second about fifteen and very pretty.

Thur. 27th At daylight found we were near the Ninepin Rock, close to the entrance to Hong Kong, but the Admiral did not wish to get in so early, so the helm was put hard aport, and we steamed round and round till it was time for the *great little* man to honour the harbour by his entrance. We anchored at 10, and got rid of the Admiral. . . .

MARCH *Sun. 16th* Webber and I, after church, took the second cutter, and picking up the girls on their way home, with a couple of their military attachés, took them for a sail across the bay. We landed on the opposite side, scrambling through brambles and over rocks, to the detriment of the ladies' dresses and poor D. [Dunlop] of the 4th M.N.I., who came down on all fours and split his continuations. He is dreadfully spoony with Miss Hickson, who was so cruel as to laugh immoderately. We afterwards saw the girls safely home, and took poor D. on board to dinner.

Mrs McKnight goes by the name of Mrs Nickleby, from her resemblance to that celebrated lady.

Mon. 17th Went to Green Island, to practise shot and shell. In evening go to a ball given by the 18th. All the beauty and fashion of Hong Kong there, plenty of old ladies and very young ones, to make up the proportion between the sexes. Ten gentlemen to one lady. Miss Hickson the belle of the room, at which her mother, Mrs Nickleby, was elated at the attention paid to all three pretty daughters, and as I took her down to supper, had the benefit of her talk under the tongue-loosening effects of champagne, when she expatiated on the virtues of her three girls. One young lady there we nicknamed Miss Jack Horner, a hoydenish lady who loved champagne, not wisely, but too well. Had a waltz after supper with my friend Bailey, who had some trouble to keep her on her legs, to the no small amusement of his messmates. After a country dance, old B. saw her safely down to her sedan-chair, and took leave of her, most affectionately, asking her on board to dinner. Captain Collinson, of the Royal Engineers, Bailey and I got into a cart drawn by a couple of Chinamen, and drove down to our boat in great style. After B. got on board he found he had worn off the Governor's cap, by mistake.

Wed. 19th Went to see my fair little patient, Alice Hickson, who is

"Scrambling through brambles and over rocks" – the excursion of March 16th

indisposed. Ladies are so scarce and doctors so plentiful, that each lady has her own doctor exclusively. Dent and I get horses and ride out to Happy Valley; call on Miss Jack Horner, who lives with her aunt, a widow of a merchant of Hong Kong. A gallant old captain of one of the frigates here is very sweet and calls her his pretty piece of velvet.

Fri. 21st Good Friday. Dent and I have been making a round of calls lately: today on Mrs Caine, wife of the Chief Magistrate – a lively little woman, full of fun, but the nicest and most ladylike woman in Hong Kong is Mrs Carr, wife of a merchant. They have a lovely house, well furnished, &c. We afterwards went out for a ride to Eastern Point, and galloping back over the bad road my horse fell over some rocks, nearly cut his eye out, hurt his shoulder and hip, and rolled over my foot, but I luckily escaped with only some slight scratches and bruises, tho' was nearly pitched into the sea.

"The Spill"

Sat. 22nd Dent and I call on Mrs Tradescant Lay, wife of the Consul at Foo-chow. She is very deaf, fortunately for me, as I mistook her for her servant. We made another mistake in entering a private house and ordering lunch, thinking it was the new hotel. The family were at dinner. They politely asked us to join them, when seeing our mistake we apologised. Thanking them we declined.

Tue. 25th A picnic had been arranged for the opposite shore of Liemoon. A lorcha, a large covered boat with a fine cabin, was hired, in case it rained, which it threatened to do. However, the ladies came on board and declared they would go, rain or no rain, and would not be disappointed of their picnic. So we started with a fair wind, under black skies, at noon. Our party consisted of the Misses Hickson, Misses Pett, Mr and Mrs Ford, Routh and Carpenter, Captain Giffard, Willcox and myself. Routh had his piano on board. Of rain and wind we soon had more than enough. We could not land for the surf on the beach, and had to beat our way back to the harbour, in time for dinner on board the *Vixen,* of which we managed to get enough for our sudden influx of visitors. The weather had cleared, so after dinner we rigged up the quarterdeck, got Routh's piano up, and our three musicians, and were soon kicking our heels up, to the delight of the girls, till near midnight, when we saw all the girls safely home.

Next day a dance at McKnight's where we met the same party, with additions.

Thur. 27th A dance at the 4th Madras N.I. Plenty of fun, but so much dissipation with the thermometer at 80° rather takes it out of one. This party was not large, eighteen ladies and twenty-four gentlemen, but kept it up till 3 in the morning. Last night we took our musicians to McKnight's and afterwards gave our friends in the town a benefit.

APRIL

Tue. 22nd Little else to record but dinners, dances and flirtations.

Wed. 23rd Willcox and I take the girls, Hicksons and Petts, in the cutter round to Chek-pi-wan, where there is a pretty waterfall, close to the sea, which I sketched. We landed and scrambled over the rocks, and made a picnic of it, as we had brought refreshments.

In the cutter near Chek-pi-wan

Fri. 25th After dinner W. and I drop into McKnight's, as we often do, to have a little music and a dance, and spend a pleasant evening. We are under orders to join the Admiral in the Straits of Malacca, which is perhaps a good thing, although the parting from our dear friends will cause a pang.

Sun. 27th I got an invite from Mr Davis,[B] Governor of Hong Kong, to dinner on Friday next. We had a large dinner on board today, including Captain Fisher, Dr Fletcher, Lieutenant Dunlop of the 4th, Dr Rows of the 2nd, Lena of the Consular Service, Routh of Commissariat, Dr Tucker of *Minden*, Captain Giffard.

Wed. 30th Willcox and I gave a dinner party on board, to Mr and Mrs McKnight, Mr and Mrs Pett, Miss Hickson and Captain Giffard. The girls came in the evening to have a dance on the quarterdeck. I fear there are not many more such pleasant evenings for us at Hong Kong.

MAY

Thur. 1st Dine at the 4th with Dunlop, and afterwards with him to McKnight's. Poor fellow, he is getting very desperate.

Fri. 2nd Dine at Government House. Meet a large party of the bigwigs, but only got a poor dinner. The Governor is said to be stingy; he is absent in manner, and not conversational, although he has written a good book on China.[5]

Mon. 5th Called at McKnight's. Found poor Dunlop had been there and popped the question; to which the lady answered No! A musical party at Mrs Caine's; some famous German performers there. Miss Hickson was to have been there, but had no escort, her mother not being able to go, so I persuaded her that it would be quite proper if she put herself under her medical adviser's care. So I walked into the room with the Belle of Hong Kong on the day she had rejected a gallant officer of the 4th. Her pretty sister Alice gave me a sly look and a flower for my buttonhole. There was a large party and some good music, champagne iced, and a capital supper, dancing and green-tea punch to finish. I escorted my fair friend home about 2 o'clock.

[5] Davis was a prolific writer as well as a linguist who had studied Chinese. The book to which Cree alludes is no doubt his successful *The Chinese: a general description of the Empire of China and its inhabitants*, 2 vols (London, 1836).

Tue. 6th The English mail arrived last night. I got letters and papers from my sister, dated Nov. 30th. As we are to leave Hong Kong tomorrow morning, I went round to take leave of as many of our friends as I could. Mrs Caine, the Petts, Hicksons, &c. We had some of the 4th dining on board, but Willcox and I got away directly after dinner, and spent our last evening listening to the music and songs of the girls, in the Hicksons' veranda, overlooking the harbour. The night was calm and sultry, but lightning and distant rumbling of thunder indicated an approaching storm, and it was time to say farewell, at all times a disagreeable word, but very much so tonight, for we don't know when, or if ever, we may meet again. There were tears in the bright eyes, but we had to hasten down to our boat. We did not get to our ship before the threatened storm broke in a tremendous crash of thunder, with lightning and a heavy squall, which lasted all night.

Wed. 7th About 9 a.m. we got under weigh, and steamed our way through the shipping in the harbour. Passing along in front of the town, we saw many of our friends at their balconies, waving their handkerchiefs and taking a last look at us. It had been a dreadful night, and now the thunder kept muttering in the distance, the skies were mournful and dropped a few tears, but were calm. We lost sight of our fair friends, and soon bid adieu to the beautiful bay of Hong Kong.

Penang

Sun. 18th Light breeze and showery, sighted Penang at 10 a.m. 40 miles off. Going in got into shoal-water, so took a native pilot and anchored off the town at 3 p.m. Found six men-of-war at anchor. The Admiral is living in a bungalow on the hill where it is cool, but it is hot enough below. Pretty scenery, high wooded hills with fine trees, the low ground planted with coconuts and nutmegs. The opposite shore of Queda, about 2 miles off, covered with forest and hilly.

Thur. 22nd As H.M.S. *Wolf* was leaving for China one of her men fell from aloft, overboard. Lieutenant Forbes jumped after him, but did not succeed in saving the poor fellow, who probably struck against something in falling, as he sank before Forbes could reach him.

Fri. 23rd Went on shore with Eatwell and had a drive through the town, and 5 or 6 miles in the country, in a palkee. Good roads through the plantations; pleasant bungalows out of town, surrounded by trees. In the town Hindu-Chinese houses; streets wide and tolerably clean; one miserable hotel, called the Punch House – hot, and poor attendance, and extortionate charges.

One shop, kept by a Chinaman, deals in everything, and rejoices in the name of Tom King. Some of the native females are good looking and beautiful figures.

Sat. 24th Queen's birthday: ships dressed and royal salutes fired.

JUNE

Wed. 4th [Mate Edward] Dent and I sallied out to make some calls, amongst other new acquaintances, on Colonel Lewis, an old Indian officer, father of a girl who goes by the name of The Silent Angel, of tallowy complexion and Malay features. Her mother is said to live in the jungle on the Queda shore, where the old Colonel has an estate. The Penang house is well furnished with every requisite for enjoying a hot climate.

We then called on Mrs Wallace and her daughter Mrs Hall, who have a large house and keep a boarding-school for grown-up young ladies, to finish their education and fit them for society, which she does by giving dancing and supper parties to whom she considers eligible. Invites naval officers, silly old woman. She is widow of an officer of the Indian Army, as her daughter also is. The young ladies are mostly of mixed breed – "Chee-Chees", as they are called here; go by their father's names, not their mother's. Some of the girls are pretty and have good expectations in nutmeg and sugar estates.

We called on a Mrs Brown at Glugar, 6 miles from the town. Mr B. is a planter and has a beautiful bungalow with a noble drawing room, well furnished and beautifully cool, with an agreeably subdued light. They are very hospitable, especially to the Navy. Mrs B. is a pleasant, chatty Englishwoman, under thirty, but Mr B. has some characteristics of a black fellow.

We had a delightful ride out and in. The country is well cultivated and pretty, the roads good; lined, mostly by bamboo hedges, well clipped. Many Chinese and Malay hamlets along the road.

Sat. 7th The *Pluto* steamer arrived with the English mail of April 7th. Robinson, Surgeon of the *Nemesis*, dined with me. He served in the *Queen* during the Chinese war. Lord John Hay,[6] a son of the Marquis of Tweeddale, also dined with us.

Tue. 10th Went to a ball given by Mrs Wallace at the ladies' boarding-school. Seventy or eighty people there, a fine display of native beauty; some really nice girls, of every shade from brown Malay, with eye of fire, to the pale-faced Anglo-tropical girl. Old Jack Rodyk, a gentleman of Dutch descent, whom I had met before, was there; also his niece, a pretty slightly brown girl, with oh! such eyes of soft dark blue, very rare in one of her complexion, and a sylphlike figure, to whom old Jack introduced me, and I danced with her so often that I was pretty well joked about it by my

[6] Lord John Hay (1793–1851), third son of the seventh Marquess of Tweeddale, had had an active naval career, losing an arm fighting the French in Hyères Roads in 1807 and commanding a squadron on the north coast of Spain during the civil war. He became Admiral of the Fleet.

"Fitting the young ladies for society" – the ball of June 10th

messmates. There was plenty of waltzing and these slight Indian girls can do that to perfection and never seem to feel the heat, although some of us were melting. After dancing till 2 in the morning, we sat down to a great hot supper. First, hot mulligatawny soup and substantials, then plenty of "kickshaws", then a wonderful pie in the centre of the table caused great amusement, for on the crust being lifted, out flew twenty or thirty small birds, all about the table, and into the lamps and into the faces. An old black gentleman got up, and after drinking the Queen's health proposed the health of a young lady who is going to leave; a pretty dark girl, whom we named the Indian Princess, but the darkie called her the "Dark Rose of Summer", which was received with uproarious applause by all the gentlemen. After such a heavy supper we could not leave without another waltz or two, so we kept it up till 5 o'clock, when we found our way down to the boats.

When I got on board I found my boots, which were of patent leather, were so saturated with perspiration that I could not get them off till I tore them off in strips, to my great relief. Certainly all the girls were not lovely, one was said to weigh 20 stone, altho' very young. I did not dance with her. Another poor girl had a woolly head as big as the rest of her body. She was only 3 feet high.

"The supper and the live bird pie"

Tue. 17th Dine at Mr Brown's of Glugar: twenty-four guests. A handsome display of plate, everything in good style. Mrs B. is an agreeable, well-educated lady, but Mr B. is half Malay, his brother half a Chinaman, but I suppose the lady thought £5,000 a year was not to be found every day. The company consisted of some of the principal residents in Penang, and naval officers. The ladies were: a sister of Mrs Brown, wife of a Dr Smith, Editor of the *Penang Gazette*, a lively little woman; Miss Rodyk, stout and thirty, but with English manners and appearance, aunt to nice little Polly Anderson; Miss De Luce and her sister Mrs Nairns from Macao, half Chinese, half Portuguese ladies, not handsome as one might fancy, but beautiful figures, as their slight clothing and the absence of stays plainly displayed, especially in the waltz, which they do to perfection, but a Chinese cast of countenance and a yellow skin are not attractive to ordinary Englishmen. After the dinner we kept up the dance till past 1, and then had a long drive down to our boats.

Wed. 18th In the evening a dance at Jack Rodyk's, a pretty bungalow where Mrs Wallace had been persuaded to bring all her elder girls, with others we had not met before. The gentlemen were mostly officers from the ships, and between them all there was a lot of flirtation. A dark brown young lady confided to me that it would be a "rāāny day for the Penang ladies when the ships went to sea. Ev'ry mother's *son* of them would cry". Poor little girls, they were very unsophisticated; many of them have never been out of Penang. They are passionately fond of waltzing, which they do to perfection, notwithstanding the heat. I had not a dry rag on me, even my boots were soaked through, and had to be taken off in strips, but the cooler skinned dark girls were quite cool. They use scented coconut oil pretty freely. We kept it up till half-past 4 and quite tired out poor old Jack Rodyk.

Fri. 20th Dent and I dine with Alexander Rodyk who lives with his eldest sister, whom I met at Glugar. He is an old bachelor and has a pretty bungalow on the beach, and gives good dinners. We dined at 4, and afterwards he drove us out a few miles along a pretty shady road in his buggy. The Rodyks are a numerous family at Penang: they are all the progeny of an old Dutch gentleman who came from Batavia, when that place was taken by the English. He is now eighty years of age and living with his granddaughter, Bella, and never drank wine or spirit in his life, nor beer. He has twenty-five children, now living, by seven or eight different mothers.

Sat. 21st We had a party on board escorted by A. Rodyk and his sister, Bella, with Mrs Wallace and a number of the pretty dark girls. Some of us escorted them on shore afterwards. Finished the evening dancing at Mr Anderson's, Sophy's father, who, very properly, stopped us at 12 o'clock and would not let us dance on Sunday morning; so we had to wish the girls good night.

Mon. 23rd Call with Bonham on Bella Rodyk and some of our "fair" friends, to take leave of them, for we expected to go to sea tomorrow. We had Mr Panting, the Colonial Chaplain, and others dining with us when the Admiral made a general signal to weigh. This caused a commotion among the ships, and we had to send our visitors on shore, where many of the officers were on leave and were left behind; Ozzard, our Purser, among the number, who was away flirting with the girls somewhere. The captains of some of the ships were almost left behind, dining with some of the Penang people, who are so pleasant and hospitable, especially to the Navy. Their peculiarities and accidents of birth, colour and education give zest to the society....

Siak River, Sumatra

JULY *Mon. 14th* ... The Admiral and Captain M'Quhae, of the *Dædalus*, came on board and we started for the Sumatra shore about 10, and got over to the low jungly coast at 5 p.m. Mount Ophir, near Malacca, still in sight as we entered the Siak River. It was a lovely moonlight night, and we continued till 2 in the morning when the moon went down. We anchored in 13 fathoms, the river being a mile in width, covered with thick jungle and large trees on both banks, the water deep all the way up, except on the bar at the mouth. The scene was lovely in the still warm night; the silence only disturbed by the cry of some wild denizen of the forest, or the plunge of some fish or alligator in the calm mirror-like water, so clear that one could not see where the water ended and land began. Alligators and other uncomfortable animals abound.

Tue. 15th 5 a.m. got under weigh and proceeded to the town of Siak, 65 miles from the mouth, where the river narrows to 250 yards. The town, which is the residence of a rajah, is merely a miserable collection of huts built on poles or stakes along the edge of the river. The place seems populous, and abounds in women and children, the former clad in one garment of blue cotton reaching from the breasts to the knees, the latter with no garment at all. The men are slight but muscular fellows, but the women have no pretensions to good looks, having wide mouths and nostrils and lips and teeth stained with betel-nut. Many of the men are smartly dressed in silk jackets of gay colours and trousers to match and handsome turbans, their waist shawls stuck full of creeses of various lengths, with handles and sheaths inlaid with gold, silver and jewels. Some carried spears. They are all pirates when they have a chance, and we came here to check some little game of that sort. The Rajah was away on some expedition when we enquired for him. We could see his wives at a distance, but the women are very shy. A ladder descends from their doors to the river, where a place is railed or staked off to protect bathers from the alligators. The Admiral went on shore, and fifty or sixty of the natives, in holiday attire, came off to see the ship. The great guns and machinery attracted their attention. They were offered to be taken a few miles up the river, which they declined. They were a formidable looking set of savages, being all armed with creese and spear.

We went on about 10 miles above the town, where the river is still nearly 200 yards across and 10 fathoms deep in the centre, and 3 near the trees. The stream runs about 2 miles an hour. We came back at a rattling pace past the town, where all the natives were looking out in wonderment. At 5.30 we reached the mouth, but keeping too near the point, ran on a mud spit and stuck fast. Our efforts to get off were unavailing, so we remained for the night.

I dined with Sir Thomas [Cochrane][7] and he gave us some amusing yarns about his experiences at Rome, Naples, &c. When we went on deck it was not quite dark; we were 40 or 50 yards from the beach, and all along close to the water sat a crowd of big red baboons, evidently discussing the great black object on their shores.

[7] Admiral Cochrane was not knighted in fact until 1847.

Wed. 16th Finding the ship would not come off the mud with the means used, a cutter with Lieutenant Bonham and ten men were sent over to Malacca for the *Pluto* steamer and *Wolverine* to come to our assistance. However, we did not remain idle, but laid out more anchors, and at high water hove her off and got outside by 9 p.m.

Brunei, Borneo

AUGUST

Thur. 7th After a fine quiet sail along the Borneo shore we arrived off the Brunei River, where we found the Admiral with the rest of the squadron at anchor inside Labuan Island.

Pangeran Bedrudin in his proa

Sat. 9th Weighed and proceeded into the Brunei River with the Admiral and a guard of honour consisting of 170 Marines, &c., to return a visit from Badrudeen [Bedrudin],[8] nephew of the Sultan of Borneo. We saw him as he passed yesterday in his boat, a long, low proa with eighteen paddles, a 4-pounder gun in the bow, red silk umbrella with green fringe, a large yellow ensign, with all the ragtag and bobtail of the place. Some of the nobs had on sky-blue jackets and yellow pyjamas, much like the worthies of Siak. The *Agincourt* saluted him with seven guns and the Admiral sent him back in the *Nemesis* steamer, which doubtless gratified his vanity much.

[8] Pangeran Bedrudin, a brother of Rajah Muda Hassim, was to defeat Pangeran Usop when Usop attempted to return to Brunei after the destruction of his fort, as described in the pages following. Bedrudin and Muda Hassim were later betrayed by the Sultan, a feeble-minded, avaricious character said to have the head of an idiot and the heart of a pirate, as a consequence of which both brothers killed themselves.

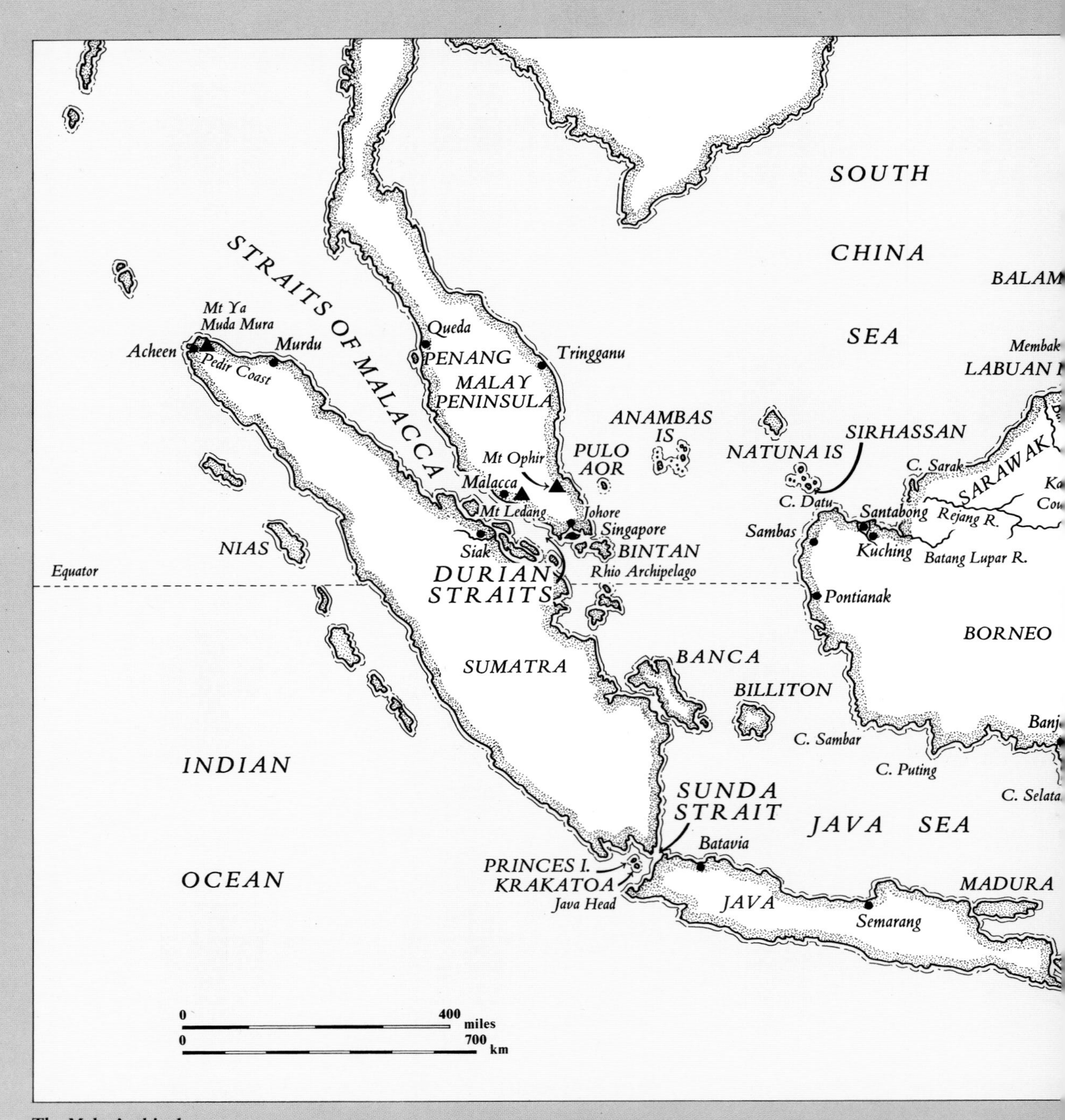

The Maly Archipelago

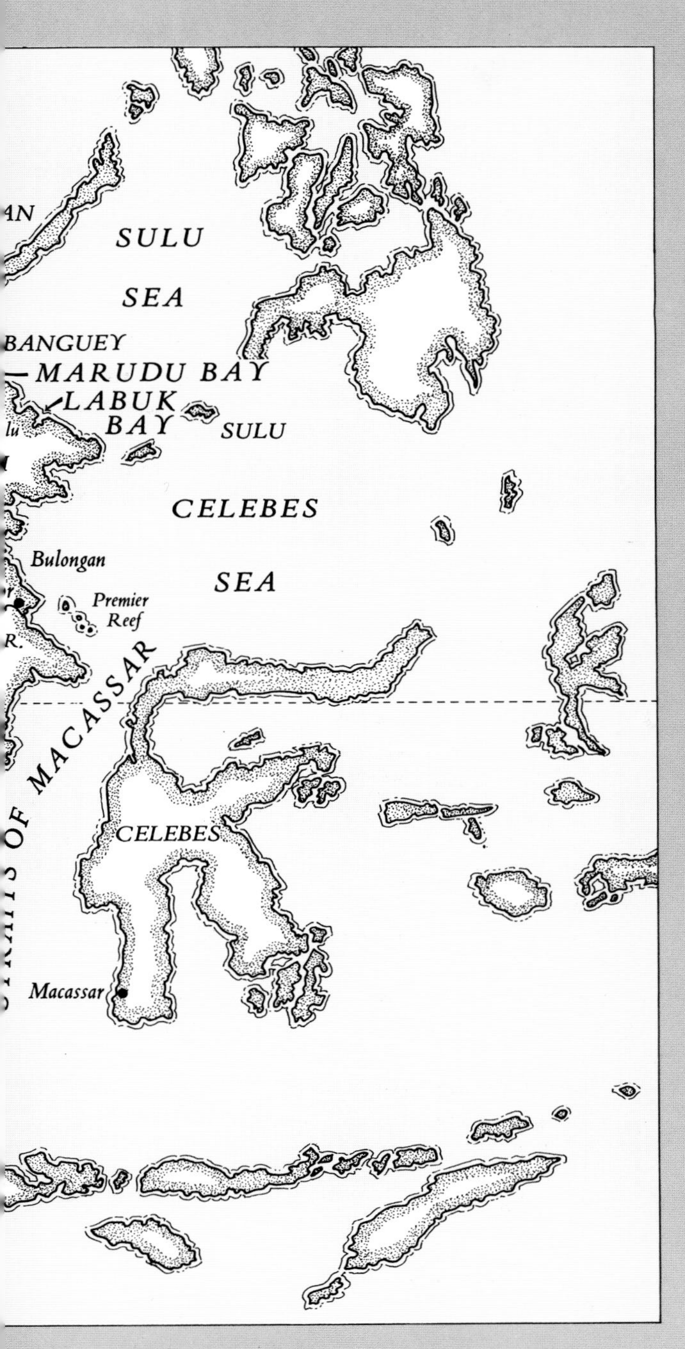

Dayak

"Brunei ladies"

Malay chieftain

The scenery is pretty up the winding reaches, well wooded with fine trees on both banks, the jungle cleared in some places by burning, leaving fine grasslands. A sudden bend of the river brought us in sight of the town, an extraordinary looking place built on piles, extending a couple of miles along sandbanks on each side of the river, generally nearly dry at low water. The houses are mean, built of wood, thatched with palm leaves. The population, about 10,000, almost live in their narrow, light canoes. We anchored about 6 o'clock in the centre of the town, in 6 fathoms of water, the *Pluto* and *Nemesis* half a mile farther up the river. The natives are fine, active Malays, light and muscular; of a light brown complexion; intelligent, but not handsome: many have a suspicious, downward look. Most of the men are smartly dressed; all are armed with creese, or spear, the former stuck in their waist belts, under the jacket. Some carry such a lot of arms that the jacket sticks out on one side. The women have good figures, but not features. They appear to wear only one garment, the sarong, generally of blue cotton, like a wide bag without a bottom. Into this they put themselves, and one end is rolled tightly round the body and tucked in. They almost live in the water.

The Admiral landed with Mr Brooke and Captain Bethune and a guard of Marines, to a conference with the Sultan of Borneo, at his house, in order to get him to sign a treaty for the suppression of piracy. It seems there is a strong party at the court of Brunei who live by piracy, at the head of which is Pangeran, or Prince, Usop, a notorious pirate.[9] On the other side is Muda Hassim, Uncle to the Sultan, Rajah of Sarawak, and Brooke's friend, who [is] interested in suppressing piracy and developing trade. The piratical party, a desperate set of fellows, threaten the Sultan, who is a weak vacillating ruler, and fears Pangeran Usop, who has a large following and a stockade about a mile up the river. The Sultan signed the treaty, so did Muda Hassim, but Usop maintained a sullen demeanour and declined to sign. After a long and late meeting, Usop was given till midday tomorrow to come to terms, or have his fort knocked about his ears.

During the day we were surrounded by canoes with natives who brought a few ducks and fowls for sale, and a mild kind of durian, which were exchanged for empty bottles, in great demand among the natives. Some well-dressed Malays came on board, probably spies. Later in the afternoon all the natives with their canoes deserted us, and we could see there was excitement amongst them on shore, for we could see a great commotion, in moving away their furniture and children. Evidently there is something up, and it was considered necessary to take precautions among a bold and treacherous set of savages. The sentries were doubled, and all were on the alert. The Admiral came on board and had his cot slung under the awning on the after part of the quarterdeck. It was a hot, still evening, and very dark. Beside our own crew, we had upwards of a hundred men from the flagship on board. As it was so hot below, the men formed into little knots on deck, yarning and telling stories.

[9] Pangeran Usop, an illegitimate son of the former Sultan of Brunei, and therefore unable to succeed to the throne, was a cousin of Rajah Muda Hassim, of whom he was intensely jealous. He had formed a murky business alliance – trafficking in stolen goods and slaves – with Serip Usman, a half-breed Arab who, without any rights to the territory, had built a fort up the Maradu River. Usop was eventually slain by the neighbouring chief of Kimanis, into whose land he fled after his defeat by Bedrudin.

We were watching the reflections in the still water, and the noiseless canoes gliding stealthily about in the shadows of the houses. We were thinking over the stories of desperate night attacks, of Malays running amok and other horrors, till we were tired. I went to bed and was soon asleep. About 11 o'clock a hurried message came off from Captains Talbot and Bethune, who were at the Sultan's with Mr Brooke, to send a party of Marines to them immediately, as they were warned by the Sultan's party that Usop intended to attack them. An officer and a guard of Marines were sent accordingly. Again all was still, and everyone wrapped in sleep, except the officer of the watch and sentries, who were supposed to be awake. About 2 in the morning I was awoke by a fearful shriek, followed by a confused sort of cry; I heard someone cry out "They are boarding us over the starboard bow". Willcox, the 1st Lieutenant, rushed on deck and sung out "Beat to quarters". My half-awake thoughts were that a desperate attack had been made on us by Malays: I seized my sword, but it having been such a peaceable weapon, it refused to leave the scabbard, being rusted in. The other officers were also rushing on deck where there was the wildest confusion, men tumbling over one another in the dark; the drummer beating to quarters, men rushing about with their drawn cutlasses, searching for the enemy, who were nowhere to be seen. We then found out that it was all a false alarm. On enquiry, it was discovered that one of the midshipmen happened to be sleeping on the deck, next to a young officer of Marines. The night being hot, they were not much encumbered with clothes. The middie was restless, and in his sleep put his cold arm across the young Marine's throat, who dreamt that a Malay was cutting his throat, and screamed out lustily; hence the commotion and panic. One of the sailors had been sleeping in the hammock netting, forward, and in his sleep turned out the wrong way, overboard into the river, which was an unpleasant way of being awoke, and might have been drowned had not there been boats full of men from other ships lying alongside. The Admiral took it very coolly and merely enquiring what was the matter. . . .

Sun. 10th A hot calm morning, therm. 89° in the coolest part of the ship. Everyone on the alert. Mr Brooke and Captain Bethune came on board. Great diplomatic work going on; messages passing backwards and forwards between the Admiral and the Sultan. The town, which before was swarming with people, was now nearly empty: the few who remained were carrying away the remainder of their furniture and property. As the refractory Rajah refused to comply with the demands, and had collected a large force of his friends and dependants, we moved higher up the river, abreast of his stockades. The *Pluto* and *Nemesis* went up a branch of the river which flanks them; the gunboats with the Marines accompanied them. We gave him till 2 p.m. and then fired a shot through the roof of his house, just as a reminder, on which he immediately opened fire from his stockade with five or six of his

Proceeding to the attack on Serip Usman's piratical nest. *Nemesis* and *Pluto* are ahead of *Vixen*, which is towing *Wolverine* and *Cruiser*. Mount Kinabalu can be seen in the background.

Ground plan of the attack on Marudu

A Enemy's stockade
1. Eight-gun battery
2. Eight gingalls
3. Burial ground
4. Serip Usman's house
B Three-gun battery
C Floating battery – no guns
D Double boom made of two tree trunks, one 7 feet and the other 5 feet in circumference, fastened to each launch by an iron chain
EEE Jungle that had been cut down and underwood about breast high
F Gardens
GG Malay town
HH High jungle

English force
1 Rocket battery
K Boats – 21 in number, eight of them with guns
1 *Agincourt*'s launch
2 *Vixen*'s pinnace
3 *Dædalus*' launch
4 *Vestal*'s launch
5 *Agincourt*'s barge
L Small ditch which before the action was supposed to be a deep branch of the river

guns, which was most ridiculous, as a broadside from our 84s and 32s sent his stockades and other defences flying in splinters and dismounted his guns. At the same time the two other ships were giving him a heavy flanking fire. However brave the chief and his followers might be, they soon found this much too hot for them; their places were soon riddled with grapeshot. In about a quarter of an hour they had cleared out, and fled into the jungle at the back. The Marines and small-arm men landed and took possession, and kept up a dropping fire on stragglers. One poor fellow had a narrow squeak as I was watching him swimming across the river under a shower of bullets. The officers had some trouble to make the men cease firing, as is always the case. We had no one hurt, as the enemy's shot went well over us, but one unfortunate man of the *Nemesis* was blown from his gun, through carelessness in loading. I don't think the enemy had many killed, as they did not stop long enough for that.

After the firing ceased, a signal was made by the party on shore for the Surgeon, so I landed at the stockade, which I found considerably knocked about, and about a dozen bodies of unfortunate Malays. I found one of our men had fainted from the heat. It was fortunate we had no wounded, as my assistant was absent in another ship. One of our 10-inch shells had pitched close to the enemy's magazine, and, fortunately for them, had not exploded. The Rajah had removed most of his valuables and his women, but a quantity of goods were found, an English calico, a sextant, chronometer and telescope. A pair of cut-glass decanters and a quantity of English crockery was found, but given over to the natives, as looting was strictly forbidden. We took away twenty-two guns of small calibre, mostly Spanish or native manufacture, two of which the Admiral kept; the remainder were given to the Sultan. A new suit of English boat-sails, charts, &c., were probably the proceeds of plunder of some unfortunate merchant vessel wrecked on the coast. A Captain and Mrs Page had been wrecked some time ago, and made prisoners by this very chief, and afterwards ransomed for 12,000 dollars.[10] We found a couple of natives of Bengal who had been made prisoners and slaves. We sent them on board the *Pluto* among their own countrymen, to their great delight. We also found a Japanese, who had been seventeen years in slavery amongst them, but he refused to leave.

Mon. 11th I went on shore with Captains Giffard, Talbot and Bethune to have a look at the enemy's quarters. The natives had completely gutted the place, nothing of value remained; they were even carrying off banana trees and betel palms from the garden. The whole place presented a sad spectacle. It reminded me of some of the Chinese houses after being sacked. We walked to the top of the hill at the back, where we had a good view of a fine, undulating country, with wood, grassland and rivers. We found the grass and low jungle so thick we could not go far, and the stench from the dead was already

[10] On January 4th 1841 the 700-ton *Sultana* (Captain Page), with a cargo of cotton, was struck by lightning in the South China Sea and caught fire, forcing the officers and crew to abandon ship. On seeking help in Brunei, they – and all their salvaged property – were seized by the Sultan, who demanded a ransom for their release. Eventually, after almost eight months' imprisonment, the captives were surrendered to the East India Company's steamer *Diana*, under the command of Captain Congleton.

beginning to be very offensive. Many wounded were found today about, and were taken charge of by the natives. We were obliged to leave the poor fellows. I have noticed how quickly the natives recover from injuries compared to our men, but they lead healthier lives. The chief is said to be deserted by most of his followers, and has fled to a village a dozen miles off.

. . . The poor Sultan was in a great state of alarm during the firing; his harem revolted, and some of the ladies escaped by swimming across the river. An officer and guard of Marines had been sent to protect the Sultan, but the ladies were disposed to monopolise all the Joeys' protection on themselves, the red coats were so attractive.

Marudu Bay, Borneo

Sun. 17th Weighed at daylight and beat up Marudu Bay in the teeth of a very heavy squall, which obliged us to shorten all sail. The squalls here are heavy and frequent: one we experienced yesterday lasted five hours. Anchored at sunset. Making preparations for landing tomorrow, to attack the fort and stockades of a notorious piratical chief, Ceriffe Hoosmaun [Serip or Sherif Usman], a desperate fellow, of Arab descent, with a following of Arabs, Malays, Illanuns and Sulu people; all pirates, who have a strong position on the Marudu River, and a fleet of piratical prahus, which scour the seas in this neighbourhood and attack all unarmed vessels they think they can rob with impunity, and murder those who give them trouble. They have many slaves, hill people and natives of Manilla, &c. The [*Guilhelm*] *Ludwig*, a Bremen merchant vessel I saw at Singapore last year, was wrecked and plundered ten months since, near this place, and others, missing, are supposed to have shared the same fate.

This is a fine deep bay, about 10 miles wide, surrounded by hilly and mountainous country; some parklike scenery, and the great mountain, Kinabalu, with his head high above the clouds, form a beautiful picture. The top of the mountain is broken into innumerable crags and peaks, some like great castles and ruins. It is very steep towards the west. I don't think it has ever been visited by Europeans.

Mon. 18th Steam up by daylight; embarked 200 Marines from the other ships, and the same number of bluejackets with their officers. The Admiral came on board with Mr Brooke and Captains Bethune and Talbot. Weighed about 8 and stood up the bay, towing *Wolverine* and *Cruiser* brigs, and seven boats with guns. The steamers *Nemesis* and *Pluto* preceded us, one on either bow to show the depth of water. We carried the Admiral's flag. We anchored at 1 p.m. about a mile from the shore, at the bottom of the bay, near the mouth of a small river, a few miles up which Ceriffe Hoosmaun has fortified himself. During the afternoon the Marines and small-arm men were embarked in twenty-five boats, including gunboats, with two days' provisions, Captain Talbot in command. The men gave three British cheers as they gave way on their oars against a nasty lop of a sea. As it was too late for any operations tonight, they anchored just outside the mouth of the river. As I was senior medical officer here, I was ordered to remain to receive any wounded sent down.

Tue. 19th During the night we could hear that the enemy were on the alert, for they were beating their gongs every few minutes. The squadron of boats got under weigh at daylight, and pulled into the river. A couple of natives of Brunei were taken as pilots: they did not relish the job, but had no choice but to do their work properly. Four or five miles up, this pirates' nest was situated, just below which a boom was thrown across the river, which was 30 or 40 yards wide at this place. The boom was made from the trunks of large trees fastened together, and to the banks by chain cables, which were clamped along the under-side. Two hundred yards above this, the river divides into two branches; on the tongue of land between is a strong wooden battery, mounting three guns, which commands the boom. At the same distance on the right bank of the river is a large stockade fort with eight guns pointing on the boom, within point-blank range. On the other side eight gingalls were mounted, but pointing in another direction. On the left branch of the river was a floating battery, but no guns mounted on it. Ceriffe Hoosmaun's house was in the large stockade, beside many other houses and stores. A flag of truce, brought down to the boom by a chief, was received by Captain Talbot, who had Williamson, Mr Brooke's interpreter, with him. The message was unsatisfactory, as they only asked for delay. The chief returned and hauled down his white flag, upon which the three-gun battery immediately opened fire on the boats which had been driven up to the boom by the strong flood-tide. Our fellows soon returned their fire with interest. The firing was hot and sharp, both from great guns and musketry. In the meantime every effort was made to cut away the boom, but this proved most formidable work under a heavy fire from the forts. It was thought that the river ran in front of the eight-gun stockade, or the Marines and small-arm men might have stormed the right of the enemy's position. The rocket party landed on the right bank and fired with good effect into the stockade.

The first few discharges from the enemy's guns told with deadly effect on our gunboats, knocking over many of our poor fellows. The enemy's guns had been so accurately laid for the dreadful boom, against which the boats were forced by the tide, that their shot ploughed along through the press, but the quick firing from our boats soon made the enemy's aim less certain, and as our shot told with more effect, their aim became less steady, and now and then, when a rocket took good effect, or a shot told well, a rallying cheer from

xen, *Pluto* and *Nemesis* at anchor in Brunei. The Sultan's palace is the largest building between the yellow and orange flags to the right.

our fellows showed that as the game became hotter the enemy's courage cooled. After a party of our men had been working desperately for fifty minutes at the boom, an opening was made near the right bank of the river, and through it rushed the boats with a true British cheer, which completely terrified the enemy from their guns. They were now seen escaping through the embrasures and over the parapets in crowds, and only one or two guns continued to fire, and these were soon silenced. The small-arm men and Marines soon rushed to the front and finished the business. Only the dead and flying were to be seen.

The action commenced at 8.50 a.m. and lasted till 9.55 a.m. Many hand-to-hand conflicts took place: a Malay in the act of plunging his spear into Captain Lyster of the *Agincourt*, his Coxwain came up and, with a sweep of his cutlass, nearly severed the Malay's head from his body. Many chiefs were killed or wounded: Ceriffe Hoosmaun and another ceriffe are said to be among the latter.[11] About a hundred of their followers are reported killed, but it is impossible to get any reliable account at present. On our side we have a melancholy list for poor friends at home: six killed and fifteen wounded, two mortally. All the killed were from round shot, dreadful wounds. The *Agincourt*'s boats suffered most, the ones in which my assistants were. In one, Assistant Surgeon Whipple amputated an arm in the boat under fire. Gibbard, a fine young fellow, a Mate of the *Wolverine*, shot in the lower part of the back, the ball passed upwards through his chest; Campbell, a Marine, with hip and thigh shot-smashed – these are the mortally wounded, and died during the night. Three of the *Vixen*'s men were wounded, but not dangerously.

[11] Usman was killed, his followers who survived the attack later forming a settlement, a peaceable one, in the south-west of the island of Palawan in the Philippines. Theirs was the last pirate settlement in Marudu Bay.

After the place had been taken, the brass guns secured and the rest spiked, the whole place was set on fire. The houses, all being of wood and thatched with palm leaves, and as we afterwards found, contained a great store of camphor, we had a terrible blaze, which lit up all the forest round.

The boats returned to the ships about 5 o'clock. I had everything ready for the reception of the wounded, and the Assistant Surgeons, Whipple and Patrick, brought all the wounded of *Agincourt* and *Vixen* to me. One poor fellow, Joshua Darlington, A.B., had his right arm terribly shattered by a large ball, which had entered at the back part of the deltoid muscle, smashing the head of the humerus and traversing the whole of the arm, lodging in front of the wrist. Nothing could be done to save the arm, so that I at once proceeded to remove the limb at the shoulder joint, ably assisted by Whipple and Patrick. Surgical operations on a crowded deck, by the light of half a dozen dip candles, with too many excited lookers on, are not done under the most favourable conditions, but one had no choice, and my patient made a good recovery. He received his wound when in the act of loading his musket.*

It is a pity some better plan of attack had not been adopted, but the nature of the ground was quite unknown, and a rough Malay chart quite misled those who had the management of the attack.

* Darlington was afterwards a pensioner at Greenwich Hospital.

The attack on Marudu, August 19th 1845 (*black and white*)

The operating theatre in *Vixen*

In the evening another party under Captain Giffard were sent to complete the destruction of this pirates' nest. They met with no enemy; the place was deserted.

Five of our killed were taken on board the *Nemesis* and buried at sea. The other poor fellow was so dreadfully mangled that he was buried from the *Dædalus*' boat, where he was killed.

Wed. 20th A party went from the ship, which I accompanied, to the scene of action. We found that the pirates had removed their dead during the night. We found a party of plunderers at work, but a few shots dispersed them. The men finished the destruction of the enemy's works except the boom, which resisted all means at our disposal in the time. It was constructed of five or six large trees lashed together with a chain cable and very cleverly constructed. We all regaled ourselves on bull beefsteaks from a fine animal we shot, and found plenty of ducks and fowls which we brought on board. Many creeses and spears were picked up and a number of curious weapons, and some more brass guns ready to have been put into the new proas burnt yesterday. We found a curious old Spanish blunderbuss, some old rifles and muskets, one 6 feet long; English books, sermons principally; crates of chinaware; boxes of silk, mostly spoilt; some hundredweight of camphor which some of our men, in their ignorance, set fire to. The brass guns were sent on board.

While our men were searching about, they saw something move in an old waterlogged canoe. On going alongside it they discovered a poor wretched

Discovery of the wounded slave-woman

native girl lying in it, with a small child in her arm. On moving her, when I arrived, I found her right elbow had been shattered by a grapeshot. She was only covered by an old mat. I gave her some water, which she drank eagerly. She had been wounded in the action yesterday, and crept in her fright into this canoe. As soon as Mr Brooke came up we got her history. She said she was a slave owned by a native of a neighbouring island. Her name is Beedean. We placed her and her child in the bottom of the cutter, carried her on board the *Vixen*, where a cot was soon rigged for her and Whipple and I took her arm off above the elbow, at which she never squeaked, but held her baby tightly in her other arm. The operation did well, and in five days she and her baby were sent on board the *Cruiser* and left at Sarawak under Mr Brooke's care. She was offered to be sent back to her own place, but would not hear of it. She said they would kill her. She was frightfully ugly, but the sailors were very attentive, and as she had no clothes to speak of, soon rigged her out in white jacket and trousers. The piccaninny was made a pet of, and it was laughable to see a rough old sailor carefully making pap out of a ship's biscuit and feeding the baby. They were sorry to part with their charges. Before we left two slaves, Manilla men, escaped to the ship.

After the amputation

Balambangan and Banguey Islands

Fri. 22nd Weighed at 10 a.m. and went over to Banguey, an island a few miles to the NE. The shore is hilly and covered with jungle. In the evening we returned and anchored near the rest of the squadron. Sir Thomas left us, returning to his flagship, at which, I think, no one in the *Vixen* is sorry, as he is at times disagreeable about dress, and very pompous. He is himself a regular old buck, and looks as if he kept himself in a bandbox.

Thur. 28th The Admiral sent us on to Manilla to announce his arrival. Parted company with the rest of the squadron and ran ahead, with all sail and steam, at the rate of 12 knots. Nearly ran on a low island in the night.

Manilla, Luzon

Fri. 29th We had a continuance of heavy rain and squalls, and in the midst of both ran into Manilla Bay and anchored a mile and a half off the town. I went on shore with some of our fellows and dined at the Gaskell's Hotel, table d'hôte. Most of the company consisted of masters of merchant ships, some of whom I had met before in China; some very lively individuals. Went out to visit some of the shops and bought some beautifully fine plaited straw cheroot cases. Cheroots are 8 dollars a thousand. A gentleman, whose name I have

The Praya Grande, Manilla

forgotten, gave me a drive in his buggy round the citadel lines, or Praya Grande; the road in wretched repair, but crowded with carriages, mostly open, with a pair of horses and a postilion, or *cochero* [?],[12] in a cutaway coat, a flat Malay hat and jackboots without feet. There was a fair display of beauty, but pale and sallow; no bonnets, but the hair dressed tastefully. We met crowds of the native factory girls, in their natty little jackets and tight sarongs, going home from their work.

[12] Cree uses the neologism "cochière" in mistake probably for *cochero* (coachman), though in fact this is not the equivalent of *postíllon* (postilion). And below he introduces the mongrel word "calesse", presumably meaning *calesa*.

In the evening Willcox, Dent and I squeezed into a *calesa* and drove to a distant part of the city, through seas of mud, for this is the rainy season, to see some native dancing. A young girl went through a wonderful fandango, with pantomimic movements, her long black hair reaching to her heels. We returned to old Blanco's Cuatros Naciones Hotel to sleep.

Cheroot making

Sat. 30th We went off to the ship at daylight in a banca, or canoe, a narrow rickety affair for rather a rough sea. I was on shore again in the afternoon and called Sturges, American Consul, a good fellow I had met before.[13] Met Diggles, a merchant, and Mrs D., living at Santa Cruz. She is a daughter of old Garling of Penang. Call on Mr Farren, English Consul.

[13] In September 1843 during *Vixen*'s previous visit to Manilla.

The Admiral and the rest of the ships arrived in the bay and were saluted from the forts. The Admiral landed in state, and was again saluted. It was a lovely evening and we took our drive in the Praya Grande, and met all the fashion and beauty of Manilla. The Spanish ladies were laughing and talking at the top of their voices, and making their remarks on *los ingleses*. Bailey was with Giles in a *calesa* ahead of us and frightened the *cochero* by telling him that Giles was lunatico. Slept at Blanco's and nearly got swamped again in going off to the ship in bad weather.

SEPTEMBER

Mon. 1st I took a stroll amongst the native shops and bought some very fine pineapple-fibre, or piña-cloth, for pocket handkerchiefs. Saw a review of some of the native cavalry: they have rather fine men, but small horses. There are said to be 7,000 native troops in Manilla, officered by Spaniards; very few European troops. In the evening went to a ball in the citadel, given by the Governor to Sir Thomas Cochrane and the British Navy. Most of the Spanish grandees in Manilla were there, the Spanish naval and military officers and

The Governor's ball

British merchants and their ladies and, of course, plenty of the fair donnas, who appeared shy and crowded together on one side of the room when not dancing. It was a good room and well lighted, and a good band. Some of the gentlemen amused us by dancing with their hands in their pockets. Met Dr Stirling, in private practice here, who introduced me to his wife and a Miss Wilson, nice looking. Met Sturges, American Consul, and his wife; also Diggles, English Consul, and others. No scarcity of partners.

The ball had to break up at the early hour of 11, as they close the citadel gates soon after, and everyone was hurried away in the midst of a pelting storm. There was great confusion amongst the carriages, someone had

"A Manilla Invincible" (*on silk*)

appropriated Dent's and mine, so we made free with someone else's and drove back to the hotel as fast as we could. There was a large number of officers from the ships. We all supped together. There was plenty of noise and many were disposed to keep it up late. There were not beds enough for all, so I thought I would secure one before there was a general rush. I found my way into a great loft with iron bedsteads all round, not much bed linen. I picked out one, but it had a pair of boots on it, which I transferred to another bed and turned in. By and by a noisy party came up to bed, but all the beds had occupants, and the owner of the boots was quite oblivious as to where he had deposited them, and vented his groggy abuse on some unknown culprit.

At Sea

Wed. 3rd 2 p.m. weighed, with the rest of the squadron beating out of the bay.

Thur. 4th Fine, hot morning, nearly calm. At 6 I was called to see one of the men and found it was a bad case of cholera. I employed all the usual remedies, but the poor fellow died at 11 a.m. At noon we had a second case, who died at 7.45 p.m. A third case occurred during the night. The former treatment of calomel and opium being apparently useless, with the other approved remedies, I gave him half a drachm of sulphate of zinc, dissolved in warm water, which did not increase his vomiting, but he improved and ultimately recovered.[14] We had five or six other cases, but they were milder and did well. All the cases occurred in men who kept the first watch last night. The officer of the watch, Lieutenant Bonham, complained of a hot wind, which blew off the land in the night, was very oppressive, with a putrid odour, and made him feel quite ill.

Fri. 5th Nearly calm. Made but little progress. No other cases of cholera.

Sun. 7th Island of Luzon still in sight. Light airs from NE. Fell in with an American frigate, the *Constitution*, Captain Percival,[B] from Macao for Manilla. As our ships were short of bread, we ran up alongside of him to ask if he could spare us some. We found him at quarters, cleared for action, as he could not understand meeting so many "Britishers" and began to calculate we were up to mischief, and "he guessed our Minister and their President Polk had been at loggerheads and were going to make a tarnation smash of it". Commodore Percival was glad to see he was mistaken, and would be happy to salute if our "Admiral Cochrane would reciprocate", so accordingly salutes were fired and he supplied us with bread and whisky, for the use of the squadron; to be returned at Rio. She is a fine big ship, but narrow; heavily

[14] Death from cholera is caused by dehydration resulting from the huge loss of fluid brought about by the diarrhoea its toxins induce. It can be very rapid. It is only in the last few decades that rehydration therapy techniques have proved effective. Cree appears not to have had any real insight into the essential pathology of the condition, nor did he have at his disposal any truly effective treatment. Then, as now, some cholera cases would recover of their own accord.

[15] *Constitution*, the first armed vessel built by the United States, and the U.S. Navy's first flagship, was constructed at Hartt's Shipyard, Boston, in 1794–7, with a displacement of 2,200 tons and an original armament of forty-four guns. Nicknamed "Old Ironsides", she was commanded by a succession of brilliant and resourceful men – Edward Preble, Isaac Hull, William Bainbridge. In 1803–5 she took part in the blockade which broke the power of Algerian and Tripolitan corsairs, and in the War of 1812 she fought with distinction against the British. In 1844–6 she was engaged on special service in the Pacific Ocean and East Indian waters, spending 495 days at sea and covering 52,279 miles. Rajah Brooke gives a clue to some of her activities in 1845 in a letter, dated May 22nd, he

Funeral at sea for the cholera victims

armed. Captain P. was polite, drinking brandy and water and smoking cigars, and spitting all about his cabin, which was in great confusion, with his furniture piled in a heap to clear away the stern guns.[15]

Later the same month at Hong Kong *Vixen* takes in $2 million, part of the ransom money. The silver, weighing about 50 tons, is packed in 500 boxes. On October 11th there is a typhoon, and on that date Cree also records that *Vixen* has now discharged her silver into *Iris* for conveying to the Bank of England. Whilst on the island, Cree is involved in the usual round of "visiting friends, flirting with the girls, country rambles and picnics", and engages in "a new dance, lately arrived from civilisation, called 'The Polka' ".

---

wrote from Brunei to his friend John Templer: "... You must know, that since we last left this place for Singapore, the American frigate 'Constitution' has been here to offer immediate protection, and a treaty of friendship and commerce, on the grounds of the coal being ceded to them, and right of exclusive trade granted. It is probable, that from the badness of their interpreter (who was formerly my drunken servant), that the demand for exclusive trade has been erroneously understood; but independently of this, had the American officers remained here longer, and been better versed in native politics, there can be no doubt that both the sultan and Pangeran Usop would have formed this alliance, or become sufficiently intimate to gain them to their party, merely out of spite and opposition to Muda Hassim and Budrudeen." – *The Private Letters of Sir James Brooke, K.C.B., Rajah of Sarawak*, Vol. 2 (1853), pp. 65–6.

Canton River/Whampoa

NOVEMBER *Thur. 20th* Beautiful weather. Keying, Chinese High Imperial Commissioner, came on board with his suite and a host of followers, executioners, barbers, cooks, valets de chambre, pages, umbrella bearers, pipe bearers, purse bearers, sedan bearers, fan bearers, and other bottle-washers and gentleman's gentlemen of various kinds, but all the common lot were sent to the *Pluto* steamer which arrived last night. We were ready to receive His Excellency at 7 this morning! He had dropped down the river during the night, with a numerous fleet of pleasure-boats, mandarin and war junks, with their long streamers and flying dragons, with their carved gilt and painted sides, making a gay scene, as they slowly got under weigh in the rising sunshine. Major Caine, as Chief Magistrate of Hong Kong, and M. Gutzlaff, as interpreter, came on board. Keying was received with a Chinese salute of three guns. He is a fine dignified Tartar, about fifty-five years of age. His style is High Imperial Commissioner; Prince of the Blood; Third Member of State; Commissioner for Foreign Affairs; Governor-General of the Kwangtung and Kiangsi Provinces. He wears the red coral ball and peacock's feather in his cap, and has the yellow girdle. Four High Mandarins are with him. Pwang-tzye-shing, or Poo-tung-qua, his personal friend, son of a Hong merchant, a red ball and peacock's feather and a blue girdle. He paid £300,000 for his rank, but he has the salt monopoly at Canton. He is building a fleet of war junks at his own expense for His Imperial Master, which will cost £300,000 more. Chaou, Doctor of the Imperial College and Inspector of the Grain Department, a pock-marked, ugly old fellow. Tung, a Manchu Tartar, candidate for a prefecture, husband of an Imperial Princess, or as old Gutzlaff calls him, "the Hūsbāānd of the Enchanted Princess". Tung, who is a merry fellow, says his wife is such a devil he cannot keep her in order and must send her back to the Emperor. Lew-tsing, Doctor of the Imperial College and Lord Mayor of Canton, or Prefect of the City. The three last wear the blue ball and peacock's feather. None of them attempted to seat themselves if Keying was present, unless invited by him. Keying was very polite and made himself agreeable on board and appears a polished gentleman.

We left Whampoa at 9 and steamed down the river at a rapid pace, with the yellow flag at the main. All the forts, war junks and military stations saluted with three guns as we passed. Keying visited the engine-room and other parts of the ship, and expressed himself much pleased with the order and regularity on board. Saw the men go to quarters and fire three rounds. He performed a great feat himself, by firing one of the 84-pounder guns, which might have proved a serious accident to him, for he got on the slide and pulled the trigger while standing close to the breach, not allowing for the recoil; fortunately the tube was a bad one and the gun did not go off. A fresh tube was brought, and His Excellency was placed at the proper distance, and he fired it all right.

We arrived at Hong Kong at 5 p.m. after a very good run. Keying and all his ragtag and bobtail landed at Commissariat Wharf, where they were received by a guard of honour. The mandarins got into their chairs and altogether formed a novel procession to the house lately built by the Parsee merchants, a great place, at Harbour Master's Wharf. We found the mail of Sept. 24th had arrived and I got two welcome letters and twenty newspapers from my sister.

Hong Kong

Fri. 21st All the authorities call on Keying. A grand review of all the troops, in the Victoria Road, before Government House, where the mandarins were, and all the Hong Kong ladies, now amounting to about fifty, in their gayest attire; the soldiers fire and march past; the field pieces fire and dismount. The mandarins dine with the Governor, who gives a ball in the evening at which I had great fun. Keying evidently admired the English ladies, especially Miss Hickson, and praised her beautiful black ringlets, and called her the Queen of Beauty.

Sat. 22nd Keying calls on the Admiral, visits the flagship: saluted with seventeen guns: dines with the Admiral, who gives a ball in the evening. The quarterdeck dressed up with flowers, flags and lamps, quite a fairy scene when the ladies arrived. The mandarins appear delighted and merry after the Admiral's dinner. Tung spoils a quadrille by dancing a hornpipe with the Chief Justice, both having partaken too freely of *simkin*. It was a laughable exhibition; Tung fat, and enveloped in his silk coats, cap and peacock's feather and satin boots, with soles 2 inches thick, and capering about like an elephant, and the Judge anything but grave, flinging his long skinny legs, encased in breeches and black silk stockings, in all directions, his long visage and protuberant nose, his bushy head and broad grin, having anything but a judge-like appearance. Keying asked if we had many more judges on the island. The polka was danced by Miss Hickson with a French gentleman, and attracted a great deal of attention from the mandarins. Keying wanted to know what Miss Hickson's bustle was made of. He took especial notice of one or two little girls there. On Keying leaving the ship, about 11 p.m., in the Admiral's barge, there was a grand display of fireworks.

Sun. 23rd The mandarins dine with the General, and some of the ladies go in the evening. Keying presented Miss Hickson with a beautifully embroidered cap, and exchanged handkerchiefs with another lady.

Mon. 24th Keying gives a dinner to all the bigwigs, heads of departments,

Tung and the Chief Justice of Hong Kong on board the flagship, H.M.S. *Agincourt*

at Hong Kong, at which about 500 different Chinese dishes were produced. The healths of Queen Victoria and the Emperor of China were drunk, speeches were made, and songs were sung. At the Governor's dinner, in the middle of it, Keying proposed as a toast "peace and friendship between the English and Chinese", but the Governor got up and said, "Time enough for that, not now", meaning it was to be drank after dinner, not at it; but it was thought to show want of tact in the Governor.

Tue. 25th Keying and suite came on board before 7 o'clock. The Admiral was waiting to receive him. On taking leave they embraced, as if they were the dearest friends parting. The Admiral presented Keying with his telescope and a brace of pistols. He had before sent the Admiral some handsome silk and other valuables. He wanted to present the crew of the Admiral's barge with 100 dollars, and the crew of the *Vixen* with 500, which on being declined he seemed annoyed, and said he would not sit down, or eat on board, if it was not accepted. So they pacified him by referring the matter to the Governor. He gave 300 dollars to the *Pluto,* which was also declined. It was explained to Keying that money presents were not allowed to be accepted in the Queen's service.

A salute was fired from the battery as we started through the Cap-sing-mun passage. On our way we were also saluted by the Chinese forts and war junks. I almost got into the bad books of Lew, the Lord Mayor of Canton, by a practical joke that Willcox, the 1st Lieutenant, played on me: he came up to

"Keying and the Admiral": the High Imperial Commissioner and Admiral Cochrane taking leave of each other on November 25th. The Rev. Charles Gutzlaff is depicted in the right foreground.

me on deck and said, "Doctor, do you know that the gunroom is full of those confounded flunkeys, and one of them is snoring in your cabin." I rushed down and saw, on my bed, a great body and a pair of legs encased in black satin boots on the pillow, the head at the other end snoring most lustily. I unceremoniously laid hold of him, and rolled him on to the floor. At the same time one of the servants rushed in and jabbered something, holding up a mandarin's cap with the peacock's feather: I immediately saw it was the great Lord Mayor I had treated so roughly. I apologised as well as I could. His Lordship, who was now wide awake, sat at the table and said something to his valet, who brought him writing materials, with which he set to work filling a large sheet of paper with neatly written Chinese characters. I thought, now I am in for a report to the Lord High Commissioner, and told Gutzlaff, the interpreter. Chaou, who was in the Purser's cabin next door, laughed immoderately. Soon the paper was handed in, and I got Gutzlaff to interpret it. I was pleased to see it was no report, but an ode Lew had been composing on his departure from Hong Kong.

. . . As we passed, the batteries were manned by the Tartar soldiers standing in a row along the top of the walls, with their banners. The commanding officers of forts and war junks came towards us as we passed to pay their respects, but we did not stop. Some of them had their bows and arrows, &c., slung on their backs, and were in full dress, with their visiting-cards ready to present.

愚弟何芳頓首拜

Card of the Lord Mayor of Canton

1846

On January 18th Cree notes: "There is a riot at Canton on account of an order from Keying to allow foreigners to enter the city, which the mob strenuously oppose." On February 4th a Tartar general arrives with 6,000 troops "to overawe the disorderly mob", and Keying (Ch'i-ying) has two Chinese arsonists beheaded. On February 7th Cree visits the city, and on February 13th *Vixen* anchors in Hong Kong harbour.

Hong Kong

FEBRUARY *Wed. 18th* Since we came back to Hong Kong my leisure-time has been spent in visiting pleasant society, and in boating and rambling about the neighbourhood. This morning, with [Lieutenant John Dalrymple] Hay[B] and Webber, start at daylight to walk to the top of Victoria Peak, a good climb before breakfast. There we enjoyed the magnificent view over the town and harbour and the surrounding mountains. In the afternoon, at Dent's bungalow, have a pleasant chat with old Chinnery,[B] the artist.

Sat. 28th All the week calling, dining and dancing with Hong Kong friends. Today we have an invaliding board on a number of sick to go home with us. For our relief, H.M. Steam Vessel [Frigate] *Vulture* arrived today from Singapore and England.

MARCH *Sun. 1st* Hurrah!! Ordered home at last!!

Yesterday, three captains with three cocked hats and three engineers went into our boilers, and after making a careful survey of the same, pronounced them to be used up, and no longer to be fit for service. So this afternoon Willcox and I make many parting calls on our friends.

Mon. 2nd Busy today hoisting in 1 million dollars, mostly in sycee silver or lumps about the size of an egg-cup, worth about 7 dollars each, packed in strong wooden boxes, hoisted up in a rope net, in case any should fall overboard. Poor John Chinaman has been pretty well squeezed by John Bull and does not like it, I fancy.

"Hoisting in the dollars", Hong Kong. The large building on the waterfront (*left*) is the Barracks, to the left of which is the officers' quarters, behind which is the General's quarters. The Governor's house can be seen directly behind *Vixen*, while the two-storey building on the hillside to the right is Albany Barracks.

There are some changes amongst our shipmates: Dent leaves to join the flagship; Hay goes to the *Vestal*. In the afternoon Willcox and I make more calls and spend the evening at West Point, and wish the dear girls goodbye. Afterwards spend the rest of the evening at the 18th mess, where after 10 there is singing and noise, with champagne and devilled bones for supper, then more songs and more speeches, and a march down to the boat at 3 in the morning, with cheers for the jolly Vixens.

Tue. 3rd Take a last sketch and look at the town. Noon, steam up and paddling out by the Liemoon passage. Stop to pick up Gransmore, the Purser of *Wolverine*, Captain Lyster, Commander Morritt, Foot [e?], of the *Plover*, and seven invalids from the squadron, go with us. Proceed at full speed till we get well outside, when we make all sail for Singapore and England, with a good breeze on the port quarter. Weather cloudy and squally. What changes have taken place in Hong Kong since I have been in China: when I first saw it, 1841, it was then a desolate rock with a few fishermen's huts on the beach; now the handsome town is spreading all over the place.

Portsmouth/Woolwich

JUNE

Mon. 29th 33 miles from the Land's End, 86 from Start Point. 9 p.m. saw the Start light.

Tue. 30th Daylight, saw Portland. 7 a.m. took in a Cowes pilot. Noon, arrived at Spithead; got pratique and 2 p.m. went into Portsmouth harbour. Went on shore, in old England the first time for nearly seven years.

JULY *Wed. 1st* The poor invalids were sent to Haslar Hospital.

Thur. 2nd Seeing old friends; all looking older; few recognised me after my long absence.

Fri. 3rd Thank God for safe return! After all. Received welcome letters from old friends at Bridport and Honiton; one from my sister which quite took me aback, for she informs me she has been married a month, by her father's wish, although she wanted to wait till I came home. But the old gentleman, Mr Melhuish, who is thirty years older than herself, was impatient, and Father wished to see her settled. I don't think she had any previous attachment; and I don't think she feels much love for her old man, who is an attorney at Honiton and pretty well off. I received a pressing invitation to go down and see them as soon as I could get away.

6 p.m. we left Portsmouth for Woolwich, to be paid off. We had a sad accident in coming out of harbour: poor McCullum, an old sailor, fell from the fore-yard and was killed on the spot. I was walking the deck at the time, and saw the poor fellow fall with a heavy thud. Sad news for his wife, who is living at Woolwich. Such are the risks of a sailor's life.

Sat. 4th 8 a.m. off Ramsgate. 4 p.m. landed our powder at Purfleet. 6 p.m. off the dockyard, Woolwich.

Wed. 8th Poor old *Vixen* nearly dismantled. In landing our heavy guns today, one of our Marines got badly hurt, his thigh being smashed: I immediately sent him to the Marine Infirmary.

Sat. 11th The *Vixen* was paid off, stripped and pennant hauled down, and most of the fellows dispersed to their homes. Poor old *Vixen* is now a melancholy object.

I got into comfortable lodgings in Woolwich, for the present, to house my baggage and loot. My dear father came to see me. I don't find him much aged; he seems still active and strong. I went up to town with him and visited old friends.

Mon. 13th Pay my visit to Sir William Burnett, the head of our department, at Somerset House, and get an order for the College of Surgeons.

London

Tue. 14th At the India House receive a cheque for £213 9. 6. for war batta and prize-money. I have also received my medal for the China War.

Certain new regulations have come out respecting certificates for operations on the dead subject, &c. Dermott's is the only school of anatomy at present open, so Webber and I went to Dermott,[B] who lives in Bedford Square, and arranged to attend his lectures and dissect, and board in his house; which we found comfortable. He keeps a good table. Dermott is one of the leading anatomists of the present time, and a good lecturer.

The breaks in the Journals from this point onwards until the end of 1846, and again almost up to the time Cree takes up his commission as Surgeon in his next ship in August 1847, are of his own making.

AUGUST

Mon. 10th Finished my work at the College of Surgeons, and at the Admiralty.

Honiton, Devon

Sat. 22nd Leave London for Taunton by the Great Western Railway, and on to my sister's at Honiton, by hired trap, and found a warm welcome.

I remained at Honiton, at my sister's, enjoying the lovely country, sketching and visiting friends, and making new acquaintances; going to Sidmouth, and wandering about.

Honiton, Devon

Percy with her first husband in their garden at Honiton

SEPTEMBER Left Honiton with Percy to visit friends at Taunton, Bridgwater, Bristol and Clifton. Introduced to a pretty cousin and some friends of my sister's at Bedminster Lodge. The number of pretty girls quite bewilders one, but like the homeopathic maxim, "Like cures like", so the spoony complaint does not take an incurable hold.

7th Return to Honiton, where I left my sister, and next day ran down to Teignmouth, as far as the railroad is carried, and on to Plymouth by coach. I had many relatives and friends to see here; cousins grown from little children to young men and women.

Bridport, Dorset

22nd Returned to Honiton, and next day went on to Bridport. Stay at Mr John Hounsell's, the dear old master.[1] The same changes in the children here: Eliza, the eldest, grown into a pretty, clever girl of nineteen, well read and accomplished; Henry, the eldest boy, commenced medical studies at London University, and so nothing remains stationary. I had hosts of old friends to see at Bridport, which was a great pleasure, but some dear ones had gone to their last rest.

[1] Cree had been tutored by John Hounsell, himself a surgeon, during his apprenticeship in the period 1829–34. He had remained on friendly terms with him ever since, regularly visiting him and his family at Bridport when he was on leave in England or serving in home waters.

Bridge House, Bridport, home of John Hounsell. The house, which still stands, was built in 1769 by the Rev. James Hooker, First Independent minister. It was once used for a spell as a Dissenting Academy.

Oct. 3rd Left Bridport by the old four-horse coach "Forrester", but in going down the hill into Winterbourn, one of the front wheels came off and we were overturned into the hedge, but no one was hurt, except a few scratches. We had to take a dogcart to Dorchester, getting to London at 9 p.m.

NOVEMBER

10th Saw my promotion in *The Times* as Surgeon R.N., dated April 4th 1843, when I joined the *Vixen* as Acting Surgeon, which is what I contended for. I got my commission on the 12th and with Webber and one or two other friends baptised it in champagne.

Edinburgh

Having determined to go on with my medical studies at the Edinburgh University, and take out the M.D. degree, I got a year's leave from the Admiralty, and on the 21st took my passage for Leith by steamer, where I arrived on the 24th and went, by invitation, to my cousin James Cree's house in Vanburgh Place. His mother and brother David were there.

27th Matriculate at the University, and enter to courses of lectures and the infirmary practice for a year. Syme's,[B] Alison's,[B] Christison's[B] and Henderson's[B] courses: so I have plenty of work for the winter, beside James Y. Simpson's[B] midwifery, and writing my thesis, the subject of which is to be "On the principal diseases to which Europeans are most liable in China". As Leith is too far from the College, I took lodgings in South Bridge, almost opposite to the College.

DECEMBER

Now I set to work in earnest, having comfortable rooms at Mrs Ironside's, who ought to have been called Mrs Eatsides, as she is such a jolly, fat old woman. She has only three other gentlemen boarding with her. She is assisted

Edinburgh from Arthur's Seat

by her niece, who sings Scottish songs to her own accompaniment on a jingling piano. However, the cooking is good, and my room is large and well warmed.

I found I could not work as hard as I intended, as the true Scottish hospitality of my cousins and their mother, whose house was always open, and their friends, that I had continual engagements to all sorts of entertainments, and at the end of the year I found myself in a whirl of gaiety and fun, and it required all my resolution to stick moderately to my studies, but I remained well and hearty, and thankful to God for all his mercies.

1847

Edinburgh

Royal Infirmary, Edinburgh

JANUARY–MARCH

While I was at the Edinburgh Infirmary I saw some operations under ether inhalations, a new method of rendering patients insensible to pain. A great blessing, but Professor Syme rather opposes it on account of the delay and the uncertainty as to the action of the ether, but the matter is still in its infancy. It seems to have been first practised by a dentist in America, in extracting teeth.[1]

I had brought home with me some things made of gutta-percha, a newly found substance, something like indiarubber. I gave a whip made of it, and a small branch of the tree, to Professor Christison, who was delighted with the specimens, although Dr Montgomery had given him some specimens from Singapore some time ago.

I was still working at my medical studies, writing my thesis, attending the infirmary practice, and lectures, five or six a day; and also joining in some of the gaieties of the season, which are very attractive in Edinburgh. I dined with Professor Christison twice, and went to his musical parties, at which he generally has some musical celebrities. He is a talented musician himself. I also dined at Professor Syme's, who has a lovely garden with hothouses in which he cultivates bananas, pineapples, &c.

[1] In 1842 Crawford W. Long of Georgia removed a tumour from a patient under sulphuric ether; in 1844 Horace Wells, a dentist of Hartford, Connecticut, used nitrous oxide to induce anaesthesia for tooth extraction; and then in September 1846 William T.G. Morton, a Boston dentist and former pupil of Wells, began using diethyl ether for the same purpose. Within a comparatively short period the method became general practice in Great Britain and Europe, the anaesthetic properties of two other drugs being discovered around the same time – namely, chloroform (1847) and ethyl chloride (1848).

APRIL *27th* First Latin examination at the University.

29th Second Latin exam.

MAY *4th* Written exam on Anatomy and Chemistry.

6th Exam in Botany, Physiology and Natural History.

12th Viva voce exam on Anatomy, Chemistry, Botany and Natural History.

JULY Written exams on Surgery, Midwifery, Materia Medica on Practice of Medicine, Pathology, Medical Jurisprudence, &c.

20th Last oral exam at the University.

31st Defence of thesis. All the examinations passed.

AUGUST *Mon. 2nd* Capping day at the University. 10.30 a.m. Chemistry classroom filled with ladies and friends of the students, Principal Lee in the chair – prayer – Latin oration from Professor Balfour. I receive the degree of Doctor of Medicine with fifty-seven others, and receive the congratulations of my friends. I had intended to take a trip in the Highlands, but my old messmate Willcox wrote to me to say he had commissioned H.M. Steam Vessel *Fury*, and would I apply to the Admiralty to be appointed to her? Which I did.

Tue. 3rd Went down to Leith, take leave of all my kind friends. Pack up, leave Edinburgh by express train and was soon rattling across the border.

London and elsewhere

Wed. 4th Arrive in London at 8 a.m. Go to Somerset House, see Sir William Burnett. Register my diploma, &c.

Thur. 5th Go to the opera, see Jenny Lind in *La Figlia del Reggimento*. Wonderfully sweet warbling, low notes distinct, clear and exquisitely sweet; high notes powerful, without effort or distortion of features. I was in the pit, but could only get standing room: a great crush, and suffocating heat; every part of the house crammed; ladies fainting.[2] In the ballet Taglioni danced "La Sylphide" with Perrot: we had also Mlle Carlotta Grisi and Louis D'Or in a *pas de deux*. Altogether it was a great treat.

[2] In its issue of August 7th 1847, the *Illustrated London News* comments: "Amongst the novelties stands pre-eminent that which render this season memorable in the annals of the Opera – the debut of Mdlle. Lind.... Her Majesty hardly missed a single performance of Jenny Lind while in town."

Fri. 6th Got my appointment as Surgeon to H.M.S. *Fury*.

Sat. 7th 9 a.m. left London by rail for Gosport. Called on Willcox and went to have a look at the *Fury*. Found her in dock, not rigged, so I got a couple of days' leave. Dined at Southampton, and went on to Dorchester, and slept at the King's Arms; going on to Bridport next morning by the mail coach.

Sun. 8th At 5 passed through and went on to Honiton, to my sister's.

Mon. 9th Returned to Bridport and stop at Mr John Hounsell's till next day, when I returned to London.

Sat. 21st At a pleasant picnic at Eypes Mount [Bridport]. The Hounsells and Colfoxes there. . . .

Picnic at Hope Rocks, Eypes Mount, Bridport

H.M. STEAM SLOOP FURY
Portsmouth

Tue. 31st The officers who have joined the *Fury* are the following: Commander, James Willcox;[B] Lieutenants, Philip W. Darnell and Edward Algernon Blackett; Master, William H. Williams; Surgeon, E.H. Cree, M.D.; Assistant Surgeon, Julian W. Bradshaw, M.R.C.S.; Purser, William Wiles; Midshipmen, Rathbone, Arthur Pennell and Massey; three Clerks; two Master's Assistants; Chief Engineer, Rumble. The *Fury* was built at Sheerness and launched Sept. 1845; is 1123 tons; carries 360 tons of coal; at full power burns from 36 to 40 tons a day; carries water, 50 tons, enough for about 100 days' consumption. Her armament consists of one 10-inch revolving gun, 84 pounds hollow shot; one 8-inch 93 hundredweight, 10 feet long, 68 pounds solid shot; four 32-pound broadside guns; two 24-pound for two paddle-box boats, and two brass field pieces. Her cost was £12,875; is supposed to steam 1.2 nautical miles an hour, in smooth water. Complement, 160 men.

Fury finally leaves Plymouth on October 4th 1847 and reaches Rio de Janeiro on November 8th. On November 13th she departs for Singapore, passing the Cape of Good Hope (3,270 nautical miles) on December 11th, and sails on via Sunda Strait and the Straits of Banca. She anchors at Singapore on January 24th 1848, having covered a further 4,660 miles. The news there is that six European clerks have been murdered in an outbreak of violence at Canton. *Fury* is ordered to hasten on to Hong Kong, which she reaches on February 6th. Cree dines there with the new Governor, Bonham. *Fury* is now ordered on to Amoy, proceeds to Shanghai and Ningpo, and returns via Hong Kong to Singapore. A visit to Penang precedes one to Bombay and environs in the period June–July. Cree takes an excursion to Poona before *Fury* continues her circuit to Madras, Trincomalee, Colombo, Singapore, and Anjer in Java Island. On December 14th *Fury* arrives at Hong Kong again, with the flagship *Hastings* in tow.

***Fury* towing the flagship *Hastings* into Hong Kong harbour, December 1848**

1849

Hong Kong

JANUARY

Tue. 9th Darnell, Martin and I went to the *Preble*, American sloop-of-war, just arrived, to call on the officers. She is a fine corvette of eighteen guns, 32-pounders; she seems clean and in good order. I fraternised with the little Yankee doctor, an intelligent man, J.L. Burtt, M.D. Dined at General Staveley's.[B] Meet Mrs S. and two Misses S., Captain S., A.D.C., Captain, Mrs and Miss Young, Captain Glynn[B] of the *Preble,* an original, funny little man, who addressed Mrs Staveley, very formally, as "Madam". Dr Dickson was there, and Mr Mclean of Jardine & Matheson's house, Vanderspar of Ceylon Rifles, Lieutenant Curme, R.N., and Captain Moore, R.M., and young Pennell of the *Fury*. The General's daughters very pleasant; one a widow of Captain Grannett, the other Mrs Jackson, lately married.

Wed. 10th The officers of the *Preble* return our call. Lunch at Dent's bungalow, meeting Captain Morgan and Dr Scott of the *Hastings*. Afterwards call on Mrs Campbell and Miss McPherson.

U.S.S. ***Preble***

Fri. 12th At a ball at Mrs Campbell's, all the beauty and fashion of Hong Kong. Amongst the élite there were the Governor [Bonham][B] and Mrs Bonham, Mrs Brain, Mrs Edger, Mrs, Miss and Captain Young, R.A., Dr and Mrs Peter Young, Miss Mclean, a new arrival with a fine English complexion, a pity it should so soon turn yellow, Miss C. Phillpotts, "the Partridge", Dr and Mrs Gordon, 95th Regiment, Mrs Cleverly, and some of our fellows; many more gentlemen than ladies, of course. A capital supper and plenty of champagne: beef-tea and green-tea punch and more dancing followed. In the small hours of the morning a party of the gentlemen wended their way down the hill; some of them what the Yankees call "swalliky".

Sun. 14th A dinner party on board: Carpenter and Tetley of Commissariat, and some of the "Arabs",[1] just arrived.

[1] "Arabs": officers of H.M. Sloop *Arab*.

Mon. 15th Hong Kong Races, first day.

Hong Kong shopkeepers

Tue. 16th Second day of Races. Dined at the mess of Ceylon Rifles: meet the Governor, General, and Admiral [Sir Francis Collier][B] there. Forty-six officers at dinner.

Wed. 17th Third day of Races. Good fun, hurdle races and steeplechases; a few tumbles. The most amusing was a race by Chinese riders.

Thur. 18th The Race Ball at the club. A gay affair and a good supper.

Fri. 19th Dine with the Chief Justice, Hulme, who has forgiven my caricaturing him on board the *Agincourt* three years ago. Meet there Thompson, Chaplain of the hospital ship; Onslow, Chaplain of the *Hastings*, and other good fellows. Whist, &c.

FEBRUARY

Fri. 2nd I am sorry to see we have a case of smallpox on board, in one of the midshipmen: I reported it to the Captain and afterwards to the Admiral, who wanted to put us in quarantine, but I found I could get him into sick quarters near the Merchant Seamen's Hospital.

Mon. 5th Scott and I walked out to call on the Judge, and afterwards dined with the Governor, where we met Colonel and Mrs Symmonds, Mrs McKean, Mr and Miss Mclean, Colonel Eyre, R.A., and other officers, Lieutenant Curme of *Hastings*, Captain Willcox, &c.

Fri. 9th At a dance given by the officers of the Ceylon Rifles, where were the usual Hong Kong society with the addition of the officers of the *Preble*, whose little fat skipper afforded much amusement by his devotion to Mrs

"The Yankee Captain introduced to the Duchess"

Symmonds, or "the Duchess" as she is usually called, from her pompous manner and her size. Miss C. Phillpotts, "the Partridge", looked very pretty, and she and Miss Mclean were the belles of the room. Little Mrs Ford looked nice and so did her protégée Miss Parkes, old Gutzlaff's niece, but too lively, fast and wild; little Miss St Hill interesting and modest; Miss McPherson not so pretty as she looked at her sister Mrs Campbell's party. The youngest daughter of old Raines of the Ordnance is pretty, with her bright blue eyes and flaxen locks. An excellent supper was not the worst part of the night's entertainment.

Mon. 12th The H.C. [Honourable East India Company's] steamer *Phlegethon* arrived from Canton with three cases of smallpox on board. I was desired by the Admiral to see if I could get them into the Seamen's Hospital on shore, as we could not take them into our hospital ship. I therefore, with the Surgeon of the *Phlegethon*, saw the House Surgeon, who took them in, but when Dr Young came next morning he turned them out of the hospital, and had a quarrel with the Admiral in consequence. At last we hired sick quarters for them.

Wed. 14th Lunched at Dent's. Met Fortune, the botanist and traveller, to whom I gave some sketches on his former visit to China. He published them in his book, but had not the decency to acknowledge. He is sent out by the Government to get tea plants to take to India, to endeavour to cultivate the tea in the Himalayas.[2]

During March–May *Fury* cruises back and forth between Hong Kong, Amoy, Shanghai and Ningpo, and then visits Singapore, Trincomalee, Madras and Acheen, Sumatra. On September 9th at Singapore it is revealed that the Governor of Macao, d'Amaral, has been assassinated by the Chinese, who cut off his head and made off with it.

---

[2] Cree had met Robert Fortune (1813–80) in Hong Kong in November 1844, some two years after he had been sent out by the Royal Horticultural Society. Fortune published several books on China, three lithographs from Cree's sketches – of Foo-chow-foo, Ningpo and the river at Shanghai – being reproduced without any credit to the artist in his *Three years' wanderings in the Northern Provinces of China*, etc. (London, 1847).

Bias Bay

Sun., Sept. 30th *Fury* ordered off in a hurry, in consequence of news brought by the little steamer *Canton* from H.M.S. *Columbine* at Bias Bay, 40 miles to the eastward, where she had been engaged with a fleet of piratical junks, and was now blockading eighteen or nineteen others in the bay.[3] The steamer had one officer, Midshipman Goddard, and four men of the *Columbine* wounded, she took to the hospital ship. Poor Goddard died as he was being hoisted out of the steamer. . . . Taking with us Lieutenant Luard, 1st of the *Hastings*, and Lieutenant Holland and 100 Marines.

[3] As a guide to the actions that follow, see the track-chart reproduced in the endpapers.

OCTOBER

Mon. 1st We fell in with the *Columbine* at 2 a.m. The junks were out of sight. They had gone up to the head of the bay, which is deep and winding, but there was not water enough for the *Columbine*, so Hay came on board the *Fury* and picked up a native fisherman as a pilot. After getting about 20 miles from the entrance a large white junk was seen, which immediately got under weigh and stood out. She was a trading junk which the pirates had recently taken. Soon after, two black junks were seen, which stood farther up the bay, then three or four more, then a whole crowd, anchored in line across the mouth of a creek. They opened fire from their whole line almost before we were within range. *Fury* was then moved to within 500 yards and fire opened

The destruction of Chui-apoo's pirate squadron, October 1st 1849, H.M.S. *Fury* in the foreground (*engraving after a sketch by E. H. Cree, reproduced in the* Illustrated London News, *February 2nd 1850*)

from the bow and starboard guns as they bore on the enemy, who returned a well-sustained fire. About twenty of their shot struck the *Fury*, but most went overhead. One struck the paddle-box and wounded the helmsman in the leg and passed through the Captain's skylight; another went through the signal-locker and gunroom round-house; another smashed the bath and harness casks in the paddle-box. Soon the nearest junks were blown up by shell from the *Fury* and a lot more set on fire. Still they sustained the action for fifty minutes. In the meantime two boats from the *Hastings* with guns took up a position from which they kept up a fire on the junks farther up the creek. There was no attempt to board, after the display of desperate courage yesterday. The firing of shot, shell and grape was too hot for the rascals and all the junks were in a blaze, and as many of the pirates as were able were swarming over the sides and swimming to the shore. Twenty-seven junks with a number of smaller vessels were destroyed. It is supposed that 400 of the pirates perished and the rest, upwards of 1,000, escaped to the shore. A party of Marines were landed to complete the dispersion of the piratical crew. There was a large village and a dockyard, with quantities of arms and ammunition, and three new junks building, which were all destroyed; the best of the guns were brought on board. At night the burning junks and dockyard made a fine sight.

Tue. 2nd It is reported that the pirate chief is Chui-apoo of Wang-na-kok, near Chek-tchu, Hong Kong. . . . It is said he is desperately wounded, but escaped to the shore.

Pirate Hunting

Sat. 6th Coaling, preparatory to another pirate hunting expedition: this time to the west, where a large fleet of pirate vessels are said to be cruising, plundering junks trading to Hong Kong, and burning villages, &c. They are supposed to be in the neighbourhood of Hai-nan Island.

Mon. 8th This piratical fleet is said to be a formidable one, commanded by an energetic Chinaman called Shap-'ng-tsai, known to the Hong Kong people as a desperate robber. Embarked fifty Marines and fifty bluejackets, Captain Moore, Lieutenant Hallilay, Royal Marines, Lieutenant Hancock and three midshipmen, and Assistant Surgeon McEwan from the *Hastings*. At 9 a.m. left Hong Kong, taking steamer *Phlegethon* in tow, to save coals, with H.M. Brig *Columbine*, Captain J. Dalrymple Hay in command, as he is *one* day senior to Willcox. Looked into some of the numerous bays on the coast and anchored for the night at the small island Cow-kok.

Tue. 9th 3 a.m. sent a boat to board some suspicious looking junks, and to gain information. 7.30 weighed and made sail, *Columbine* and *Phlegethon* in company. Coast barren and mountainous. 6 p.m. anchor with the other vessels.

Wed. 10th 3.30 a.m. weighed and made all sail. Proceed under sail with the others along the coast, searching all the bays. 6 p.m. anchor at Ty-foong.

Thur. 11th 3.30 proceeded under sail. 10 mustered at quarters, loaded all the guns with shot. Many junks in sight. Proceeded into Now-chow under steam: a small town and mandarin station; a fort on a low sandy island. Anchored for the night. We were soon surrounded by a multitude of sampans, with curious natives, miserable and dirty. Here we got a pilot to take us through the Straits of Hai-nan.

Fri. 12th Captains Hay and Willcox went on shore to call on the mandarin and brought him off to see the ship. He wears a white crystal ball on his cap, and a dragon embroidered on his coat. Not a very intelligent looking person. He brought his second in command with him and twenty common looking fellows. We saluted him with three guns, and showed him round the ship, but he expressed no astonishment at what he saw. They never do.[4] He informed us that Shap-'ng-tsai paid him a visit a few days ago, attacked his fort, took away all his guns, and demanded a ransom for the place. We find he has gone towards the Gulf of Tonquin, and we must follow. Having secured pilots to take us through the sandbanks at the entrance of the straits, which we had to put off till next day, in daylight, we procured some fine shrimps here.

[4] Cree was unaware maybe that expressions of astonishment were considered ill-bred by the Chinese.

Sat. 13th A number of junks anchored near us last night. We found they were opium traders and had passes from the clippers at Cum-sing-mun.

We started at daylight with *Columbine* and *Phlegethon* in tow, and twenty junks in company, for protection. We went through a passage bounded by reefs and sandbanks, on which the sea broke violently. On the right the flat, sandy shore of the peninsula of Lui-chew [Lui-chow] rises only 50 feet above the sea-level: some low hills farther inland, some villages along the coast, with fruit trees and green crops. A few coco and palmetto palms.

Noon, distant hills on the island of Hai-nan in sight and the Poo-chin pagoda. Three suspicious looking junks in sight. We cast off the tow and gave chase, on which they set more sail, trying to get away among the sandbanks, but we sent a shot from one of our long 68-pounders. The first shot fell short, but a bigger charge sent the next over her, which brought them all up. They only proved to be honest traders in a funk.

3.30 anchored off the large town of Hoy-how, in Hai-nan Island. The straits are about 12 miles wide, a low coast on each side, with a few scattered conical hills. A good sized river enters by many mouths separated by long spits of sand. The town of Hoy-how is well built for a Chinese place. We saw three forts on the beach, an old pagoda, a big square pawnshop, and a few large houses belonging to mandarins; some coconut palms which don't flourish well on the mainland. A salute of three guns from one of the forts was answered by the *Columbine*. Captains Hay and Willcox went on shore to call on the Governor. They found the streets and shops cleaner and better than any Chinese place they had been in. The Governor received them with much civility and offered to render any assistance in destroying the pirates, who had been a terror to the whole coast. A naval commander, Wang-hai-quang, an Acting Major-General in the Chinese service, is to go with us. We saw many well-dressed natives going about in wheelbarrows, which are the cabs of many of the Chinese towns. The wheel is in the centre; a person can sit on each side. Shap-'ng-tsai was here with a great fleet of junks three weeks ago: he beat the Chinese naval force sent against him and burnt a village on the opposite shore. He anchored here and then sailed into the Gulf of Tonquin. Geese, ducks, fowls, pigs and goats were brought off for sale, and afterwards a present was sent by the Governor, consisting of roasted pigs and goats, beside oranges, pomelos and musk-oranges, a small kind with a fine flavour.

I could not go on shore as my poisoned ankle obliged me to use crutches.[5]

[5] The previous month, whilst sketching on a plantation outside Singapore, Cree had been stung by what he took to be a scorpion.

Sun. 14th Wang-hai-quang, the naval mandarin, came on board. We sailed at 3 p.m., the *Columbine*, *Phlegethon* and eight war junks in company. General Wang brought his Secretary, Lieutenant, and some servants with him. He is a fat, good-humoured but active looking Chinaman of about forty. He expects to get his promotion if we catch Shap-'ng-tsai. Of that he may, I think, make sure. The Chinese sailed in two lines, keeping position very well. General Wang acted as pilot.

6 p.m. Kamee [Camez] Point NW 7 miles. Anchored at 8 with our now augmented squadron.

Mon. 15th 6 a.m. weighed and proceeded, towing *Columbine* and *Phlegethon*, the squadron of junks in company. 1.30 p.m. saw the islands of Wy-chow and Chy-ung. The former terminates at the west end by an abrupt cliff, and at the east tapers off to a low point, covered with grass. At 6 we entered a snug cove which has a remarkable rock at the entrance. Here we anchored for the night, and received intelligence, from some fishermen, whom Wang boarded, of the pirates being at Pe-long with a squadron of sixty or eighty junks. This island is only inhabited by some priests who have a josshouse in a cave in the cliff. We outsailed our Chinese friends, who have not yet hove in sight.

Tue. 16th 2.30 a.m. weighed and proceeded to Pe-long Bay, at the head of

Major-General Wang-hai-quang

the Gulf of Tonquin, in lat. 21° 10′ N. Mountainous scenery extending all along the northern shore of the gulf.

4.30 p.m. we suddenly, from 8 fathoms, ran on a sandbank, and the *Columbine* being astern ran into us, damaged a gig and some of the stern-work, and left part of her bower-anchor sticking into our quarter. The shank broke off. The two Captains with General Wang went off in the *Phlegethon* to overhaul a boat, to gain information, and found that the pirates had been here a week ago, with seventy junks and beached them, to scrub their bottoms. They robbed the poor natives of all they possessed, and killed those who resisted, and carried off many of the young women. They are gone down the coast in the direction of Pirate Islands, or to Go-to-shan, on the Tonquin Coast, SW.

Managed to get the *Fury* off by laying out an anchor.

Wed. 17th At anchor off Chuk-shan. Some junks being seen over a point of land, the *Phlegethon* and three boats were sent away to examine. The Captains with the General and some of the others landed at a fishing village, where the information of yesterday was confirmed. The junks were found to be only fishing-craft. Our mandarin sharply reprimanded the head man of the village for not coming off to see what we wanted. The people went on their knees to beg us to go after Shap-'ng-tsai, who keeps the whole coast in a state of terror. It is settled that we go on tomorrow to the Pirate Isles, where it is said Shap-'ng-tsai has gone to take and plunder five junks laden with rice.

Thur. 18th 5.30 weighed and made sail; rounded Go-to-shan Point.

Noon, hove to in a pretty bay with sandy beach and fishing village, backed by wooded hills whose sides were cultivated with the sweet potato, a kind of convolvulus. The day was cloudy and pleasant, with a fresh breeze, and we enjoyed the sail along this beautiful coast lined with picturesque little islands. A high range of mountains of about 8,000 feet are seen far inland, lower ones near the coast, with serrated tops like enormous teeth.

On turning the point of another island the *Columbine* suddenly came on a fast boat, which Wang pronounced to be one of Shap-'ng-tsai's fleet. We immediately gave chase and all had long shots at her. She made all sail and got out her long sweeps and got away into shallow water, where we could not follow. The *Phlegethon*, which drew less water, followed her into the bay, putting some shots into her. She attempted a narrow passage between the islands, but seeing the steamer gaining fast upon her, ran her aground. All her crew escaped up the hill, which was covered with jungle, where a party of men searched in vain.

On returning to the junk she was found to be stowed with smoke-balls, small arms and ammunition, and carried six guns, but no cargo, showing her character, so we set her on fire and she continued to blaze away all night on the beach.

We anchored here in the bay; it came on to blow and rain – a dirty night.

Fri. 19th Wind NW fresh, raining. Weighed at 6.30 and stood along the coast, which is here thickly studded with extraordinary rocky islets, myriads of them, like buildings, as churches, castle and chimneys, &c. The mainland, the same on a larger scale, looks as if an enormous chopper had been at work to chop it up into great junks. The tops and sides of those, not too steep, were clothed in verdure. Altogether the scene was strange and beautiful. We saw no signs of inhabitants except a few deserted huts on one of the islands, not so steep.

Sat. 20th Weather much cooler, therm. 78°; a fine bright morn. The *Phlegethon* was inshore of us. At 7 a.m. she signalled "Numerous strange sail to the SW". From our mast-head they could be just seen far away on the horizon. We soon got under weigh, towing the *Columbine*; the *Phlegethon* ahead sounding. The junks, which could now be counted to the number of twenty-four, were coming before the wind towards us, now put about and stood towards the mouth of a large river.

We could now count fifty junks, some very large, carrying red-and-blue flags; the wind fell light, and the junks got out their sweeps. A fire on the beach looked like a burning village. We beat about, trying to find a channel amongst the shoals and small islands. We got a pilot from a town on a low island ahead of us, Fo-foong, and crossed the bar of the river in 3 fathoms. The water soon deepened to 5 and 7 fathoms. As we neared the piratical fleet, the largest, an immense junk carrying forty-six guns, fired a broadside and was soon seconded by others, but their shot fell short. We now gave them a taste from our bow guns, throwing a 68-pound shot close to the big junk. We cast off the *Columbine* and opened fire, from all the guns that would bear, with shot and shell. The *Columbine* and *Phlegethon* had to fire over us as we were nearer in. The big junk carried a red and blue ensign and all the junks were decorated with numerous flags, and were all firing away as fast as they could, but it was wild, and none of their shots struck us; some went one side and some another, but most of them fell short. We sent one of our shells right into the stern of the big junk, which must have exploded in her magazine, for there was immediately a great red flash with a tremendous report and a dense volume of smoke mixed with pieces of the junk, masts and men. Her sides appeared to open. When the smoke cleared she was seen to be settling down, only her lofty stern and the mizen-mast with the pirates' red-and-black flag floating proudly over the wreck. Just before she blew up, we could see her people crowding

The attack on the pirate fleet of Shap-'ng-tsai in the Tonquin River, October 21st 1849, by (*left to right*) *Columbine*, *Phlegethon* and *Fury*

(with two boats of ***Hastings***). **Shap-'ng-tsai's junk is seen exploding after a broadside from *Fury*.**

over her sides into the water. The other junks got into confusion; some caught fire, and as they came into collision with one another the fire spread and some others blew up. I saw a shell from the *Phlegethon* pitch into the centre of another large junk and she blew up. Still many of them would not give in and kept up the firing, and endeavoured to escape up the river. Most of those on fire exploded as the fire got to their own gunpowder, and burnt to the water's edge.

There were some dreadful sights as the wretches crowded into a small fast junk and endeavoured to run the gauntlet, but would not give in. We could not allow them to escape, so fired into them with grape and musketry till they ran her into a mangrove swamp and all, not killed, jumped overboard and hid among the mangrove bushes, to be afterwards killed by the enraged Cochins. This junk was afterwards visited: on her deck were found a heap of dead, so she was set on fire and soon after blew up in a succession of explosions. Many of the men who got away from her were stark naked. The Cochins were chasing the poor wretches in their sampans and spearing them in the water.

We then followed those who had gone up the river, driving them ashore and setting them on fire, till it was too dark to venture any farther up the river, as the channel is intricate amongst the sandbanks; so we anchored for the night and sent the boats away to burn a few deserted junks stranded near us. So, the whole neighbourhood was lit up all night by the burning pirates.

This is one of the mouths of the Tonquin River. The city is said to be 60 miles farther up. Our charts are all wrong, so we have to be wary. There is a town, Chok-am, near us; the walls of which have been lined with Tonquinese soldiers carrying little flags. There is a large fishing town on a low island near the mouth of the river, but the natives are in such a state of alarm that we could not get them to sell us any of their fish.

Sun. 21st Therm. 80°, wind NNW, calm and hot. 5.30 weighed and proceeded cautiously up the river. *Phlegethon* and *Columbine* were ahead. Thirty-four of the junks still have to be accounted for, which have made their way up the various branches. The boats being sent away to search found many deserted and saw the crews of others getting away in small boats. After going about 10 miles farther, the river made a sharp turn to the right and became too shoal for the *Fury*, so we had to anchor. But all our boats were sent on and Lieutenant Hancock had, with one of the paddle-box boats, a pretty little fight with three junks which blocked the passage and opened fire on him, which he soon returned from his bow gun and musketry; after which the pirates deserted and were dispatched by the Tonquinese, who were armed with swords and long spears, which I could see them using pretty vigorously against the unfortunate wretches in the water. Our boats brought back some prisoners. Our old General, Wang, showed some pluck in jumping overboard from one of the boats and swimming to a junk and capturing three of the

Cochins spearing survivors from Shap-'ng-tsai's fleet

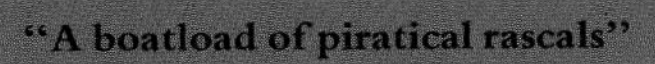

"A boatload of piratical rascals"

Decorative fragment taken from Shap-'ng-tsai's junk

pirates himself. They were so frightened at seeing one of their mandarins that they made no resistance. As we returned towards Chok-am we set fire to all the deserted junks within reach.

The country appears to be thickly inhabited; numbers of cottages peeped out from among the trees. Chok-am looks pretty on the side of a hill rising from the river. We saw a few large roofed buildings over the wall, on which soldiers were ranged in single file with flags, short swords and long spears. A number of others appeared to be marching about in search of pirates who had escaped to the shore. The chief, Shap-'ng-tsai, is said to have escaped before his junk blew up, in a fast boat with forty of his followers and his second in command and 8,000 dollars. His agent, Phat-ping, who had just arrived from Hong Kong, he suspected of treachery, and when we hove in sight beheaded him. A police agent of Sew, Viceroy of Canton, who had come to make proposals, was decapitated at the same time. This information was obtained by Wang.

At dusk all our boats returned laden with spears, swords, flags, josses, &c.

Tue. 23rd All the piratical fleet being destroyed except six, two large and two small junks, which escaped through some other branch of the river, we prepared to return to Hoy-how and Hong Kong. The following is the account to be sent to the Admiral:

Junks destroyed – 58; 6 escaped.

Killed, Chinese pirates – estimated 1,700; escaped to the shore, to be captured, or killed, by the Tonquinese – 1,000.

Prisoners – 49: women 8, children 6; most of the latter kidnapped from Hong Kong and the coast. (I fear there were many women destroyed in the junks, unfortunate prisoners of the pirates, who had been plundering and burning the villages along the coast.)

We received 40 prisoners from the mandarin at Chok-am, who had given themselves up to the natives. Forty guns taken are to be given to the Governor of Hoy-how.

Hoy-how

Fri. 26th 6 a.m. weighed and proceeded to the anchorage off Hoy-how, with *Columbine* in tow. 7 a.m. stop, and anchor in 4 fathoms. Our friend General Wang went on shore, and it was arranged that the Captains and other officers should visit the Ta-jin or Governor.

We left the ship at 10 in six boats. We had a pull of 3 miles to the shore; it was blowing hard with a heavy sea. We entered the harbour between low sandbanks: a couple of old circular forts, without guns, on each side, except three saluting guns, which were fired as we approached and a red flag hoisted. A few large war junks, which appeared to be laid up in ordinary, were anchored here, and as we passed the man in charge commenced beating a gong vigorously. On the left great water-buffaloes were feeding in the swampy meadow; on the right, the suburb extended down to the water, a collection of small mean houses. At the landing-place great crowds of Chinese had assembled to see the conquerors of the dreaded pirate who had threatened to plunder Hoy-how on his return. The crowd were very respectful, and made way for us as we passed through two gateways, where we found chairs and ponies to convey us to Wang's house, where we were to meet the Governor of Hai-nan and the rest of the mandarins. The narrow streets we passed through were lined on each side by a curious but respectful crowd: there were Government servants and police amongst them. Wang and some of our party were mounted on little Tartar ponies, the rest in sedan-chairs. The streets are cleaner than in most Chinese towns, and not so smelly; perhaps they had been purified for the occasion. The open shops on each side were stored with wares and provisions, baskets of fowls, eggs, pigs and goats, &c.

As we approached Wang's house salutes of three guns were fired and a squeaking Chinese band struck up the usual monotonous tune. The centre gates were thrown open and we were ushered through two entrance halls, mere sheds of places, then a courtyard with a stagnant ditch on each side the central paved walk. In the farther hall of reception, the Governor and two other mandarins approached to meet us, shaking their own fists in the usual Chinese manner of salutation. Ho, the Governor, is a dignified, intelligent looking man of about fifty, wears a red ball and peacock's feather. A little ugly man with a brass button appeared to be next in rank, but with a thoughtful, European expression of countenance. Then General Wang and a host of lower mandarins appeared. After we were all seated in chairs round the reception hall, no one occupying the bench of honour at the upper end of the room, tea was handed round, hot, in little cups. Numbers of Chinese crowded into the room and stood at the backs of the chairs, making the place hot and smelly. Our unfortunate prisoners were marched past to a dirty shed in one of the wings of the mandarin's house; they were tied by a stout cord, and by the resistance they made to being thrust in, did not appear to relish their quarters. Much confusion and noise made in getting them into the prison. The band struck up; three guns were fired; the centre gates thrown open; the Governor rose from his seat to usher in a tall, jolly looking mandarin with beard and mustachios. He wore a blue button and peacock's feather, and was attended by some others of inferior note. As soon as he entered he commenced at one end of the line shaking hands all round, with the Fanquis, and then said in Chinese, "Does no one recognise me?" – which, being interpreted to us, Willcox, Hay and I recognised as Tung, the Tartar Prince we brought down in the *Vixen* from Canton, in Keying's suite, in 1845. He is a Manchu Tartar, married to an

"Does no one recognise me?" Tung, the Tartar Prince, with Cree (on crutches), Hay and Willcox at the Governor of Hainan's reception.

Imperial Princess. He was pleased at being recognised, and put us in mind of his getting drunk on board the *Agincourt* and dancing with the Chief Justice of Hong Kong, and a few other freaks. He also asked about the pretty black-haired girl, Miss Hickson, and was not surprised when I told him she was married.[6] After staying some time longer we took our departure and had a rough and wet sail off to the ships. Notwithstanding the bad weather, Ho, the Governor, politely came off to the ships to return our calls, and took tiffin on board the *Fury*, inspecting the guns and engines. Wang and only two others accompanied him. He preferred to go ashore in one of our boats, so he was sent in one of the cutters, but he got a thorough wetting, as it came on to blow harder and rain, in fact a regular gale, so we did not go to sea but struck topgallant and lower yards, and the brig her topmasts.

[6] Cree attended the wedding of Alice Hickson on March 25th 1848 in Hong Kong. She married (Lieutenant) E. (Edmund W.) Sargent of the 18th Regiment, then A.D.C. to the Governor.

Sat. 27th Blowing a gale, so we could not venture through the junk channel and amongst the sandbanks. We remained at anchor and I employed myself sketching our late actions to send to the *Illustrated London News*.

Sun. 28th The weather having moderated, we weighed and proceeded with *Columbine* in tow. . . .

November–December: Hong Kong – Singapore – Trincomalee – Bombay. At Hong Kong, Admiral Collier dies of apoplexy. At Bombay, the bottom of *Fury* is found to be much damaged, with a large part of her keel missing. Repairs are duly effected.

Bombay/At Sea

JANUARY

Tue. 1st Celebrated New Year's Day by a great dinner at the Indian Navy Club: all the "Cambrians" and "Furys" there and a lot of the soldiers and Indian Navy at present in Bombay. It is a good thing we are going to sea soon, as this sort of life rather tells upon one in the tropics.

Wed. 2nd ... In the evening Darnell and I drove out to Mazagaon, by invitation of a native merchant who was giving a "nautch", which kept us out till very late, and is generally rather a stupid affair, with monotonous squeaky music. The dancing girls were not bad looking and much more clothed than our London opera dancers.

Thur. 3rd After breakfast at the club packed up my belongings, and with Darnell and Ross went on board to dinner, but found the ship anything but pleasant after one's luxurious quarters on shore, the smell of fresh paint, new oilcloth, &c., no table, no chairs; but there is no help for it as we have to go to sea tomorrow. After a time we got the table set up and borrowed chairs from

The nautch

the Captain's cabin, and then procured a dinner out of old Yeo, our cook, who is a capital man in an emergency.

Trincomalee

Mon. 14th Anchored in Trincomalee harbour before dark.

Tue. 15th Mr Pett came down to the dockyard and drove me back to my delightful quarters in Fairy Hall, where the pretty little Fairy was looking more bewitching than ever.[1]

[1] Cree had of course first met Mr Pett, Ordnance Storekeeper, with his wife and two of their daughters, in Hong Kong in February 1845. He again met Mr Pett, and his daughter Emily, "the little Fairy", in Madras in 1848, Mrs Pett having returned now to England with their other children and Pett himself having been transferred to Trincomalee. Cree describes Emily then as "a pretty girl of eighteen, lively as a cricket, and plump as a little partridge", and is evidently made very welcome by her and her father at their house, which he dubs "Fairy Hall", on subsequent visits to Trincomalee in June–July and November 1849.

Thur. 31st Every morning before sunrise the boy has called me and brought a delicious cup of coffee. Soon the ponies were at the door and Mr Pett and I went off for a gallop, before the heat of the day, then returned to bath and breakfast. I generally went down to the ship and afterwards sketching; or in the carriage with Emily calling on some of our numerous Trincomalee friends, with whom we often spent an evening, with music and dancing. Altogether a delightful time.

Trincomalee harbour

FEBRUARY

Fri. 1st I went on board the *Fury* to arrange about a picnic on Sober Island; called on the Commodore [Plumridge][B] and returned to an early dinner. Took Emily and her father over to the island, where we found all the others assembled, males and females, in the upper bungalow. We mustered about thirty and strolled through the woods till dark, tho' there was a lovely moon. We then assembled round a cold dinner and afterwards a dance. The bungalow was prettily fitted up with flags and Chinese lanterns, and being all open at the sides, with a pleasant breeze blowing through, it was delightful,

Outside the bungalow, Sober Island

and with the bright moonlight, and the trees, with the scent of the flowers, it was like Fairyland, as one of the young ladies observed, who probably had been there, as she was an accomplished flirt. However, there were bright eyes and pretty faces. Dancing was kept up with great liveliness, before, and again after supper, and then a burst of sky-rockets and blue lights with very pretty effect, to light us down to the boats. Had a row back to the dockyard in the bright moonlight with songs and music. Found the carriages waiting, then three cheers and a drive home at 3 in the morning.

The picnic at the bungalow

Sat. 2nd Went to call on the ladies and found them all delighted with their entertainment.

Sun. 3rd Our stay at Trinco drawing to a close. In visiting the Commodore this morning he told me we should have to sail in a few days, alas! Took some of the ladies, Miss Pett, Misses Tranchell, Mrs Warrington, &c., off to the ship, to church, and afterwards a drive round Tee Esplanade. The Garrison Church in the evening.

Mon. 4th A pleasant gallop out to the jungle, in the evening, with E., but driven in by a thunderstorm. Twenty inches more rain falls in a year at Trinco than at Madras, hence the luxuriance of the vegetation.

Wed. 6th On horseback before daylight, to have a gallop out on the Jaffnapattan Road, to see the sun rise over the rock of Trincomalee.

Thur. 7th A parting dinner at Colonel Cochrane's. Most of the Trinco ladies there, some of them showing their amusing peculiarities – no scandal!

Bay of Bengal/Straits of Malacca

Sat. 9th Alas!! I had to tear myself away from my pleasant quarters at Fairy Hall and bid adieu to the pretty little Fairy. The old Commodore, who has just taken to himself his third wife, in the shape of one of the Trinco beauties, a sister of Captain Skinner of the Ceylon Rifles, ordered us off to Singapore, determined that none of the other officers should commit matrimony at present. We therefore left Trincomalee before daylight and a cruel fair wind soon blew us away from Fairyland and rattled us across the Bay of Bengal.

Fri. 15th A dead calm, with a hot, coppery sky. At noon we fell in with a large Malay proa with a crowd of poor Chinese coolies on board, who were making signals of distress, being entirely without water or food. We ran alongside and filled one of their casks, poor wretches! How they fought and struggled for their first taste of the water, spilling most of it in their eagerness. We also supplied them with a bag of bread, for which they were profuse in their chin-chins. In the afternoon we fell in with a large steamer which proved to be the Hon. E.I. [Honourable East India] Company's steamer *Feroze* with the Marquis Dalhousie,[B] Governor-General of India, on board, on his way to Singapore. We soon got another boiler at work and left His Highness behind.

I forgot to mention that the Commodore, Sir James Plumridge, and his new lady are with us for the passage to Singapore. Her Ladyship has become several inches taller in her own estimation since she became Her Ladyship.

In the period February–March *Fury* is anchored at Singapore, proceeding in early April to Moulmein, Burma, from where she sails to Trincomalee. On April 26th, at the end of a pleasant week there, Cree bids farewell to Emily Pett and her father for what is to be the last time, *Fury* leaving for Singapore early the following morning.

"Recollections of Trincomalee, April 1850" – Emily Pett, "the little Fairy"

Singapore

MAY

Fri. 24th Her Majesty's birthday. The Admiral[2] and Flag-Lieutenant came on board at 6 a.m. and we got under weigh, taking the *Hooghly* with the Governor and all the consuls in tow. At 9 we picked up the *Ayrshire* with forty freemasons on board, also taking them in tow. At 11 came to off Pedra Branca, a small rock in the passage to Singapore on which they are going to build a lighthouse. The authorities landed and the Governor laid the foundation-stone, with the deposit of coins and publications of the day, with a parchment scroll containing a financial account of the colony of Singapore, &c. At 2 we started on our return; the Governor entertained the Admiral and rest of the party on board the *Hooghly*.

We got back to our anchorage soon after sunset: the freemasons cheered us when we cast them off.

In the evening at a ball and supper at Government House. All the beauty

[2] Rear-Admiral Charles Austin, who had replaced Collier as Commander-in-Chief.

and fashion of Singapore there. We lent our fiddlers, for lack of better music, but there was more fun in consequence.

Mon. 27th Dined at Mr Jackson's to meet Rajah, Sir James, and his nephew, Captain Brooke. Mr and Mrs McDougal there. Sir James is preparing to go on a mission to Siam on some diplomatic matters.

AUGUST *Sat. 10th* Our last day at Singapore, and in the East. The ship in confusion, filling up with coal and stores for our long voyage, embarking invalids, many of the poor fellows never destined to see their homes in this world.

Took in 225 tons of coal, and plenty of sundries, amongst others our linen, supposed to have been washed, but the rascally dhobies had merely dipped them in dirty water and not dried them; but they do not expect to see us again.

At Sea

Sun. 11th 6 a.m. weighed and proceeded out of Singapore. Passed St John's Island and out through the Straits of Durian, the same passage we took in the *Vixen*.

Mon. 12th Crossed the equator in the night, rain with thunder and lightning. Midnight, anchored in the Straits of Banca.

Tue. 13th Our first poor invalid died – H. Douglas, A.B., dysentery, and was buried at sea. Through the Banca Straits; anchored for the night.

Wed. 14th Another victim of dysentery, T. Webber, Seaman, died and was buried at sea.

Anjer, Java Island

Thur. 15th 9 a.m. anchored in Anjer Roads. Captain Willcox and I went on shore, landed under the Big Tree; called on M. Le Man, the Governor, who came to his door and gave us a hearty welcome. Since we were here before, he has married a young Dutch lady, twenty years his junior, to whom we were introduced. She is brisk looking and speaks English tolerably; was dressed in a white morning wrapper, and wears no stays; her dark hair drawn back in a knot, and [shows] symptoms of an increase in the Harbour Master's establishment. We soon had to take leave of the good-natured Dutchman and his young wife and get back to the ship, while the stewards were replenishing the hen-coops and a supply of turtle, which we found plentiful. We were surrounded by boats and canoes with birds and monkeys, so that the ship became crowded with pets of various sorts – few men who had not got one or two, and very few will survive beyond the Cape of Good Hope.

We got under way about 1, and steamed out of the Straits of Sunda between Princes Island and Krakatoa, on the Sumatra coast. . . .

9 p.m. we were clear of the Straits of Sunda; disconnected our engines and set sail with a fresh sea breeze.

***Fury* passing Krakatoa in the Sunda Strait, August 15th 1850**

Fury anchors in Plymouth Sound on November 17th 1850, and Cree spends that evening at Stoke with Mr and Mrs Hancock and their daughter Eliza. On December 5th he reports to the Physician-General, Sir William Burnett, who grants him a year's leave to help him recover from his dysentery. Weak and ill from his Eastern service, Cree recuperates at his sister Percy's in Honiton, where he is reunited with his father. In January 1851 Percy (whose old husband died in 1849) becomes married for the second time – to John Cox, another lawyer. In June Cree visits the Great Exhibition in London, and then takes a trip to Europe, travelling through France and Savoy to Switzerland, down the Rhine to Frankfurt, and finally through Brussels and Antwerp to Rotterdam, accompanied most of the way by a bizarre looking American called Jonathan Hale, from Salt Mills, Virginia. In December, whilst Cree is staying with relatives in Edinburgh, his father Robert arrives ill with bronchitis. Robert Cree dies on the 20th, shortly after his sixty-seventh birthday. In March 1852 John Cox dies, and whilst Cree is at Honiton taking care of his sister's affairs he receives an order from the Admiralty, dated June 9th, appointing him to the frigate *Spartan* and directing him to Devonport.

1852

H.M. FRIGATE SPARTAN

Devonport

JUNE

On arriving at Devonport I found the *Spartan*'s probable destination was China. As I had been out on that station nearly ten years, and had suffered from chronic dysentery ever since, I determined to apply to be superseded. In the meantime I joined, and did the duty, inspecting and examining newly raised men. Our rendezvous was at a tavern near the dockyard gates, where men who had volunteered for the ship were examined and, if found fit, entered on the books. The ship at the same time was being rigged and the guns got on board. A good set of officers had joined: Sir William Hoste, Bart, Captain; Charles Fellowes, 1st Lieutenant, a smart officer. We had beside the usual complement of a 36-gun frigate.

While the ship was fitting we were supposed to live in the hulk, but when not on duty I found greater attraction at Somerset Cottage, Stoke, where cousin Lizzie Hancock was the bright pole-star towards which I was attracted, although she was not a cousin, but the only child of Mr Hancock's second wife, the first being my father's sister. I soon began to think that all my former love affairs were mere flirtations, but this had more meaning in it, and that I had got to an age when, if I intended to marry at all, I should not put it off any longer. I had long had a great admiration for Eliza Hancock, and I fancied she encouraged it, so to bring affairs to a crisis I proposed and was accepted.

JULY/AUGUST

About the middle of the month an order came down for me to be surveyed by a Medical Board, at the Naval Hospital, where I was pronounced unfit at present to serve on the China station. Therefore I was superseded from the *Spartan* July 19th, after having belonged to her forty days.

I was then again on half pay, but my own master. Of course I spent most of my time at Somerset Cottage.[1] As I had a great objection to a long engagement, we agreed to get married early in September. I therefore went back to Honiton to arrange matters with my dear sister. She poor girl appeared glad at the prospect of my forming a home in which she might still be happy, with my wife for a friend and companion, having known Lizzie all her life and admired her. Mrs Hancock invited Percy there for a change, so I took her down. There were lots of arrangements to make; a house to be taken and furnished. We fixed on a small one in Alfred Street, Plymouth, near the

[1] Somerset Cottage, while its exterior has been greatly altered since Cree's day, is still standing. Two other houses where Cree was to live in Stoke, as well as the house he was to occupy on his return from his honeymoon, look much the same as they must have done when he lived there in the 1850s and 1860s.

Plymouth Sound from the Hoe. Drake's Island, standing at the entrance to the Tamar River, was long a fortress and a principal defence of Devonport.

Somerset Cottage, Stoke

Dockyard Gate, Fore Street, Devonport. (This area was destroyed by German bombers in the Second World War.)

The wedding procession, September 7th 1852

The start of the wedding trip

Hoe, being in a cheerful neighbourhood. Percy agreed to live with us, having her own apartments and sitting room, &c. We were consequently very busy moving.

At the end of August I took my sister to Exeter where she went on a visit to friends.

The Wedding Trip

SEPTEMBER

I returned to Honiton to finish our arrangements there, returning to Plymouth the first week in September. I put up at the Royal Hotel, but spending most of my time at Somerset Cottage, till the eventful day arrived, 7th September. The morning was fine, but it soon came on squally with heavy showers; in driving to Stoke Church we met a large funeral. This was considered the first unlucky omen; however, the Rector, old St Aubyn,[2] got through the ceremony all right, assisted by our friend Mr Bazeley,[3] but we were delayed some time afterwards by the weather, thunder and lightning, six bridesmaids and a large party of friends and relatives. However, at last we got into the carriages and drove back to Somerset Cottage and the inevitable breakfast, speeches, congratulations and leave-taking, amidst showers of rice and old slippers. To avoid curious friends at the railway station, we drove off to Plympton and took the train there for Torquay, where we arrived about 5 at Hearder's Hotel, on the Strand, and ordered dinner and rooms, then drove out to the pretty village of Babbacombe, where we strolled along the beach. After a dinner of a very tough duck, Lizzie thought the hotel people would not know we were a newly married couple, but the chambermaid said to her, "Does the gentleman require hot water to shave with?" Lizzie quite innocently referred her to me, thus letting the cat out of the bag.

[2] The Reverend William John St Aubyn (1834–94), Rector of the parish church of Stoke Damerel and Prebendary of Exeter, was the third son of Sir Edward St Aubyn, Bt, of St Michael's Mount, Cornwall. The St Aubyn family are still patrons of the living.

[3] Francis Ley Bazeley, the officiating minister, was Rector of St Dominick's in Cornwall in the period 1835–53. He continued as patron of the living after giving up the rectorship.

Wed. 8th After sauntering about Torquay, the cliffs and signal station we returned to the hotel and a dinner of tough beefsteaks, so shall not recommend this hotel to future wedding parties. At 4 p.m. we left by train for Bristol; between Taunton and Bridgwater we were delayed for an hour while the line was being cleared from the wreck of the express down train. We saw the engine half buried in the bank and a luggage-van turned over. A gang of men were at work, but we could not learn many particulars, except that the engine-driver had been killed and several passengers seriously hurt. It was late when we arrived at Bristol, so had to put up at the Railway Hotel. Unlucky omen number 2!

Thur. 9th Fine weather; we stroll about Bristol, to Redcliffe Church, &c. At noon, went on to Bath, where we had lunch. At 3, left for London. I had generally stopped at the Tavistock Hotel, not remembering it was only a bachelors' house, so we shifted to the Piazza Hotel, Covent Garden, comfortable but somewhat crowded with fleas.

Fri. 10th As Lizzie had not seen much of London before, we spent the day sightseeing – Somerset House, Wyld's Great Globe in Leicester Square.[4] Get an Italian dinner at Bertolini's and then go to the Haymarket Theatre: saw Mrs Keely as Jack Sheppard, Paul Bedford as Blueskin; afterwards Wright as Paul Pry, at which Lizzie screeched with laughter. She had been brought up so strictly that she had never been in a theatre before! However, she appreciated this.

[4] Mr Wyld's Great Globe, which occupied the centre of the square, was removed in 1864.

Sat. 11th The new Coal Exchange, Billingsgate Market, Tower – Armoury, Jewel House. Steamer to Hungerford Market; Horse Guards; Whitehall; Admiralty. Dinner at a restaurant in Piccadilly, find questionable company. Return to our hotel, and afterwards pay a visit to Cremorne Gardens, where we were weighed, and had a laugh about Lizzie weighing as much as I did; then the Cirque – horsemanship, nigger songs, Madame Celeste, dancing, fireworks, Siege of St Sebastian, &c.[5]

[5] Cremorne Gardens: this pleasure-ground in Chelsea offered among its many and diverse attractions concerts, balloon ascents, dancing at dusk and firework displays. Cree alludes to the last named when, later, he is in the Crimea.

Sun. 12th Morning at St Paul's. After, at Westminster Abbey.

Mon. 13th Morn at the British Museum, afternoon to Newhaven. Put up at the Railway Hotel, where Louis-Philippe stayed when he fled from France in 1848. We had procured our passport.

"Attempted Abduction" – the altercation outside the Custom House, Dieppe

Tue. 14th 8 a.m. leave by steamer for Dieppe; had a fine passage across. Arrive at 1, disembark at the Custom-House where we were detained till too late for the next train. I was in the Douane looking after our luggage and Lizzie got into an omnibus to wait for me, but they commenced to drive away, taking her off *nolens-volens*; but she so strongly objected to be taken to Paris without me that her British pluck was raised, and she upset the little French conducteur at the door, as he opposed her passage. She rushed over to the Douane, where a gendarme prevented her with fixed bayonet from getting in, or me from getting out.

The Strand, Torquay

Torquay from the Rock Walk

Dieppe

Thur. 16th . . . Start at 3 [from Rouen] for Paris, express train. Get there at 5: another examination of luggage. Go to the Hôtel de Normandie [on the Rue St Honoré], where I stayed last year. Paris is very full, all the hotels are crowded, and we could only get a little cupboard of a place at the top of the house, up about a hundred stairs, and a bed about 3 feet wide. We were in time for the table d'hôte, but the table was full, so with six others we had to squeeze in to a small room, at a round table. But we were all very jolly, especially a "Professor of Irish", a Mr Moffat, who with his wife kept us all in a roar of laughter. After dinner went to the Palais-Royal, Place de la Concorde, Champs-Élysées; and visit one of the café concerts and took our coffee under the trees. Tired enough when we got back, especially after our climb up to our sky bed under the roof; like sleeping in the maintop.

Fri. 17th Wet, went to the Louvre, the picture galleries and sculpture, then a déjeuner at the Restaurant Orléans, in Palais-Royal. In the evening to the Théâtre Lyrique, *Si J'étais Roi*. We got a better apartment this night with the bed in an alcove, but somewhat stuffy.

Sat. 18th Lovely weather. We walked in the Tuileries Gardens, out to the Arc de Triomphe, L'Étoile, Champs-Élysées; ascended to the top of the Arc and had a magnificent view over Paris and the neighbourhood. On our way back went into the Madeleine Church, the Boulevards, and back to table d'hôte, and afterwards to Théâtre de Variétés in Boulevard St Martin. Got back to our apartment tired enough, but it is now on the first floor, so we have not such a climb.

Sun. 19th Notre Dame in forenoon; déjeuner in Palais-Royal. Afterwards by rail to St Cloud, a truly elegant place: the château is open to the public while Louis Napoleon is away on a tour. We were stopped by a heavy shower. After visiting the apartments we went to the gardens, where the Fête of St Cloud was being held: shows, whirligigs, mountains de Russe, noise and fun of various sorts. One show or theatre in particular arrested our attention, which would have shocked the good orthodox people at home. The whole life of Christ was dramatised by a set of gaudily dressed, common looking fellows! Nothing sacred in their appearance, but it is sanctioned by the clergy, so it is all right I suppose. The Virgin Mary was well rouged and wore a very low dress, in fact she looked very low altogether. Joseph had a cast in his eye and looked a thorough blackguard. Herod was a meek, respectable character. We soon had enough of it and went into the gardens to see the Grand Jet d'Eau, in the centre of a circular pond. A single jet shoots up to 140 feet; tops all the high trees; it can be seen from all parts of the grounds, high above the trees, and falls like a shower of silver. Then we saw it between us and the setting sun, a lovely sight. The grounds were crowded by thousands of gay Parisians.

"That Wicked City"

Grande Cascade, St Cloud

"The Sky Bedroom"

"A drive through the forest of Fontainebleau", September 24th (*from Cree's original notebook*)

Tue. 21st ... It being a lovely moonlight night, we strolled out to take a last look at some of the scenes near. Visited some of the shops in Rue Royale, back through Rue St Honoré to our hotel to pack up before turning in.

Tue. 28th Very wet morning; railway station at 8. Plenty of confusion – dripping passengers looking for their packages and lost friends. After getting our luggage ticketed, we ensconced ourselves in the corner of a first-class carriage. Two other passengers soon came in, a French Senator and an English M.P., so we guessed. We whisked away towards Rouen, where we arrived at 11. The weather cleared up and we had a pleasant run to Dieppe, which we reached at 1 p.m. Found the *Wave Queen*, a long, narrow, iron steamer we had noticed on our first crossing over, ready to start. After much turning ahead, backing, and bumping against the piers, we got out of harbour about 2, meeting the *Paris* steamer going in. The weather looked squally and it soon commenced to blow in heavy squalls, with lightning and hailstorms. We had between fifty and sixty passengers, most of whom were sick enough from the ugly motion of this wavy craft. All of them in Tee Saloon (a glass-house on the deck, which I thought the sea would smash in). It soon became very close and smelly, as the doors and windows had to be kept closed. The weather continued to get worse, heavy squalls from SE and SW. We were both sick, I worse than Lizzie.

7 p.m. Beachy Head Light in sight. Blowing a gale. The tide not being sufficiently high to enter Newhaven piers, we stood out to sea again; the ship rolling her paddles under. The vessel, from her great length and small power, would not come round to the sea. A shocking scene in the overcrowded saloon, passengers all sick, ladies fainting, screaming, praying, the wind howling, and the sea striking the glass sides of the saloon with great violence, I thought would smash it in. Everything rolling about, crockeryware and glass smashing. To add to the confusion we had a raving lunatic on board who was screeching the most outrageous nonsense, the old steward and stewardess trying to pacify him, and endeavouring to quiet the frightened ladies, although they did not seem very comfortable themselves.

At 9.30 stood in again towards the shore, and I could see the white line of breakers. We tried to run in between the piers, but in the heavy sea the vessel would not steer and we drifted broadside into the breakers and took the ground to the eastward of the harbour. Then she bumped heavily, and the sea made a clear breach over us. I managed to scramble out to see the situation. I saw the crew getting over the bow and getting on shore by a rope, so I scrambled back to the cabin and got Lizzie to scramble out after me, dragging herself along by the ropes, for no one could stand. The vessel twisted about so, I thought she would have broken in half. We got forward to the bows. There was no one there, all the crew had gone. I saw a stout hawser hanging from the starboard bow and a lot of coastguardmen below, so I got Lizzie to scramble over the bulwark and slide down the hawser to the coastguardmen, who were ready to receive her, but just then a wave took her up to the neck, but a sturdy coastguardman caught hold of her and dragged her up on the beach. I followed and we got into the boat-house, but of course we were soaked to the skin. The rest of the passengers soon followed.

"Cast ashore at Newhaven"

We then had to scramble along the embankment, which was so slippery we were nearly blown into the canal as the storm continued. After crossing the harbour in a small boat, we got to the hotel in a pretty plight, about midnight, and as our luggage was in the steamer, we borrowed clothes from the chambermaid and waiter, regardless of fit, they were both small people. However, we soon turned in to a comfortable bed. Where the other passengers were stowed, I do not know.

Wed. 29th The storm was over; all our baggage, which was left to the mercy of the winds and waves last night, was got out of the vessel this morning, which was left high and dry on the beach as the tide receded. We lost nothing, thanks to the coastguardmen, for whom we got up a subscription amongst the passengers. They deserved it.

We left for London by the 1 p.m. train and got to town between 3 and 4; but our mishaps were not yet over, for we picked up a drunken cabby at the station, who ran us against all the omnibuses and cabs he could, and in the middle of London Bridge we had to get out and get into another cab, while a policeman took charge of the first one. At last we got to the Piazza Hotel and ordered dinner and enjoyed the mulligatawny soup, &c. We were too tired to go out.

The drunken cabby on London Bridge (*from Cree's original notebook*)

On their return to Plymouth, Edward and Lizzie Cree are expecting Percy to join them in their new home near the Hoe. On October 14th, however, Percy dies suddenly. On December 22nd Cree is appointed to the paddle steam frigate *Odin* (16), "a big lump of a ship, but not handsome", commanded by Captain Francis Scott. Throughout 1853 she is based chiefly at Lisbon, returning to home waters on March 1st 1854 with orders to refit and prepare for sea as soon as possible. Cree sees Lizzie briefly with their first child, William (b. June 1st 1853), before *Odin* departs on March 19th for the Baltic. France and Great Britain are on the brink of war with Russia, and the overall task of the British fleet in the months ahead (allied with a smaller French fleet) is to prevent Russian ships from leaving the Baltic and to protect Danish and Swedish property. Finland at this point in history is a constitutionally governed Grand Duchy within the Russian Empire.

1854

H.M. Steam Frigate *Odin*

H.M. STEAM FRIGATE ODIN

Kiel Bay

MARCH

Wed. 29th 5.30 Observed the fleet at anchor.* We anchored ahead of the *Duke of Wellington*. 2.15 Weighed and proceeded with the fleet. 3.40 H.M.S. *Lightning* arrived from England. 6 p.m. anchor.

Thur. 30th Fog; too thick to move; coaling, the *Lightning* alongside.

Fri. 31st 8 a.m. clearer. Got under weigh with the fleet, took the *Neptune* in tow, *Monarch* in tow of *Gorgon*. Standing in towards Kidge [Koge] Bay in Zeeland, south of Copenhagen.

Off Copenhagen

APRIL

Sat. 1st 4 a.m. anchored on account of the fog. *Princess Royal* ran into the *Cressy* and carried away her fore-yard. 9 a.m. fog cleared and the fleet got under weigh; we towing the *Neptune*. 3 p.m. anchored in two lines, Copenhagen just in sight. The *Conflict* just joined from England.

Sun. 2nd A Danish steamer with a large party of the good folks of Copenhagen steamed round the fleet, cheering as they went by some of the

* British men-of-war now in the Baltic – names, denominations, guns: *D. of Wellington*, screw (131); *Neptune*, sail (120); *Royal George*, screw (120); *St Jean d'Acre*, screw (101); *Cressy*, screw (90); *Princess Royal*, screw (90); *Monarch*, sail (84); *Blenheim*, screw (60); *Hogue*, screw (60); *Ajax*, screw (58); *Edinburgh*, screw (58); *Euryalus*, screw (50); *Impérieuse*, screw (50); *Arrogant*, screw (47); *Amphion*, screw (34); *Tribune*, screw (30); *Dauntless*, screw (24); *Leopard*, paddle (16); *Odin*, paddle (16); *Valorous*, paddle (16); *Conflict*, screw (8); *Bulldog*, paddle (6); *Dragon*, paddle (6); *Gorgon*, paddle (6); *Lightning*, paddle (2); *Vulture*, paddle (6).

Copenhagen

ships. The War Minister arrived at the flagship from England with the declaration of war. Hurrah!

Mon. 3rd Cold and raw, heavy squalls; struck lower yards and topmasts, the *Neptune* lost a man in the process. H.M. Steam Vessel *Hecla* joined and the screw *Archer*, 14 guns, from England. Rear-Admiral Plumridge[B] in the *Leopard*, H.M.S.s *Impérieuse, Tribune* and *Dauntless* sailed to the eastward to search for three Russian frigates said to be outside the ice. The declaration of war was read to all the ships' companies and the Admiral, Sir Charles Napier,[B] hoisted the following signal: "Lads! War is declared with a numerous enemy. If they are bold enough to offer battle you will know how to dispose of them." There were enthusiastic cheers from all the ships.[1]

[1] France and Great Britain had declared war on Russia on March 28th.

Thur. 6th H.M.S. *Cæsar* joined and the steam vessel *Basilisk*. Captain Scott[B] was signalled for "Steam to be got up". Sir Charles Napier and Rear-Admiral Chads[B] came on board. 10 started for Copenhagen. H.M.S. *Desperate* joined, having left Spithead last Saturday. H.M.S.s *Cruiser* and *Alban* joined. Met my old messmate, Ozzard, now Secretary to Sir Charles Napier. Anchored off Copenhagen at 2 p.m. Saluted. Found H.M.S. *Dragon* here; Willcox came on board.

Fri. 7th Blowing too hard to go on shore. A queer old codger is our Baltic pilot; a Hull skipper called Armstrong; a jolly old fellow like an animated beer-barrel.

Sat. 8th Still blowing hard with snow squalls.

Sun. 9th Took a cargo of water out to some of the line-of-battle ships, our decks lumbered up with great water-casks. In evening it came on to blow heavily while we were at anchor amongst the fleet. Parted two anchors, got up steam and went for shelter near Dago Light, and anchored.

0 200 miles
0 400 km
NORWAY
SWEDEN
FINLAND
Tornea
Skelleftea
CARLO I.
Uleaborg
Brahestad
Bjornklubb
Ratan
HOLMONIN I.
Raita
Gamla Carleby
Jakobstadt
Arno Sound
GULF OF BOTHNIA
Hudiksvall
Soderhamn
Bjorneborg
Nyastad
Lake Ladoga
Viborg
Gefle
ALAND IS
Abo
Helsingfors
Kronstadt
Oregrund
Grisselhamn
Hango
Bomersund
Sveaborg
St Petersburg
DAGO I.
Reval
Stockholm
GULF OF FINLAND
GOTTSKA SANDO
ESTONIA
FAROE I.
LIVONIA
GOTTLAND
Riga
Denmark
BALTIC SEA
KURLAND
Copenhagen
Memel
RUSSIAN EMPIRE
Koge Bay
BORNHOLM I.
Danzig
PRUSSIA
River Elbe
POLAND
LH

The Baltic

Mon. 10th 4 a.m. up anchor and finished our work, watering the big ships.

Thur. 13th We have been two days dragging for the anchors we lost during the gale. We have secured them now. Nearly all the large ships have left for the Gulf of Finland. The *Alban* had got ashore, we went to help.

Fri. 14th Good Friday. We had church service on board. In evening went to Copenhagen for supplies. I put up for the night at the Hotel d'Angleterre, where I had a comfortable little room and sat over the stove.

Sat. 15th Slept heavily, but restless and hot, for I had an eiderdown bed on top of me as well as the one underneath, and both were much too short, so I had alternate fits of heat and cold.

Cruising in the Baltic

Wed. 19th Passed north of Faroe Island and fell in with the fleet. Cruising between Faroe and Dago, in three lines. We ran down the lines delivering our mails and packages to all the ships. Friend Scott came on board for his supplies for the *Royal George*.

"England's Might"

Thur. 20th Cruising with our own squadron towards the small island of Gottska Sando, which is low and covered with wood. Some of our lieutenants went boarding strange ships.

Fri. 21st Stood to the NW. Made Landsort Lighthouse on the coast of Sweden and stood into a deep bay far amongst small rocky islands covered with firs and pines, 20 miles Elgsnabben harbour, about 30 miles south of Stockholm. Saw a few wooden farmhouses and a signal station on a hill but few other signs of inhabitants. A curious rarefaction of the atmosphere and refraction, causing the ships to look distorted into all shapes and sizes, some upside-down and some cut in two.

Sat. 22nd Threatening snow and very cold. Some of our fellows landed for a ramble on one of the little islands but met none of the inhabitants except some cows and sheep. They brought off a quantity of juniper berries.

Sun. 23rd Very cold and snowing occasionally. We have got amongst a lot of islands at the entrance of the Stockholm River. Three or four small steamers crowded with people came to look at us. The English Minister and some of the officials came to visit the Admiral. We are ordered to proceed to the Aland Islands. After taking a pilot we steamed through some intricate passages between the islands, which are very much alike, rocky, covered with firs and pines. Passed a few good sized villages, from which the natives flocked to see the strangers. Scenery pretty, but it was too cold to stop long on deck.

Mon. 24th Anchored off a small village during the night, where we had to take another pilot to take us through the mass of islands, the passage in many places not being double the width of the ship, sticks being placed to mark out the passage; scenery being all the same, rocky islands covered with pine. About noon got out of this labyrinth of islands and anchored off a town on the coast, Arholma, where we got another pilot and continued our course up the coast of Sweden, abreast of the Aland Islands, and anchored for the night off Grisholm [Grisselhamn?].

Tue. 25th Got under weigh at 4 this morning and stood across Alands Hoff to Ekero, one of the Aland Islands, but a violent snowstorm came on which prevented us from seeing the entrance of the harbour, so we put back and anchored at Arholma. Yesterday we took our first prize, the *Njarden*, a new schooner of about 160 tons under Russian colours, empty, from Aland. It was afterwards sold for £1,008.

Wed. 26th Got under weigh at 4 a.m. and stood along the Swedish shore to the north; difficult navigation between rocky islands and reefs, the shore all granite rock with forests of fir and pine as far as one can see. At noon anchored at Oregrund, a small port and village of about a hundred wooden houses, in lat. 60° 20′ N. on the Swedish coast. I landed in the afternoon with Mould and Hay to explore the place, which we found very clean; most of the houses painted red, with white window-frames and shutters; a tall wooden clock-tower; a church built of stone without a steeple, surrounded by a graveyard; enclosures of little gardens about the houses; the currant bushes and apple trees just budding. The young girls wear black pants like those I have seen in

"The cocky 1st Lieutenant and big Marine officer" – Lieutenants William Mould and Arthur Lewis

Swedish housemaid cleaning a doorstep in the traditional way

Normandy, regular young bloomers. Nothing appeared to be going on in the little place, streets silent; one or two little shops for the sale of groceries, drapery, &c., like we find in country villages at home. I got some gingerbread and rusks at a baker's shop, and a cake of their black rye-bread, with a hole in the centre to hang it on a pole. The people very civil and clean, all with blue eyes and sandy hair. Capercailzie, or cock-of-the-woods, appear plentiful, as we bought ten for about 2 shillings each, weighing about 10 pounds apiece. Some blackcock were also purchased. Beef or mutton we did not see, but a very wild looking hog. Eggs and milk are plentiful and cheap, corn brandy and nice bread-cakes.

Thur. 27th Under weigh at 4 a.m. Standing across the Gulf of Bothnia for Bjorneborg on the coast of Finland.

4 p.m. observed the ice ahead; 4.45 tacked, running along the edge; 5 shaped course to WSW lat. 61° 21′, the ice was broken up, not in a solid field, and extended as far as the eye could reach. We saw the high land of Finland beyond. The air felt chilly and atmosphere hazy.

Fri. 28th Lay to at noon off Grisselhamn, on the Swedish coast, while the Captain landed, saluted the Governor with four guns. Proceeded on our course towards Gottska Sando.

Sat. 29th Snowing and blowing ENE wind and an unpleasant sea, sighted Gottska Sando, but did not find the Admiral there. Fell in with H.M.S. *Ajax* and saw the *Euryalus* and one or two of the other men-of-war. Stood away towards Elgsnabben, blowing hard; hove to all night.

Sun. 30th Not much improvement in the weather. Sighted Landsort Lighthouse and ran up to Elgsnabben, where we found the Admiral and the rest of the ships. We were sent off again, but I got a letter from Lizzie and was able to write a hasty letter in reply by friend Ozzard, the Admiral's Secretary. By noon we were again on our way to Gottska Sando, where we arrived about 8 p.m. On our way we fell in with the *Ajax* and *Euryalus* and afterwards with the *Austerlitz*, French, 98 guns.

MAY *Mon. 1st* 6 a.m. weighed, fell in with H.M.S. *Hecla*. Took our Russian prize the *Njarden* in tow for Faroe Sound; saw H.M.S. *Magicienne*; dined with the Captain; heard the sad news of the drowning of Captain John Foote, of H.M.S. *Conflict*, the medical officer and boat's crew, by the boat capsizing off Memel. In evening it came on a dense fog, which prevented our getting into Faroe.

Wed. 3rd Anchored in Faroe Sound, the weather having cleared, but all yesterday we had to stand off the land on account of the fog. Ran into a narrow strait between the islands of Faroe and Gottland, with green fields and farmhouses on each side of us, a happy change from fields of ice and dense fogs. We also got some fresh stock, although the beef was indifferent and no mutton.

Thur. 4th H.M.S. *Amphion* arrived with two Russian prizes she had cut out from Riga. H.M.S. *Rosamond* arrived from England bringing a welcome supply of letters and papers. Wrote home by our prize which sails for England tomorrow.

Fri. 5th A lovely warm morning. Got under weigh, but came to again to assist the *Amphion* which has got ashore, but we soon got her off. H.M.S. *Impérieuse* arrived and brought a report that the Russian fleet had put to sea. We took the mail-bags from the *Rosamond* and started in search of the Admiral. Fog came on; we fell in with some of our ships off Gottska Sando.

Sat. 6th Saw Landsort Lighthouse, but it came on too thick to go on: blowing hard and heavy sea. Stood out and fell in with H.M.S. *Duke of Wellington* and the rest of the fleet off north end of Gottska Sando. We were ordered back to Faroe.

Sun. 7th Anchored at Faroe Sound, H.M. Ships *Leopard* and *Porcupine* came in. We commenced coaling and took in 60 tons before midnight.

Mon. 8th 8 a.m. went out with our collier in tow. In evening fell in with the fleet and at midnight saw some strange sail and beat to quarters, but they proved to be only some of our own ships.

Tue. 9th Passed Svarklubb Lighthouse. Ran into Oregrund for the night, with H.M.S. *Leopard* and our collier.

Wed. 10th Left Oregrund at 6 a.m., H.M.S. *Leopard* in company. Stood over towards the coast of Finland.

Thur. 11th Fog, but when it cleared found we were on the north side of Aland Islands. Saw a steamer ahead, supposed to be Russian, gave chase and cleared for action, but lost her in the fog amongst the islands. Passed Enskar Lighthouse. Saw the ice along the coast of Finland; altered course towards the west. Curious mirage and sun-blinks; the sea-water quite fresh.

Fri. 12th Fell in with H.M. Steamers *Valorous* and *Vulture*, who had been cruising amongst the islands and captured a Russian bark laden with salt and also destroyed some Russian gunboats, their crews escaping on shore.

Bombardment of the Russian dockyard at Brahestad

Sat. 13th Very thick fog: we found ourselves amongst the ice in great lumps all round the ship; we stood back towards the Oscar Lighthouse.

Sun. 14th Lat. 61° 20′, long. 18° 19′.

Mon. 15th Tried to find our way amongst hundreds of rocks and shoals into the harbour, or sound, in the Aland Islands. The *Valorous* got on shore and also the *Leopard*, so after tugging them off we gave up the attempt for the present and stood up the Gulf of Bothnia, chasing five vessels, but finding they were Norwegian, returned to the senior officer. Found ice all along the Finnish coast.

Wed. 17th Standing along the coast of Finland, *Leopard*, *Valorous* and *Vulture* in company. Plenty of ice about: observed several signal fires along the Finnish coast: hove to for the night.

Thur. 18th Standing under easy sail to NW. Boarded a Norwegian schooner laden with salt.

Fri. 19th Standing north, towards the head of the Gulf of Bothnia. In evening anchored off the island and town of Holmonin, lat. 63° 44′.

Sat. 20th Sent a boat on shore with the stewards, who managed to pick up some fine salmon, and milk, eggs and potatoes.

Uleaborg

Wed. 31st Anchored at 4 this morning off the island of Carlo; sent boats to sound the passage. 11 a.m. weighed and stood on towards Uleaborg. At 2 p.m. anchored off the beacon and sent boats farther in to sound the passage. *Valorous* joined us with wheels smashed in the ice.

JUNE *Thur. 1st* My boy's first birthday, which we celebrated by a tremendous bonfire, such an one as the Vikings of old occasionally lit on our own shores, in the olden time.

We got into the river and anchored off the town of Uleaborg about 8 p.m. Boats away, manned and armed. Here were great stores of tar, hemp, timber, &c., for shipbuilding, belonging to the Russian Government, of which we soon made such a blaze as illuminated the country for many miles round, destroying many thousand pounds' worth of the Russian Emperor's property, and crippling his shipbuilding in the Baltic, beside a great many vessels on the stocks building and in the dock, all consumed. A more destructive fire than at Brahestad.

Fri. 2nd Wet. Our party all got safely on board about 8 this morning, wet, dirty, and tired, after destroying all the public property and stores on shore. One unfortunate casualty happened to a man of the *Vulture* who discovered some spirits in one of the storehouses, got drunk and was burnt to death. No resistance was made; a party of twenty-five Cossacks had bolted when we appeared in sight. Some fresh provisions were sent off to the ship, which showed that the Finlanders had no ill feeling against us.

Sat. 3rd Wooding the ships. Got under weigh about 11 p.m. and left Uleaborg, anchored off the island of Carlo at 2 a.m.

Sun. 4th At anchor off Carlo. 4 p.m. weighed and proceeded down the coast, after leaving Admiral Plumridge in the *Valorous* on their way to Tornea.

Mon. 5th Lat. 64° 25′, long. 23° 27′. Tankar Beacon SW 31 miles.

Gamla Carleby

Tue. 6th Standing offshore after sighting Gamla Carleby, a small town on the coast of Finland where the Russian Government had a depot and store: the

Sun. 21st Lat. 64° 6′. Anchored off Raita on the Swedish coast, where we procured a pilot for Bjornklubb, about 40 miles farther up the gulf. Daylight nearly all night, sunset at 10 p.m. when we anchored in the harbour of Bjuroklubb, quite landlocked. Surrounded by rocks and pine forest, where were able to fill up with water.

Tue. 23rd Lat. 64° 28′. Weighed at 9 and stood out to sea.

Wed. 24th Stopped by the ice in our progress farther north; found the ice extending all along the Finland shore and blocking up the head of the gulf; lat. 65° 4′. Forced our way through some of the floating masses of ice, but compelled to turn our head to the southward.

Thur. 25th Floating masses of ice all around.

Fri. 26th Lat. 64° 35′, long. 23° 11′. Amongst the ice.

Sat. 27th 9 a.m. anchored off Tankar Beacon, a lighthouse on a small rocky island; *Leopard, Valorous* and *Vulture* in company. 11 weighed and stood to the NW. Standing up the gulf, overhauled two Norwegian vessels.

Mon. 29th Beautiful weather, detached lumps of ice all about. The Captain turned the hands up and made a speech to the men, informing them we were about to attack the town of Uleaborg on the Russian coast, which speech was cheered by the men, who were tired of accomplishing so little.

Brahestad

Tue. 30th Pushed through the ice with the loss of some of our paddle-floats. Left the *Valorous* behind and anchored in clear water about a mile off the little town of Brahestad, where the Russians had a small dockyard. Our boats manned and armed were sent on shore and informed the Russian authorities that we were come to destroy all Imperial property, but if the peaceful inhabitants made no resistance, private property would be respected. We found ten new vessels, intended for gunboats, on the stocks; these were very soon in a blaze, beside a quantity of wood, tar and other stores. Great destruction of property, but it was in order to assist in crippling the enemy. The unfortunate people fled to the country, for there was no resistance. The blaze was tremendous, an awful and cruel sight, but such is war. After this destruction the boats returned to the ship and we stood out to sea and along the coast.

The attack on Bomersund – (*left to right*) *Valorous*, *Odin*, *Hecla*

next place destined for attack, but this time unsuccessfully, and we were destined to sustain a sad disaster.

In the evening we sighted the coast of Sweden and then returned to Gamla Carleby and anchored.

Wed. 7th About 4 miles from the town about 8 p.m., the water being too shallow to go farther in. H.M.S. *Vulture*, Captain Glasse, was with us and was senior officer. About 8 p.m., a fine clear night, broad daylight, the boats, two paddle-box boats, pinnace, cutter, and gig, were called away, manned and armed, and with the *Vulture*'s boats pulled in to the landing-place. The officer in command demanded a parley; there was no suspicion, foolishly, of the place being quite prepared to resist a boat attack. Afterwards we found they had two Russian regiments of infantry, with artillery, there. Our poor foolish Jacks and Marines were taking it easy, smoking their pipes, their muskets and carronades not even loaded, when a sort of wooden barricade was suddenly thrown down and a company of Russian soldiers poured in a volley, and two of their field pieces opened fire within a couple of hundred yards. Our men pushed off a little way, loaded as quickly as they could, and returned the fire with interest; but the Russians had stone walls to get behind, and one of the *Vulture*'s boats, with a gun and twenty-eight men, was sunk by the Russian fire. Poor Lieutenant Carrington, my friend and frequent companion, was killed by the first volley, with Montagu, a mate, and three sailors, one a petty officer; poor little Athorpe, Mid., mortally wounded by a shot through his chest and abdomen; Magrath shot through his thigh; and fourteen of our men wounded. Our big Lieutenant of Marines had a near shave by a rifle-shot taking off one of his mustachios.

We could see there was a hard fight going on, but were too far off to render any assistance. At last, finding our men were falling fast without being able to get at the enemy, the smashed boat had to be abandoned; the survivors had been made prisoners. Our poor fellows sorrowfully returned to the ship, bringing our killed and wounded with them. My turn now came to do the best I could for the poor sufferers; my assistant was away doing duty in another ship. However, there were no serious operations to be performed: extracting a bullet from Magrath's thigh and dressing the other hurts, mostly gunshot wounds, not dangerous, except poor little Athorpe, who was becoming unconscious and asking for his mother, poor little fellow. It was 8 in the morning before death released him from suffering. It was some time after that before I had finished.

Thur. 8th We had all the main deck for our sick-bay: everything had been got ready for the reception of the wounded before they came on board. We were anxious to know the fate of the *Vulture*'s men, so Captain Glasse sent a boat with a flag of truce to the Russian commanding officer to enquire into the

Gamla Carleby, June 7th 1854: the boats going in

fate of the *Vulture*'s boat's crew, but no answer was returned or information of any sort; so we concluded that the survivors, if any, were marched off to a Russian prison. Nearly all our boats were penetrated by Russian rifle bullets, and it is a wonder we had not a larger list of killed and wounded. However, we were thankful there were no more. We mourned the three officers much, they were such nice young fellows: Carrington was about twenty-four, Montagu twenty-one, and poor little Athorpe fifteen. In the evening we stood out to sea.

Gulf of Bothnia

Fri. 9th Stood in again towards the Russian shore. Sighted Jakobstadt and Nye Carleby, then went out to sea again to consign our six poor shipmates to a watery grave. Our Chaplain, Fred Smith, performed the service. Of course all the crew attended, and I saw many tearful eyes amongst the rough sailors. Smith read the service impressively. The Marines afterwards fired three volleys.

In the evening we were joined by *Leopard* and *Valorous*.

Sun. 11th Standing down the gulf towards Oregrund under sail.

Mon. 12th Up steam, proceeded into Oregrund and anchored for a few repairs, H.M.S.s *Leopard, Vulture* and *Valorous* in company, the two latter ordered to join Sir Charles Napier.

Wed. 14th Our wounded going on well. In evening a stroll through the town and had supper at the only hotel, a primitive place, but they were able to give us some blackcock nicely cooked. Supplies are plentiful and cheap – milk, fish, eggs, butter, and sheep.

Thur. 15th The weather has become quite warm. I took a walk over the island, to a pleasant wood amongst the pines, and laid down in the deep, soft moss, and fell asleep. The scenery very pretty, so quiet and rural. A farmhouse was near, where I got a basin of new milk. Met the Surgeon of the *Leopard* and returned by the skiff to dinner.

Fri. 16th Crowds of natives came off to see the ship, men and women, high and low, pretty and ugly.

Sun. 18th 3 a.m. anchored in Arno Sound, a snug creek about 80 miles north of Oregrund, surrounded by pretty hilly and rocky country, covered with forest and dotted with lakes abounding in fish; a stream of good water from which we filled up our tanks. Numbers of the natives, male and female, came off to see the ship and brought milk, potatoes, and fish, for sale.

In the afternoon I went for a ramble up amongst the rocks and laid down in the heather with Gibbon's *Decline and Fall* till it was time to return on board. The weather has become pleasantly warm and the air soft, at night as well as by day.

Bomersund

Wed. 21st Fell in with H.M.S. *Hecla*, Captain Hall, whom I knew when he commanded the *Nemesis* in China in 1842. The *Valorous* also joined us and we three steamers started for Bomersund, a Russian fort in the Aland Islands;[2]

[2] Bomersund was one of the four main defensive points guarding the Gulf of Finland, the 200-mile-long sea route leading to the Russian capital, St Petersburg; the others being Sveaborg, Reval, on the Estonian coast, and finally the fortified island naval base of Kronstadt.

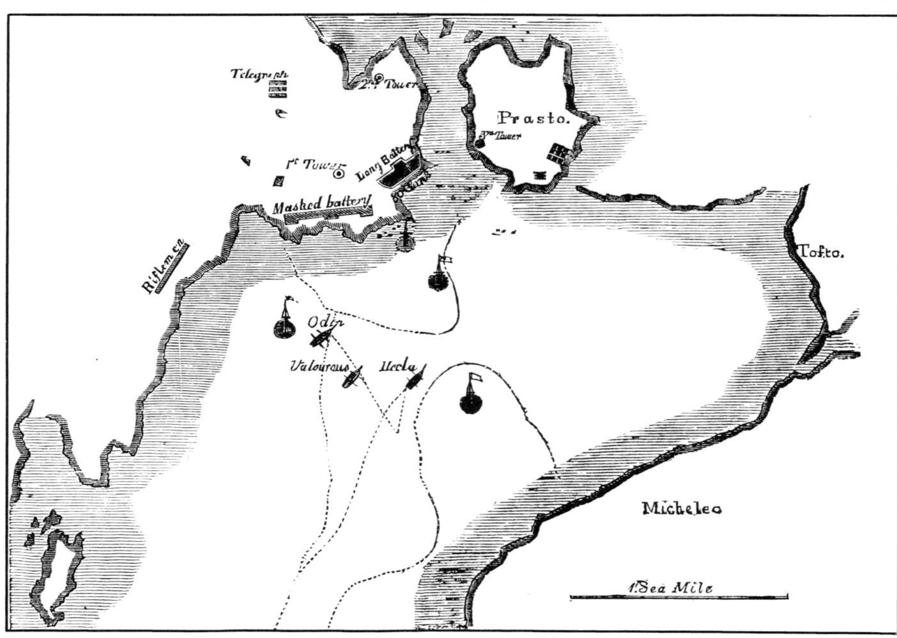

Plan of the fortifications and positions of the ships at Bomersund, June 21st 1854 (*from the* Illustrated London News, *July 8th 1854*)

an intricate navigation amongst the numerous islands and rocks, as we found it before, but we had a good pilot now, and cast anchor at 4.45 about a mile from the great circular fort, on which we all opened fire and found with our long guns our shot would search the fort pretty well. They soon returned our fire, but their balls fell short. A small fort or Martello tower soon joined in with her guns which had greater range as it was on a hill, but fortunately the shot went over us. We continued to ply them industriously with shot and shell; then we were favoured with some balls from the wood on an island on our left, where the Russians had a masked battery amongst the trees, and also some sharpshooters. We were struck in many places on the port side by round shot and rifle-balls, and one of our Marines had a bullet through his thigh. We should have suffered more but we got up defences with hammocks and screens, which were pretty well peppered. Soon we saw smoke and then flames rising from the storehouses at the back of the great fort and the fire from their guns slackened, and as we were expending all our shot and shell we also ceased. The fire at the Russian storehouses continued to blaze away, when we hauled off about midnight, everybody tired out.[3]

Beside the Marine shot through the thigh I had a few trifling accidents to attend to. The ship was struck in many places: a 30-pound ball had entered one of the portholes and gone right through the Captain's cabin, smashing a window, but none of his valuables, as they had been all stowed away before the firing commenced. We left the fort on fire in two places. We steamed out again amongst the islands and anchored outside.

[3] It was in this action that Mate Charles Davis Lucas (1834–1914), of Clontibret, Co. Monaghan, was reported to have flung a live shell overboard *Hecla*. He was made Lieutenant from the day of the attack, and for his bold action later (in 1857) became the first recipient of the Victoria Cross. He rose to the rank of Rear-Admiral.

Thur. 22nd At anchor all day repairing damages. Captain Hall dined with us. The *Valorous* was sent on to Oregrund.

Fri. 23rd We were joined in the evening by *Leopard*, and *Cuckoo*, gunboat, and a French frigate which we took in tow and steamed away towards Oregrund.

Gulf of Bothnia

Sat. 24th Swedish coast in sight. 2 p.m. anchored in Oregrund with the French frigate *Andromache*.

Sun. 25th Stood up the coast to the north and anchored at Gefle. Afterwards, in the cutter, went 8 miles to the town. Passed a small fort, off which the merchant ships take in their cargoes of wood. Scenery pretty, hills covered with pine forest on each side, pretty country houses, green fields, little wooded islands. Before we arrived at the town we passed the public gardens, crowded with gaily dressed natives, who cheered us on passing.

JULY *Mon. 10th* About 1 o'clock in the morning sighted Malorn Lighthouse, on a small, low island at the head of the Gulf of Bothnia, in North lat. 65° 31′, our farthest north, not far from the Arctic Circle. The sun had just risen above the horizon, red and fiery, but the weather might be called "a rosy morn". We were near the mouth of the Tornea River. As we could not go any farther north we turned to the SW and soon came in sight of the Swedish coast. It came on misty and wet.

Skelleftea harbour

"The Landlady"

At 2.30 anchored in Shilleftia [Skelleftea] harbour. Went on shore for a walk through the pine forest, along a sandy path. The moss, dry leaves and wild flowers gave some lovely tints. Some of our fellows, after a deal of trouble, procured a country cart and drove to the town 9 miles off. I met Pottinger, Surgeon of the *Hecla*, and we went to the inn, such as it was in this out-of-the-way place, and got a cup of very good coffee. It was so good that we accepted the invitation of the landlady, a Swedish countess by-the-by, to breakfast with her next morning. Her Ladyship was fat and over fifty, I should say, but very amusing and spoke French well. She gave us wild strawberries and cream.

After a ramble through the forest, returned to the hotel to dinner, which consisted of veal cutlets, pickled salmon, sour milk thickened, pancakes, and country beer. The Swedish air gives one an appetite and no mistake; nothing in the shape of food comes amiss.[4]

After returning to the ship we went out of harbour and parted company with the *Hecla*.

Wed. 12th At 3 a.m. anchored off Ratan harbour. Left again about 2. Soon after fell in with the *Leopard*. Returned to Ratan and left again at 6 p.m., then at

[4] In March of the following year Cree found his weight had increased from 136 pounds to 168 pounds in the previous twelve months. He attributed this expansion to "cod-liver-oil and the Baltic climate".

9 p.m. anchored in Sika harbour. From Ratan we had given a passage to a Swedish gentleman, his wife and daughters, very pleasant people, who live about 3 miles from Sika. He is the owner of some ironworks, a thriving man. He sent an invitation, after we got into the harbour, to come up to his house, and sent his carriage. A party of our officers went up and were most hospitably entertained at dinner and afterwards kept it up dancing till early morning. Sika harbour is a snug little place. We came in to get some coal which had been left for us.

The Collector of Customs, Ratan

Fri. 14th Left Sika harbour at 4 p.m. and soon fell in with our friend the French frigate outside.

Fri. 21st Anchored off Ratan at noon. The fat old officer of Customs came on board to welcome us and brought a party of his friends with him. After we got rid of our visitors we ran to the south and entered the Hudiksvall River, 9 miles below the town. Found the *Virginie*, French frigate, there. We received an invitation from the Burgomaster and Corporation to a ball in the town. Fellowes, Apgeorge, the interpreter, and I went up to the public rooms: about 200 people, twenty-five officers from the French frigate, all the principal inhabitants of the place were there. A goodly show of the fair Swedish ladies and plenty of dancing, polkas, quadrilles and waltzes. A cold stand-up supper, consisting of cold veal in thin slices, bits of salt fish, force-meat balls, hashed veal, dried reindeer, custard pudding, radishes, bread of various kinds, ices, punch, ale and porter, claret and corn brandy in plenty. Four gentlemen sang glees; rooms very hot, dancing kept up till 4 in the morning; the Frenchmen were as lively as usual and insisted in seeing all the ladies to their own doors. Only two or three spoke English, and not much of that. I met a young doctor of the ship and fraternised, a very pleasant fellow, but as my French is defective we were unable to have much conversation, and he could not speak English. Two Swedish merchants named Frisk were very attentive. It was broad daylight when I got back to the hotel and to bed, which I found comfortable and clean.

Mon. 24th Breakfast of tea, reindeer flesh, raw and dried, eggs, dried fish, cucumber, cold veal and wild strawberries. The charges were very moderate, 3 rix-dollars and 24 skilling, or 4/-6 each, for tea, bed, breakfast, and attendance. The little town is clean, silent, and well built. I found a good apothecary's shop, the only one.

We left at 10.30 and got back to the ship at noon. Found them busy coaling from a brig alongside; took in near 300 tons by 9 p.m. We received a visit from a gentleman with his family of sons and daughters who were at the dance. They came in their own boat, and the ladies showed themselves to be expert at the oars.

"Rusticating in the Aland Islands" – Cree and messmates taking a siesta ashore

Tue. 25th Some wild raspberries were brought on board, but we could get no vegetables – none to be got in this part of the country now. Gooseberries, currants, and wild strawberries were procured. At noon we left and sailed towards Oregrund, weather squally with thunder and lightning.

Fri. 28th We were ordered to proceed through the islands towards Bomersund. Saw the fort on the hill, but directly after struck on a rock and there we stuck fast. Captain Giffard [now commanding the steam frigate *Leopard*] was with us and the *Basilisk* and *Porcupine* and two small surveying steamers in company. Our men were at work all night trying to get the vessel off – one of our poor fellows was killed in a cutter under the bows of the ship by one of the anchors slipping and crushing out his brains.

Sat. 29th We got off the rock by the assistance of the other vessels. Afterwards anchored near the *Hecla*, about 5 miles in rear of Bomersund, to intercept, with the assistance of 5,000 French soldiers, any troops or supplies being sent to the Russians, for they intend to take and destroy the forts that we with two other steamers had the audacity to attack and managed to burn their stores. But I fear we only showed them their weak points which they have had time to repair since, and I think the "Brave Nemesis Hall" got a reprimand from the Admiral instead of thanks.

Sun. 30th Three Russian deserters came off to the *Odin*. They stated that they were in the fort when we bombarded it, and that, if we could have continued our fire for three hours longer, it would have been deserted by the

Russian garrison. Ten of their people were killed and amongst them their surgeon. Another deserter swam off to the ship. But one cannot put much faith in what these fellows say, as they only wish to conciliate their new friends.

AUGUST

Tue. 1st We captured an old yacht belonging to the Governor of the Aland Islands. Some of our boats went away reconnoitring. We hear that 5,000 French troops have arrived in English ships. General Baraguay d'Hilliers[B] to command them and assist in taking Bomersund.

The weather has become very warm. A woman came off from one of the islands with milk and butter for sale. She soon disposed of her stock.

Woman selling milk and butter, Aland Islands

Fri. 4th In the afternoon [Chaplain F. W.] Smith, [Lieutenant T. H. B.] Fellowes and I paddled our canoe to a little uninhabited island astern of the ship, where we enjoyed a siesta amongst the soft heather with a novel and a cigar each. In the evening we saw a great fire in the direction of Bomersund, caused we heard by the Russians burning their storehouses, &c. We soon afterwards moved in nearer the forts and watching the passages.

Bomersund

Sun. 6th Moved up nearer the forts at Bomersund, the steamers concentrating round the point of attack.

Mon. 7th A transport with 300 French soldiers passed us to a point of landing. *Hecla, Gorgon, Basilisk, Leopard, Alban, Porcupine* and other steamers all here.

Tue. 8th Sent back to our old station, 3 miles to the northward. Captain the Hon. H. Keppel dined with us; his ship [*St Jean d'Acre*] is away towards the Gulf of Finland. Heavy firing we heard in the direction of Bomersund, but we cannot see what is going on. During the night an expedition went from this ship to destroy a Russian signal station on a hill, and had a troublesome march of 5 miles over rocks and bogs.

Thur. 10th Another expedition went to destroy a building used as a prison. Great excitement about some Russian troops said to be landing on the north end of the island.

Fri. 11th The *Locust* steamer got on a rock and we were all the morning getting her off. Moved to near a small village. The *Penelope* got ashore too near the forts and was fired upon with red-hot shot, by which three of her men

Bomersund, August 1854: (*left*) Fort Notvik, in ruins, and Fort Prasto; (*centre*) the chief fort before it was blown up; (*right*) a French picket and, on the hillside, the destroyed western fort.

were killed, and she was on fire for a time. One of her midshipmen did a plucky thing: one of the red-hot shot came through the ship's side and lodged in his sea-chest; he coolly picked it up with a shovel and placed it on three cold-shot till it became harmless. The *Hecla* had been sent to the assistance of the *Penelope* and got considerably damaged by the shot, and had three men wounded. The *Valorous* and *Lightning* also went to her assistance; and in the meantime the other ships kept up a fire at the forts with shot and shell. They then lightened the *Penelope* by throwing all her guns overboard, when she floated and was towed to a place of safety, tho' much damaged. We could not see much of this as we were kept on the other side of the point of land, to intercept any of the enemy attempting to escape to the mainland.

The Russians now burnt everything that was inflammable in the neighbourhood of the forts. There were many great explosions and firing away on both sides. At last the Russkis, after displaying a great deal of bravery, had to give in, and haul down their flags and march out prisoners of war, a large number having been killed.

H.M.S. *Penelope* on shore at Bomersund under the Russian guns, August 10th 1854

The French and English flags now float over what remains of the forts. All the ships at the outposts were now recalled and we went into the inner harbour.

Thur. 17th I went on shore and landed at the great fort, which has been pretty well battered. Next morning I went to the hospital ship *Belleisle* to call on Dr McKechnie, Inspector of Hospitals, to look over the hospital. I found everything very nice and clean, but pretty full of our sick and wounded, beside the worst of the Russian wounded; very bad some of them are. Afterwards went to the large fort and visited the Russian hospital, filled with their poor wretched wounded, whom I found sorely plagued with flies, but the poor fellows seemed very grateful for the attentions they received from our medical officers. I looked into the dispensary where one of the Russian surgeons was killed, a shell had burst amongst the bottles, an awful smash.

Stockholm, November 1854

On December 11th at Copenhagen *Odin* is ordered to Woolwich to refit. She arrives there nine days later.

1855

In February Captain James Willcox (formerly of *Fury*) takes command of *Odin*, which is destined shortly for the Crimea, where the war against Russia is still raging. The peninsula was invaded by the French and British in September 1854 with the purpose of taking pressure off the Turks, who had been fighting the Russians on the Danube and in Asia Minor since October 1853, and of capturing the great Russian naval base of Sebastopol. In 1854 three major battles were fought: Alma (September 20th), a victory for the French and British in their drive from their NW base for Sebastopol; Balaclava (October 25th), in which the Russian march towards the landlocked harbour of Balaclava, base for the British army engaged in the siege of Sebastopol, was halted; and Inkerman (November 5th), a bloody affair in which the Russians, aiming to break the allied siege of Sebastopol, were defeated with heavy casualties. On November 14th a tremendous storm lashed the peninsula, sinking many British transports with cargoes of essential winter clothing and supplies. This was the preface to a winter of fearful hardship and administrative chaos. By early 1855, however, provisions and clothing delivered via the Crimean War Fund (organised by *The Times* of London) had brought many comforts to the demoralised and much depleted British army, and administrative order had been largely restored. Florence Nightingale's tireless work among the once deplorably neglected sick and wounded had also taken effect.

Spithead

MAY

Tue. 22nd In the afternoon Her Majesty passed through the fleet, close under our stern, so we had a good view of her. She looked very well: she was in the *Fairy* on her way to Osborne. Royal salute, manned yards, full dress.

Fri. 25th Went alongside the *Neptune* and took on board three 13-inch mortars. Embarked Royal Marine artillery, policemen, their wives and families; the ship crowded.

At Sea

Sun. 27th Noon, weighed, with three mortar-boats in tow. Proceeded round the east end of the Isle of Wight and down channel.

Mon. 28th Rain and misty; blowing hard from SW. Passed the Start about 5 p.m. and Plymouth soon after, and looked with longing eyes towards my loved ones there, God bless them!!

Tue. 29th Lat. 49° 2′, long. 5° 51′. Blowing hard and much sea. In the evening our mortar-boats broke adrift and we soon lost sight of them, but picked them up next day.

The Dardanelles – Constantinople – The Bosphorus

JUNE *Fri. 22nd* Lofty mountains of Greece in sight, their tops covered with snow. In the evening we passed through the Cerigo channel and by Cape Matapan; many vessels in sight.

Sat. 23rd Passed SE of Zea and through the Doro passage.

Sun. 24th Passed Mytilene and inside Tenedos, saw the Plains of Troy and Mount Ida. Entered the Dardanelles at 5 p.m.

Mon. 25th In the Sea of Marmara, met H.M.S. *Gorgon* on her way home.

Noon, Constantinople in sight with its minarets and domes, a lovely and interesting scene. Anchored at 2 p.m. above Seraglio Point: crowds of shipping; palaces and mosques, trees and picturesque houses on each side, steamers crowded with Eastern looking people, caiques gliding about manned by bearded Turks. H.M.S. *Albion* here has bad news from Sebastopol: poor Captain Lyons, son of the Admiral, killed, or died of a wound in the calf of his leg from a splinter of a shell. Repulse of an assault on the Malakoff with heavy losses to English and French.

6 p.m. went on to the Bosphorus and anchored about 6 miles above Constantinople. Lovely scene in bright moonlight, palaces, kiosks and gardens on the steep hillsides, a Turkish military band was playing some wild tune in front of a beautiful white marble palace; there were lights among the trees, a fairy scene, while the light caiques glided over the glittering water.

The Bosphorus – Black Sea – Sebastopol

Tue. 26th Weighed at 5 and proceeded through the beautiful Bosphorus.

Constantinople

The Bosphorus: *Odin* towing mortar-boats into the Black Sea

Passed Therapia, where we saw the *Mæander* frigate with her mizen-mast gone and figure-head shot away; some French men-o'-war, transports and other vessels in great numbers. All the beauty of the scene vanishes at the mouth of the Bosphorus, which we reached by 8 o'clock. The shores of the Black Sea, which we now entered, are bare and dark, and the scene was anything but cheering after the lovely shores of the Bosphorus. A large fleet of ships extended in a long line on their way to the seat of war, with supplies and more victims.

Thur. 28th Daylight: high mountains of the Crimea in sight ahead. It came on to blow from NW with a good deal of sea. Our mortar-boats broke adrift, but were able to make sail, which delayed us off the entrance to Balaclava, for which I was not sorry, as I was able to get a sketch of the narrow entrance, hemmed in by frowning cliffs, crowned by the ruins of an ancient Genoese castle and numbers of tents of Marines and Highland regiments, under my old shipmate Sir Colin Campbell,[B] of Chin-kiang-foo celebrity. Crowds of ships were anchored outside, there being no room inside. We took the *Flamer* in tow and proceeded towards Sebastopol. We rounded the low point on which the tall white lighthouse of Chersonese stands, and ran in amongst the ships blockading Sebastopol. The *Royal Albert*, with Sir Edmund Lyons'[B] flag, and about a dozen other line-of-battle ships, beside French, and a hundred other ships jammed close together in two little bays near the lighthouse.

We anchored about 2 miles outside the formidable forts at the entrance of the harbour of Sebastopol, and had a good view of the tents of the allies and the Russians each side. A terrible battle was then going on, the booming of the big guns and continual rattle of small arms were audible enough, but the white clouds of powder-smoke rising behind the great forts obscured the view in that direction. I watched the shells flying between the Malakoff, the Redan, and the Mamelon and the town, till late.

We were soon visited by the guard-boat, whose officer gave us the news. The worst was that Lord Raglan[B] was dying. He died at 5 this evening. The fact is that His Lordship's health had been visibly failing for some time – the worry and vexation after the failure of the last two bombardments and assaults on the Redan and Malakoff, in which so many of his officers and men were killed, on the 6th and 18th of this month. Lord Raglan's death will be a terrible loss to the British, who will find it impossible to supply his place out here. General Estcourt,[B] the Adjutant-General, died on the 24th. The following superior officers are knocked up: Generals Sir George Brown,[B] Pennefather,[B] Codrington,[B] Buller[B] and Estcourt. General Pélissier[B] had become French Commander-in-Chief, General Canrobert[B] having resigned the first place to him, Pélissier, who is a more determined man and prosecutes the siege with greater vigour. Many important points have been captured from the enemy

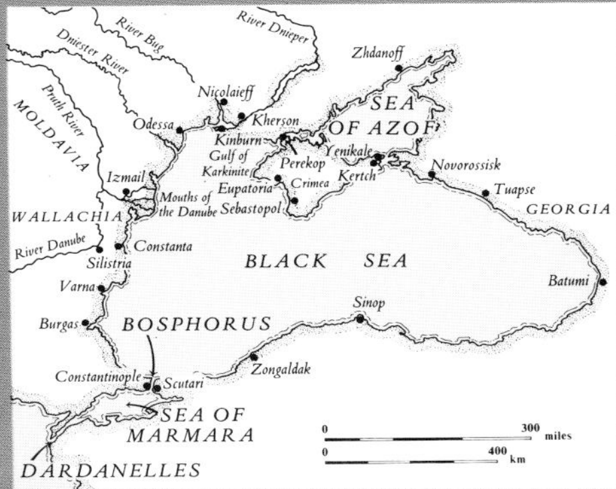

The Black Sea

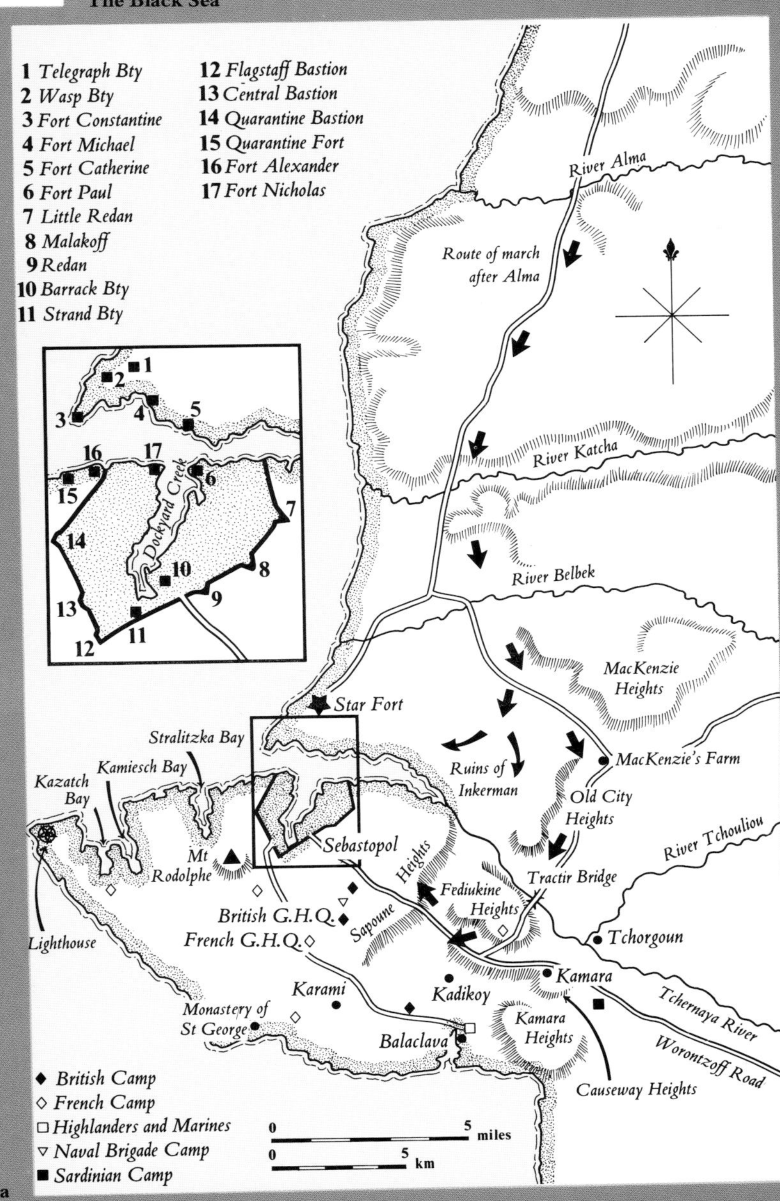

The Chersonese Peninsula

Landing-place at Kazatch Creek

after hard fighting and much slaughter on both sides. There are rumours that Pélissier and the Emperor are at loggerheads, but that the former won't be interfered with in his plans.[1]

A successful expedition to Kertch and the Sea of Azof has returned.[2] There was a great bombardment of Sebastopol on the 6th and 7th of this month, and assaults on the town, which were repulsed. The Malakoff had been nearly captured after stubborn fighting. The Quarries had been captured.[3] In these affairs it is said the Russians lost 5,000 men, killed and wounded, the French 5,500 and the English 700 and 47 officers. A fourth bombardment on June 18th with 600 siege-guns, which nearly ruined the enormous Russian works, but they were able to repair them during the night. In this assault there were 1,500 Russians killed and wounded, 3,500 French and 1,505 English. The famous Russian General, Todleben,[B] the great engineer in the defence of Sebastopol, was wounded in the head and disabled for the time.[4]

Sebastopol

Fri. 29th Received our letters from home and visits from many of our friends in the ships near, amongst them Lieutenant Fellowes, Captain Giffard,[B] Chaplain Thompson, and Surgeon Willcox, the Captain's brother, who said Lord Raglan died from exhaustion after diarrhoea of a few days. I went with Fellowes to his ship, the *Royal Albert*, and saw my friend Brien the Surgeon, then to H.M.S. *Rodney*, then landed in Kazatch Bay. At a wooden shed there, got a fine pony belonging to Fellowes and had a ride out round to Kameisch and wondered at the crowds of ships jammed close together in the narrow bay or creek, then passed through the French wooden town, a queer place all bustle and noise – French cafés and shops, French girls in some of them. Went on to a camp on rising ground towards Cathcart's Hill, to try and

[1] General Pélissier – called "tin head" by his men – was a man of independent spirit and fiery temperament and, unlike his predecessor Canrobert, showed a cavalier disregard for the Emperor Napoleon III's plans and opinions, which he considered quite valueless. Napoleon did in fact send him a letter of dismissal, but at the last minute it was withdrawn, the Emperor having been prevailed upon by Pélissier's supporters in Paris to change his mind.

[2] The raid on Kertch, conceived by Pélissier and Lord Raglan for the purpose of opening the Sea of Azof to allied ships, the British contingent being led by Sir George Brown, was made on May 24th/25th. The Russian batteries having been destroyed, the Anglo-French squadron moved in and sank 200 Russian supply-ships, landing-parties destroying the factories. An orgy of looting and violence by the raiders followed, the Turkish troops running amok amongst the women and children.

[3] The works in front of the Great Redan, known as the Quarries, were taken by less than a thousand British troops and held despite repeated counter-attacks by the Russians. The Mamelon, the redoubt screening the fortress called the Malakoff, was taken by the French after a fierce Russian counter-attack and considerable French casualties. The assault which followed the allied bombardment on June 17th, by which it was intended to take the Redan and the Malakoff, proved to be a military fiasco, through misunderstanding among the French generals and lack of co-ordination between the French and British commanders.

[4] Todleben's rank at this point of time was Lieutenant-Colonel.

get a view of the front, but could not see much beyond smoke from the guns in the front: the undulating ground covered with great patches of tents, distance very deceptive, no landmarks, the hills all alike over the whole plateau, strings of mules and wagons laden on their way up to the camp. Constant firing renders the view indistinct over the town.

Returned to Kazatch tired and hungry about 7. Found the *Odin* had got into the creek amongst the crowd.

Sat. 30th The *Odin* hauled alongside the *Rodney* and hoisted out the 13-inch mortars we had brought to help in the destruction of Sebastopol. I went on board to see Dr David Deas, now Inspector of Hospitals, and my China friend Surgeon Kinnear, and dined with them. There was no lack of good things or wine there. The *Rodney*'s lower-deck guns were out at the front with most of her men.

JULY

Sun. 1st After church took a walk a few miles towards Headquarters; tents and soldiers everywhere, and smoke obscuring the view. It is fatiguing work tramping over these dusty, barren hills in this hot weather.

Mon. 2nd Therm. 75°, a hot wind. We were coaling alongside an American ship and were half smothered in coal-dust. In afternoon walked out with Captain Willcox and his brother to the left attack, to see the practice from the 13-inch mortars, into Sebastopol. We were in shelter of one of the trenches, as the Russkis did not omit to send a few of their shells in return. While we were there a couple of wounded soldiers were carried past to the rear from a trench more in advance.

"Getting a mortar ready", July 2nd 1855: the Sailors' Battery No. 2, showing a wounded Marine being carried off on a stretcher

Tue. 3rd Went on duty to H.M.S. *Royal Albert* and *Rodney*. Met Rumble, late Chief Engineer of *Fury*, and Surgeon Brien. In evening the body of Lord Raglan was brought down from Headquarters on a gun-carriage, escorted by nearly all the Cavalry and Artillery and Guards, to the *Caradoc* steamer for conveyance to England. General Pélissier and the principal officers of our allies were there, as well as the chief naval officers. Met Captain J. Dalrymple Hay [now commanding H.M.S. *Hannibal*] and a Major de Courcy I had met before at Strangways':[5] he is now in the Turkish contingent.

[5] Cree had first met Tom Strangways (whom he described as "Captain the Hon. Strangways" and as being a kinsman of the Earl of Ilchester) when the latter was a passenger aboard *Firefly* in the Mediterranean in 1838. He continued seeing him over the years on his visits to London, and he and Lizzie had met him last in February.

Wed. 4th On board the *Rodney* – the bombardment going on slowly in the day, but plenty of firing during the night.

Thur. 5th On board *Rodney* with Surgeon Peters to examine Assistant Surgeon —— who has suddenly become insane. In evening a walk round Kazatch Bay with Captain Willcox and his brother.

Fri. 6th Weather very hot and sultry. The *Odin* came out of Kazatch Creek and anchored near the *Royal Albert* off Fort Constantine, at the mouth of the harbour. There was much firing all the evening, but probably we shall not know the cause till we see it in the English papers.

Sat. 7th Captain Digby and Lieutenant Hewett, R.M.A., left us. They have command of our mortar-boats in Stralitzka Bay.

Sun. 8th ... Lt-General James Simpson[B] has now assumed the chief command of the English army out here, since Lord Raglan's death. People don't seem to expect much from him. Our right attack, over by Inkerman, has been given over to the French. More the pity!

Mon. 16th After breakfast landed abreast of the ship, with Hay and [Master William?] Ellis [of *Agamemnon*?]. Walked up to the batteries in the front. First visited the left or French attack, then crossed the ravine to No. 9, Sailors' Battery, and to No. 10, where a party of the 67th [South Hampshire] Regiment were. Remained there some time looking at what I could see of the town – not much! as the firing was getting rather hot and we were obliged to keep our heads low, well below the sandbags. We were about 800 yards from the Redan; shells were flying overhead and bursting beyond, but we could generally see them coming and lay down close till they had burst. Rifle-balls gave a sharp disagreeable ping! ping! every instant; prevented one from looking even through a crevice between the sandbags. A thunderstorm came on, with lightning and heavy rain, which soon wet us through and we had a long traverse through the trenches on our way back, hungry enough, but we found our way into a French restaurant in the camp, and got a doubtful sort of stew, tho' not bad in flavour, with plenty of good bread and a bottle of *vin ordinaire* and a cup of *café*. The storm was over. We did not get to the ship till 10 p.m.

Tue. 17th Weather very fine now, therm. 72°, very few sick.

Wed. 18th On shore with Hay and Ellis. Walk up to the left, or French attack, then across the country to the picket-house, where I had a good view of the Mamelon, Malakoff and Redan, the field of the Battle of Inkerman, and the hills and ravines beyond. We then went across to Cathcart's Hill, where are the tombs of General Cathcart[B] and many of those who fell at Inkerman. I met Surgeon Kinnear, now of the *Rodney* and serving in the trenches. We then walked through the English camp, then up to the French observatory and back, returning on board tired and thirsty, about 8 o'clock, having walked 18 or 20 miles.

Thur. 19th In the afternoon with the Captain landed in Stralitzka Bay, where our mortar-boats are moored and intend opening fire into the Dockyard Creek at the next general bombardment. We walked up to the left attack and stayed till after sunset, watching the firing. We started a hare, which made off towards the trenches, soon I expect to find his way into a French cooking-pot. A seaman of H.M.S. *Queen* was killed in the trenches not far from us – a shot through his head, poor fellow! Captain H. Keppel now commands the Naval Brigade in the trenches.

Sat. 21st Had a call this morning from Surgeon Kerr and Paymaster [Master Benjamin J.] Hooper, of H.M.S. *Highflyer*, old China friends. In the evening Captain W. and I walked up to the mound, to look at the firing along the lines.

Tue. 24th Sultry sirocco weather, afterwards a thunderstorm. Heavy firing at night from a sortie near the Little Redan, in which the Russians were driven back with heavy loss.

Wed. 25th Showery. Captain W. and Hay and I walked up to the French lines. Met one of their officers who spoke English. He said they lost four officers in the sortie last night.

Sun. 29th Captain Willcox and Major Inglis of 4th Dragoons, brother-in-law to our Lieutenant Douglas, dined with us. He appears to be disgusted with the mismanagement of the war, due in great measure to the divided command.

Mon. 30th Hot and thundery weather, therm. 83°. A squall brought up a waterspout, which travelled close to us and afterwards broke near the "Wasp", Russian battery.

AUGUST *Wed. 1st* Heay rain and squalls. A good deal of firing all night from both sides. It is very interesting and exciting to watch the shells after dark, but the volleys of musketry are far more deadly, these fireworks beat hollow the ones at Cremorne Gardens!! The same sort of work goes on night and day more or less continually. At present there seems no chance of it ceasing, and the daily list of killed will be greater as we work nearer to the Russian lines.

Sat. 4th About 10 p.m. the Malakoff roused up with great fury firing against the French trenches.

Sun. 5th A great fire in Sebastopol which lit up all the surroundings. Saw a great funeral on the north side, some distinguished officer, by the large procession of officers and men, but the heavy firing was not slackened.

Tue. 7th On board H.M.S. *Rodney* to see Dr Deas.

Wed. 8th 10 a.m. got under weigh and anchored nearer in the harbour mouth, but 5,000 yards from the Wasp Battery. We had a better view of the town, the Russian ships, dismantled, and moored across the mouth of the harbour, the lines and camps of the allies round the south side of the town.

Tue. 14th Cooler, NW wind. All very busy with Captain Digby, getting our mortar-vessels into right position for firing into the Quarantine Battery. They seem very snug here sheltered under a high bank about 3,000 yards from the Quarantine Battery. Great news has arrived from the Baltic: Sweaborg has been bombarded, but with what result we have not heard.[6]

Wed. 15th We opened fire this morning from our mortar-vessels, the shells falling right into the Russian battery. That is good!

Thur. 16th We are favouring the Russkis with a shell about every ten minutes, just to keep them out of mischief in other directions, for we hear a battle is going on on the other side of the plateau, near where the Sardinians are encamped. There was a signal early this morning "No leave today", so something important is expected. We hear heavy guns and see clouds of smoke rising from behind the right attack. In the evening came news that the French and Sardinians had been attacked by 60,000 Russians in the Tchernaya Plain, and advanced over the little stream, but were driven back by our brave allies with great slaughter, upwards of 1,300 killed and 600 prisoners. I have not heard what our losses have been, but I fear heavy also.

[6] On August 9th–11th 1855 Admirals Dundas and Pénand had led a naval bombardment of the heavily defended congeries of fortresses called Sveaborg, occupying part of a group of small islands lying ESE of Helsingfors (Helsinki). The attack had been staged largely for prestige purposes, and although the damage inflicted was said to be considerable, it appears to have had little or no adverse lasting effect upon the Russians against whom it was directed.

Mortar-boats at work before Sebastopol, August 15th 1855

Fri. 17th The weather keeps fine. Heavy firing all day from the Malakoff and the Mamelon [Redan] and all the right attack. Signal again from the Admiral, "No leave today". We are still sending our little presents into the Russians in shape of 13-inch shells, to which they reply, but if they don't burst in the air they drop harmlessly into the water outside of us. One of our Marines was wounded in his leg today by a piece of shell which burst over us.

Sun. 19th Not a quiet Sunday; heavy firing still going on, principally against the Redan and Malakoff. In the afternoon I was able to get on shore with the Captain. We walked over to the Tchernaya to view the battlefield, where parties of Turks, Sardinians and French were busy burying the dead which lay thickly amongst the grass and low bushes. The stench was rather powerful. The sight brought back to my recollection some of the battlefields I had seen in China. We had a long and dusty walk back and did not get on board till near 10 p.m.

Weather fine, cooler, but we have an increase in our sick-list, principally from dysentery. Many of our men got chilled during the late stormy weather: thirty-seven on the sick-list today.

Wed. 22nd We anchored farther inshore; we have now six mortar-vessels in Stralitzka Bay. While we are firing, either I or Hamilton, my assistant, is on board one of the vessels in case of accidents.

Sat. 25th Lord Stratford de Redcliffe[B] arrived to hold a chapter of the Order of the Bath, for which a salute was fired at 1 p.m. This is reward before the accomplishment of the task.

Mon. 27th In afternoon with 1st Lieutenant Pickard to our mortar-boats, then landed at the French camp and walked to the battery facing Quarantine Fort. Active shelling going on, but we kept low behind the sandbags.

Wed. 29th Beautiful weather now, cloudless skies. There was a tremendous explosion of one of the French magazines near the Flagstaff Battery, said to have killed 40 men and wounded 100.

Thur. 30th Through my glass today I noticed that a statue that used to stand in front of what we call the Clubhouse in Sebastopol has been removed, and furniture being carried over the bridge of boats to the north side. A promising sign!

Fri. 31st On shore in the evening to see a theatrical performance at the Headquarters of the Naval Brigade. The following was the bill of fare: "Deaf as a Post", "The Silent Woman", and a farce, "Slasher v. Crasher" – "God Save the Queen" and "Rule Britannia". The scenery was very well painted by a man on board the *London*. A ballet girl was represented by a young boatswain's mate. The Duke of Newcastle[B] and Lord Rokeby[B] were present and applauded lustily. Now and then a dropping shot from the Russian batteries came inconveniently near, especially if it happened to be a shell. However, we got on board safely at midnight.

The Russian generals commanding are now Gortschakoff,[B] Liprandi[B] and Osten-Sacken.[B]

SEPTEMBER *Sat. 1st* In a letter from home there came a bit of scarlet geranium and a piece of southernwood from Somerset Cottage. Our men are all busy making flannel cartridges against the next bombardment.

Sun. 2nd In afternoon the Captain, his brother and I landed at Stralitzka and walked up to the old Genoese fort, from which we could look down on the Quarantine Battery.

Mon. 3rd On board the mortar-vessels all day. We were firing into Sebastopol as fast as we were able. Admirals Lyons, Houston Stewart[B] and Fremantle[B] came on board to see the mortar practice. Our mortars are slung in chains, a new plan which appears to meet with approval.

The firing very hot from the enemy, very hot, and as the trenches get nearer the loss of life is greater. Thirty shells are fired in a volley; a fine show at night, but not pleasant to be near.

Tue. 4th On board the mortar-boats all day. Each mortar was firing a 13-inch shell every ten minutes. All the other batteries are pouring in shot and shell as fast as possible. Such an infernal din as I never heard before, from 5 or 6 miles of big guns. Nothing but smoke to be seen. We occasionally get a return shell over us which falls harmless into the water. One of our Marines was badly wounded by a splinter of a shell and had to be taken on board the ship. Many of the Russian shells fall short, and many burst high up in the air. It is very exciting work. The French batteries near us we can see hard at it. This is the greatest bombardment Sebastopol has sustained yet and I hope will be the last.

Wed. 5th Still on board the mortar-vessels. We hear the forts are to be assaulted today. The French battery near this is firing away heavily, but nothing to be seen but smoke. As I was returning to the ship about 4 p.m. I saw one of the Russian frigates on fire. The firing appeared to be slackening. After we got on board the *Odin* we could see the Russian frigate in a blaze from end to end; the masts soon fell overboard and continued burning till 4 in the morning.

A mortar at work

Thur. 6th Heavy firing from the English and French batteries. While we were at dinner flames were seen to issue from another Russian frigate, on the north side, and burnt to the water's edge.

Fri. 7th Rumoured that we are going into action tonight. We are making preparations, but there is no getting any reliable news. We can see two large fires in the city.

Sat. 8th We have had fine weather till yesterday, the wind changed to NW and blew hard. Blowing very hard this morning. Signal from the

Sebastopol: destruction of the south side, September 9th 1855

Admiral: "Do not intend to weigh. French have possession of the Malakoff, we hope." A great deal of heavy firing, great quantities of shell and continuous volleys of musketry. We are also hard at it plying this end of Sebastopol with our big shells, which are bursting well in the Russian dockyard. An infernal din, nothing to be seen but smoke and the continual flashing of big guns. The assault of the Redan is now taking place. Oh that it may be successful! The French, we hear, have got into the Malakoff; the Russian ships are also firing into the Malakoff, so that shows that the Russians have been driven out. Our ships ought to have gone in, but they say there is too much sea to enable their fire to be effectual. I am afraid there is a want of enterprise which has been the case all through this war; the old pluck of Benbow and Nelson has departed.

In the evening we hear that our attack on the Redan has failed from the want of efficient support; somebody in command lost his head. It is disgraceful after the French succeeded! I hear our attack was badly planned, but we shall

know more about it tomorrow.[7] In the evening the fire slackened, but our mortar-vessels continue to pound away. A great fire is raging in the town itself and explosions are frequent. No going to bed tonight, too exciting work going on.

Sun. 9th The wind has gone down, but there is a thick haze. The whole of Sebastopol seems to be on fire; terrible explosions in the great forts all night; all their ships are sunk and the bridge of rafts across the harbour is disappearing. We hear that the Redan was evacuated at 2 this morning; no thanks to our generalship. There has been terrible slaughter on both sides. We in the *Odin* have only one wounded Marine. I offered to assist on shore amongst the hosts of wounded, but the authorities don't want it. There is no going on shore yet, so I had to be satisfied with remaining on board and watching the volcano-like blaze reaching to the clouds and the volcano-like explosions of the forts and magazines, which went on all this terrible Sunday.

[7] The morale of British troops had fallen to a low ebb under the command of the reluctant General Simpson. Those assaulting the Redan were mostly raw recruits and old soldiers with tattered nerves. When they reached the parapet, their officers could not induce them forward, and under withering Russian fire they fled in panic back to their own lines. Without the Malakoff, however, Prince Gortschakoff, the Russian commander, considered he could no longer hold Sebastopol, and the Russians thereupon set about destroying the arsenals, barracks, magazines and docks.

Mon. 10th After I had written home, I landed at Stralitzka and walked up to the Central Bastion, or what remains of it, still burning and exploding; through the Garden Redan; up into the Great Redan. What a sight was there: the wounded had all been removed, but most of the killed were lying in heaps; the smell was horrid and the sights heart-rending. The ditch we crossed had been cleared, only to get at the living underneath the dead. We had just got out of the Garden Redan in time to avoid an explosion, which killed a private of the 19th [1st Yorkshire North Riding] Regiment and wounded two others. We then climbed up to the Malakoff, which had been cleared of the dead, but it had been terribly knocked about, smashed gabions, guns and gun-carriages. The Russian guns had been now all turned round pointing down towards the town. We then came down to the Russian hospital which, although cleared of all the living, exhibited signs of what it had been, and smelt – oh, how it smelt! We then visited the long barracks and arsenal and got covered with fleas in some of the Russian shelter-holes. We went to see where we had pitched our 13-inch shells. Not a building was standing, nothing but great holes surrounded by broken stones, broken furniture and crockery. I met two old China friends, Carpenter and Routh, of the Commissariat, who hold important posts here. Rejoiced to meet them.

We were well tired and made the best of our way on board. Saw a Russian steamer on fire, which I think must be their last in Sebastopol.

Kinburn

OCTOBER

Sun. 14th A fine bright morning. Weighed at 10 a.m. and proceed with the fleet towards Kinburn, keeping about 3 miles off the shore backed by high cliffs and downs, in fact the steppe. We passed many Russian signal stations and companies of Cossacks on the look-out. We saw a couple of ladies get out of a carriage and have a good look at us, and then go on their road towards Nicolaieff. We anchored at 4 about 3 miles off the main fort of Kinburn.

Mon. 15th Therm. 66°. A fine bright morning with a light breeze from SE. 6 a.m. up anchor and went to breakfast, then towed the mortar-vessels into position, about a mile from the fort. Our troops were landed on the beach south of the spit of sand on which the fort is situated and cut the Garrison off from the mainland. Some of the gunboats had gone round the end of the spit, so as to cut the Garrison off on that side. The gunboats were fired upon by the batteries at the end of the spit, but without being hit. The forts opened fire at 10 a.m., then the ships engaged the forts at the end of the spit at long range, as the shoal-water would not allow of their getting closer in. About 2 p.m. our mortar-vessels opened fire, in which we joined with our long 64s, throwing shot and shell into the fort, which they returned in a plucky manner, although their range was indifferent, their shot dropping short, or going over, except one shot which destroyed the boat of the mortar-vessel *Camel*. Most of our 13-inch shells fell – burst – inside the large fort, and must have done immense damage, but the enemy would not give in, although they must have seen how useless was their resistance to such an overwhelming force as we brought against them. One of their storehouses in the fort was in a blaze, and as they saw the troops advancing against them on the land side they set fire to the village outside the fort. I admired the pluck of one Russian artilleryman serving a gun on the parapet over the main gateway, alone: the other gunners appeared to have been swept away, but he continued to load and fire till we sent a shot which knocked over his gun and himself too, I suppose, as after the smoke cleared away nothing was seen but dust and rubbish.

Tue. 16th Fine, but too much sea to do anything with the mortars. Some gunboats ran the gauntlet of the forts on the spit and with those inside kept up the fire on the forts; the big ships were too far out to fire effectually. The French pickets advanced to the village.

Wed. 17th Overcast and misty, but less sea. 7.30 a.m. the Russians opened fire from the large fort on the French troops. We got the mortar-vessels into position again and sent our shell into the large fort. In the meantime three French floating batteries had arrived, great square-looking iron boxes with eight or ten heavy guns of a side, came crawling up slowly against the large fort, which fired away vigorously against them. It was strange to see the shot striking their iron sides and flying off again, generally split into pieces. By 9.40 the batteries had steamed into position and then opened a terrible fire, in volleys, which brought down the outer wall of the fort in cartloads at each volley. It was a fine sight for us, but not to the poor Russians, the volleys from the heavy guns crumbling away the wall by tons, our shells bursting in the fort. Ten of the buildings on fire in the fort. At 10.30 the Russian flag was shot away and their fire began to slacken. The gunboat *Arab* near us had burst her two Lancaster guns and signalled "Two men hurt and no medical officer", so I had the Captain's gig and went on board the *Arab*. Found two of her Marines had been hurt by the bursting of the guns – contusions, but nothing very serious. I attended to them and then returned to my ship as the *Arab* retired out of range, for shot and splinters were falling all around.

The enemy's fire now began to slacken, necessarily, for most of their guns were disabled and they must have had a large number killed. The batteries on the sand-spit still kept up the fire, against which the big ships were near enough to deal. Admiral Houston Stewart, in the *Valorous*, with other steamers went round the point, inside. At 2 p.m. the firing ceased, and soon after a flag of truce was sent in and the enemy surrendered. Some hundreds of prisoners marched out.

The bombardment of Kinburn, October 15th–17th 1855, *Odin* in the foreground

Thur. 18th ... At noon I went on shore with the Captain and [1st Lieutenant] Studdert [, R.M.]. We landed at the second spit battery and then walked to the main fort to examine the destruction there. All in ruin, as bad as Sebastopol on a smaller scale; scarcely a gun remained serviceable, some capsized and broken, their carriages smashed; scarcely a square yard untouched by shot or shell. I cannot imagine how they escaped with only 45 killed and 187 wounded, but they had fine casemates quite bomb- and shot-proof, in the fort, which we visited and found they stank as bad as most Russian retreats. In the lower part of the fort we saw some good mortars and new guns, not mounted, and tons of shot, shell and ammunition. We then climbed on the wall which had been nearly breached in many places by the fire of the floating batteries. From the fort we walked along the spit to the remains of the burnt village, another evidence of cruel, cruel war – a baby's cradle, a bedstead, books and furniture, half burnt, showing how little warning the poor natives had to quit their homes.

We passed a little cemetery beyond the village, and walked on to our lines to see the Russian prisoners, who poor fellows were like a flock of sheep all huddled together, surrounded by our Royal Marine sentries. The prisoners were mostly fine looking men, all in their long grey coats and flat caps, the officers in the same, but a green uniform underneath. The Russian General is on board the French flagship, drunk. The spit spreads out here to about a mile in width, across which our troops have entrenched themselves. The sand is

covered with fine turf and heath, a promising place for wildfowl in winter. Our boat met us here and we went off to dinner with the Captain, tolerably tired and hungry.

Wed. 24th It being a fine day, went on shore with the Captain to get a little shooting beyond our pickets. We came upon a deserted fishing station where we found some casks of salted mackerel and some nets. We let our boat's crew take what fish they liked, but it proved too high for their tastes. As we went on through some flat, sandy country with stunted oak trees and a few deserted huts, we started a few hares, curlew and quail, but did not bag any. We went on 5 or 6 miles south of Kinburn, as far as we thought it safe from prowling Cossacks. The country got more wooded with dwarf oak; we met no natives. Got back to dinner at 6.

Fri. 26th Received a box of good things from home. We sent a foraging party away, who bagged two turkeys, a goose, and netted 500 mackerel, a shoal of herrings and a few small sturgeon.

Our mail arrived. Got a welcome letter from Mr Hancock, announcing the birth of my second boy.[8] All well, thank God! It is a dense fog. Lieutenant Beresford, a cousin of Douglas, and Lieutenant Grills, of the gunboat *Fancy*, dined with us on turbot and turkey, the produce of yesterday's chase. The health of my wife and new son were drank in champagne.

[8] Cree's second son was born on October 10th. He was christened Percy Kinburn.

1856

Eupatoria

Tue., Jan. 22nd The news seems to be confirmed that Russia is exhausted and has agreed to terms of peace. . . .

Kazatch

FEBRUARY *Wed. 6th* Fine, bright and cold. We left Eupatoria at daylight; anchored at Kazatch at 10 a.m. Received our letters from home. Another great explosion of remaining forts and docks on south side of Sebastopol.

Sebastopol: the last explosion in the destruction of the docks, February 6th 1856

Thur. 7th The ship filling up with coal to be ready to sail. I am feeling weak and ill, the old Chinese chronic dysentery has troubled me for the last month and more, so I applied for a medical survey. The result was the recommendation that I should be sent home by the first opportunity.

Homeward Bound

Mon. 18th . . . In the afternoon we got a signal from the senior officer: "I have your orders for Malta. Come on board when weather moderates." This put us all in good spirits.

Tue. 19th The therm. fell to 10° during the night, with cutting NE wind, which was fair for the Bosphorus. The mail arrived and brought me a welcome letter from home, the last in the Black Sea. At 6 p.m. we started, and bid farewell to the dismal snow-covered heights of the Crimea, on which the moon was shining brightly, a scene I don't wish to visit again; although many dear friends sleep there in death.

Edw H. Cree

H.M.S. *Odin* passing Eddystone Lighthouse, March 1856

Edward Cree made the last stage of his journey, from Malta to England, along with other invalids from the Crimea, in the steam transport *Andes*. Disembarking from the ship at Plymouth Sound, he arrived safely home in the early hours of Saturday, March 15th. Fifteen days later the Treaty of Paris was signed, bringing the war in the Crimea to an end.

Appendices

1 Details of E.H. Cree's ships 1839–1856

Note: These details have been culled from the Rupert Jones List in the National Maritime Museum. No more detailed listing of H.M. ships of the period is available. The number of guns is given in parenthesis after the name of the ship. Measurements are in feet and inches. The tonnage given is B.O.M. (Builders Old Measurement), a calculation based on dimension not weight. Tonnage based on weight (i.e. displacement tonnage) was not introduced by the Royal Navy until 1872.

1839–1843

RATTLESNAKE (28), 6th rate.* Built at Chatham by Surveyors of the Navy 1822. 113.9$\frac{1}{2}$ length. 94.6$\frac{7}{8}$ keel. 31.11$\frac{1}{2}$ breadth. 8.9$\frac{1}{4}$ depth of hold. 503 tons. Draught: 9.8 forward, 11.10 aft. Grabusa Harbour January 31st 1828; China as troop-ship 1839–42 (2 guns), then as surveying ship (2 guns). Broken up 1859/60.

* The size and number of guns decided the rating of sailing-ships, i.e. from 1st to 6th rate.

1843–1846

VIXEN (6), steam paddle sloop. Built at Pembroke by Sir William Symonds. Launched February 4th 1841. Indicated horsepower 280. 180.0 length. 155.9$\frac{3}{4}$ keel. 20.11$\frac{1}{2}$ breadth. 1054 tons. Draught: 7.9 forward, 8.0 aft. East Indies/China 1842–6; Borneo 1845; Serapaqui 1846; stationed in Pacific during 1854. Deleted 1860/4.

1847–1850

FURY (6), steam paddle sloop, wood. Launched at Sheerness 1845. 190.0 length. 166.0$\frac{3}{4}$ keel. 36.0 breadth. 21.0 depth of hold. 1124 tons. Draught: 8.5 forward, 8.5$\frac{1}{2}$ aft. East Indies/China 1848–50: assisted *Columbine* and *Phlegethon* to destroy a fleet of Chinese pirates October 20th/21st 1849; Crimea 1854; Second China War 1856–7: boats at Fatshan Creek June 1st 1857; China 1858–9. Deleted 1864/9.
See also additional data given by Cree in his entry for August 31st 1847 (pp. 187–8).

1852–1856

ODIN (16), steam paddle frigate. Built at Deptford by Mr Fincham 1846. Horsepower 560. 208.0 length. 187.1$\frac{1}{2}$ keel. 37.0 breadth. 24.1 depth of hold. 1326 tons. Baltic 1854/5; Crimea 1855–6; Peiho forts August 20th 1859. Deleted 1864/9. Cree gives this breakdown of guns: 6 on the upper deck, 4 being 10-inch, 2 8-inch on bow and stern; 10 32-pounders on the main deck, broadside.

2 Summary of E.H. Cree's naval service 1837–1869

Note: The date of appointment is not necessarily the date of his joining a ship.

Appointed	*H.M. Ship*	*Description*	*Station*
(Appointed Assistant Surgeon June 8th 1837.)			
June 8th 1837	*Royal Adelaide*	flagship	Plymouth
July 28th 1837	*Princess Charlotte*	flagship	Mediterranean
Aug. 18th 1837	*Ceylon*	receiving ship	Mediterranean
Oct. 14th 1837	*Firefly*	steam vessel	Mediterranean
July 10th 1839	*Excellent*	gunnery ship	Portsmouth
Sept. 18th 1839	*Rattlesnake*	troop-ship	East Indies/China
(Promoted Surgeon April 4th 1843.)			
Apr. 4th 1843	*Vixen*	steam sloop	East Indies/China
(In the period November 1846–August 1847 studied at Edinburgh University for his M.R.C.S. and M.D.)			
Aug. 6th 1847	*Fury*	steam sloop	East Indies/China
(Shortly after his return to England in *Fury* in November 1850, granted a year's sick-leave, resuming his duties in *Spartan*.)			
June 9th 1852	*Spartan*	frigate	Devonport
Dec. 22nd 1852	*Odin*	steam frigate	Lisbon/Baltic/Crimea
Dec. 15th 1856	*Eagle*	frigate	Falmouth (coastguard service)
Feb. 1st 1858	*Russell*	screw steamship	Devonport (coastguard service)
(From June 1st to October 10th 1860 served as Private Medical Attendant to the Earl of Mount Edgcumbe, based in Plymouth.)			
Oct. 22nd 1860	*Orion*	screw steamship	Mediterranean
May 10th 1862	*Saturn*	4th rate	Pembroke Dockyard

Promoted Staff Surgeon December 10th 1862. Served at H.M. Dockyard, Portsmouth, from September 5th 1864 to July 12th 1869, when he retired with the honorary rank of Deputy Inspector-General of Hospitals and Fleets.

Selected Biographies

Abbreviations

C.B. *Companion of the Bath* D.C.L. *Doctor of Civil Law* F.R.S. *Fellow of the Royal Society* G.C.B. *Knight Grand Cross of the Bath* G.C.M.G. *Knight Grand Cross of St Michael and St George* K.C.B. *Knight Commander of the Bath* K.C.H. *Knight Commander of the Hanoverian Guelphic Order* K.C.M.G. *Knight Commander of the Order of St Michael and St George* M.R.C.S. *Member of the Royal College of Surgeons*

ALISON, WILLIAM PULTENEY (1790–1859), physician, was Professor of Medical Jurisprudence at Edinburgh 1820–2; Professor of "Institutes of Medicine" (i.e. physiology and also pathology) for twenty years; and Professor of the Practice of Medicine 1842–56. Appointed First Physician to Her Majesty for Scotland. As highly respected as he was popular, did much to help the poor in Scotland, advocating reform in the system of public relief. Published *Outlines of Physiology* 1831.

BARAGUAY D'HILLIERS, ACHILLE (1795–1878), son of Louis Baraguay d'Hilliers, one of Napoleon's generals. Commanded the French military force of 10,000 men which, with a contingent of 1,000 British under Brigadier-General Jones of the Royal Engineers, successfully stormed the fortifications at Bomersund, Aland Islands, in August 1854. Napoleon III considered him the victor of the operation and consequently made him a Marshal of France.

BARTLEY, ROBERT (1787–1844), became an ensign in 1806 and served in the American War of 1812–14, being severely wounded in the action at Chrysler's Farm (SW of Montreal) in 1813. Served at the Cape of Good Hope 1821–8 and in Bengal 1828–40. Commanded the 49th (Princess Charlotte of Wales's or the Hertfordshire) Regiment at the capture of Chusan in 1841 and the 3rd or Left Brigade of the expeditionary force at Chin-kiang-foo in 1842, following which was made K.C.B. Died at sea whilst travelling back to England from India.

BEAUCLERK, LORD AMELIUS (1771–1846), third son of the fifth Duke of St Albans, entered the Navy in 1782 and served at the blockade of Toulon in 1794. Held chief command off Lisbon 1824–7 and at Plymouth 1836–9, becoming full Admiral in 1830. A.D.C. to William IV and to Queen Victoria.

BELCHER, EDWARD (1799–1877), grandson of William Belcher (Chief Justice and later Governor of Halifax) and great grandson of Jonathan Belcher (Governor of Massachusetts, New Hampshire and New Jersey), entered the Navy aged thirteen. Surveyed the coasts of North and West Africa, Ireland, western America, China, Borneo, the Philippines and Formosa 1830–41. Made Captain and C.B. in 1841 and knighted in 1843. Irascible and quarrelsome (Cree found him an amusing dinner companion), was yet a brilliant surveyor and gave valuable service in operations against the Chinese in the First China War. His accounts of his voyages in *Sulphur* and *Samarang* were published in 1843 and 1848. Commanded expedition to the Arctic in 1852 and became Admiral in 1872.

BONHAM, SAMUEL GEORGE (1803–1863), after service with the East India Company was Governor of Penang, Singapore and Malacca 1837–47, and in 1848 became Governor of Hong Kong as well as Plenipotentiary and Superintendent of Trade. Made K.C.B. in 1851, and on his return to England in 1853 was created a baronet.

BREMER, JAMES JOHN GORDON (1786–1850), after engagements with the French was made C.B. in 1815. Fought in the First Burma War (1824–6), made K.C.H. in 1836 and in 1837 went to Australia for the second time, establishing a settlement at Port Essington (Cobourg peninsula, N.T.). Commanded expedition to China 1840–1, for which made K.C.B. in 1841. Rear-Admiral in 1849.

BRIGGS, THOMAS (1780–1852?), son of Stephen Briggs, formerly Chief Surgeon at Madras, entered the Navy in 1791. Served as lieutenant in 1797 in *Ville de Paris,* flagship of Earl St Vincent, and commanded the brig-sloop *Salamine* (16) at the reduction of Genoa in 1800 and in subsequent actions against the French. In 1800 captured the privateers *Guadeloupe* and *Susanna* when in command of the frigate *Orpheus* (32), which in 1807 was wrecked on the Jamaica station. In 1823 nominated Resident Commander of the Navy at Bermuda. Served at Malta 1829–30, becoming Rear-Admiral and Superintendent of Malta Dockyard in 1832. Made G.C.M.G. in 1833 and retired as Admiral in 1850.

BROOKE, JAMES (1803–1868), ran away from school in Norwich and at sixteen became an infantry cadet in Bengal. Served in the First Burma War (1824–6), in which he was wounded. In 1834 sailed in a small brig to China, inheriting a fortune on his father's death the following year. In 1838 sailed in his private schooner *Royalist* to Borneo, whence he proceeded to Sarawak. Following his aid to Muda Hassim in quelling the revolt there in 1839–40, was invited to take over the government of the province, becoming the first white rajah. Made K.C.B. in 1847 and became subsequently British Commissioner and Consul-General of Borneo and Governor of Labuan. His last action in 1849 against pirates in Sarawak was strongly criticised in some quarters, but he was exonerated by an overwhelming vote in his favour in the House of Commons.

BROWN, GEORGE (1790–1865), fought in the Peninsular War and after various staff appointments was made Lt-General in 1851 and K.C.B. in 1852. Commanded the Light Division in the Crimea, and led the British contingent in the raid on Kertch in 1855. In the period 1860–5 served as C.-in-C. in Ireland.

BULLER, GEORGE (1802–1884), served in the Kaffir (1847–8) and Boer (1852–3) Wars and as a brigade commander in the Crimea, being wounded at Inkerman in 1854. Made K.C.B. in 1855 and General in 1871.

BURNETT, WILLIAM (1779–1861), served as naval surgeon at St Vincent (1797), the Nile (1798) and Trafalgar (1805). Physician to the Mediterranean fleet 1810–13 and at Chatham in 1814. Physician of the Navy 1824–41; made K.C.B. in 1831.

CAMPBELL, COLIN (1792–1863), son of a Glasgow carpenter named Macliver, became an ensign in 1808, serving first in Portugal under Sir John Moore. In 1810–13 fought with great bravery in the Peninsula, and served subsequently in the West Indies 1819–26, China 1842–6, and India 1846–53. Made K.C.B. in 1849 and Major-General in 1854. Commanded the Highland Brigade at the Alma, Balaclava and Inkerman. C.-in-C. in India 1857–60, during which time he suppressed the Indian Mutiny. Created Baron Clyde in 1858 and made Field-Marshal in 1862.

CANNING, STRATFORD (1786–1880), diplomatist, served at Constantinople 1808–12, as Plenipotentiary to Switzerland 1814–20, then as Envoy to Washington 1820–4, St Petersburg 1824/1833, and Constantinople 1825. M.P. for Old Sarum 1828, Stockbridge 1830 and King's Lynn 1835–41. Subsequently British Ambassador in Constantinople in 1842 and again in 1848 and 1853, and in 1847 Envoy to Switzerland. Created Viscount Stratford de Redcliffe in 1852.

CANROBERT, FRANÇOIS CERTAIN (1809–1895), served for twenty years in Algeria and supported the future emperor, Napoleon III, in the *coup d'état* of 1851. In 1854 commanded the French 1st Division in the Crimea under Marshal St Arnaud, being wounded at the Alma. On St Arnaud's death, assumed command of the French. The British thought him far too cautious, nicknaming him "Robert can't", and, harassed by directives from the Emperor, he became increasingly indecisive. Superseded in 1855 by Pélissier (q.v.), having pleaded incompatibility with Raglan (q.v.). Commanded the French 3rd Division in the war in Italy against the Austrians. Became Marshal of France and in his later years was active politically, serving the Bonapartist cause in the senate of the Third Republic.

CATHCART, GEORGE (1794–1854), younger son of the first Earl Cathcart, whom he served as A.D.C. in 1813–14, becoming A.D.C. to the Duke of Wellington at Waterloo. C.-in-C. in South Africa 1852–4 at the defeat of the Basutos and Kaffirs. Made K.C.B. in 1853. Commanded the 4th Division in the Crimea and killed at Inkerman.

CHADS, HENRY DUCIE (*c.*1788–1868), served in operations leading to the capture of Mauritius in 1810. In 1812, whilst serving in the frigate *Java* (38), was taken prisoner by the American frigate *Constitution*. Served subsequently in the West Indies and Burma. Commanded *Andromache* (28) and then *Cambrian* (36) in the East Indies 1834–45. Rear-Admiral in the Baltic 1854–5. Made K.C.B. in 1855 and Admiral in 1863.

CHINNERY, GEORGE (1774–1852), English landscape and portrait painter, abandoned his family in 1802 and went to live in India before moving to Canton. In 1825 quit Canton for Macao, to escape debts and his wife who had by now followed him. Notable for his pencil sketches, wash drawings and water-colours, and drawings of European and Chinese merchants, occupies a unique place among Victorian painters, being the only notable European artist of the time to live and work in the Far East.

CHRISTISON, ROBERT (1797–1882), toxicologist, was House Physician to Edinburgh Infirmary 1817–20 and 1827; Medical Professor in Edinburgh 1822–77; Medical Adviser to the Crown 1829–66; and President of the Edinburgh College of Physicians 1839/1848. Created baronet in 1871. Published various works, including *Treatise on Poisons* (1829).

CLINTON, HENRY PELHAM FIENNES PELHAM (1811–1864), succeeded his father as fifth Duke of Newcastle in 1851. Served as Chief Secretary for Ireland in 1846, then as Secretary of State for War and the Colonies 1852–4, and Secretary-at-War 1854–5, visiting the Crimea when holding the last-named office.

COCHRANE, THOMAS JOHN (1789–1872), eldest son of Admiral Sir Alexander Forrester Inglis Cochrane (youngest son of the eighth Earl of Dundonald), entered the Navy in 1796. Present at the Battle of San Domingo (1806). Commanded the frigate *Ethalion*, the frigate *Jason* from 1806 until the end of the war against the French, and then *Forte* in the West Indies until 1824, when he served as Governor of Newfoundland for eleven years. Made C.B. in 1839. Became Rear-Admiral in 1841, succeeding Admiral Parker (q.v.) as C.-in-C. East Indies station in 1843. Made K.C.B. in 1847 and G.C.B. in 1860. Appointed Admiral of the Fleet in 1865.

CODRINGTON, WILLIAM JOHN (1804–1884), second son of Admiral Sir Edward Codrington, of Navarino (1827) fame. Not in action thitherto, but fought commendably as a brigade commander at the Alma and at Inkerman. Superseded General Simpson (q.v.) as C.-in-C. in November 1855, holding command at Sebastopol until it was evacuated in July 1856. Made K.C.B. in 1855 and General in 1863. Governor of Gibraltar 1859–65.

COLLIER, FRANCIS AUGUSTUS (*c.* 1783–1849), second son of Vice-Admiral Sir George Collier, entered the Navy in 1794 and in 1798 was appointed to *Vanguard*, which bore Nelson's flag in the Mediterranean and at the Battle of the Nile, afterwards serving with Nelson in *Foudroyant*. Appointed Rear-Admiral in 1846 and to the command of the East Indies station in 1848 on the death from sunstroke of Rear-Admiral Inglefield.

DALHOUSIE *see* **RAMSAY**

DAVIS, JOHN FRANCIS (1795–1890), came to Canton in 1813 in the service of the East India Company. In 1816 accompanied Lord Amherst on his unsuccessful mission to see the Emperor in Peking. In 1834 became second Superintendent of Trade. In 1844–8 served in the roles of Plenipotentiary and Chief Superintendent of Trade as well as Governor and C.-in-C. at Hong Kong. Created a baronet in 1845 and made K.C.B. in 1854. A writer as well as diplomat, published a number of works on China.

DERMOTT, GEORGE DARBY (1803–1848), son of a medical practitioner who became a Wesleyan minister, studied in London under the celebrated Joshua Brookes, becoming an M.R.C.S. in 1822. Started his first private anatomical school in Little Windmill Street, Soho, changing the site several times until establishing a school of medicine in Charlotte Street, Bloomsbury. In 1845 moved to Bedford Square. Eccentric and outspoken, wielded a genial influence over his pupils, and is described in an obituary in the *Medical Directory* as "the last of the great anatomical teachers".

DICKSON, DAVID (1780–1850), youngest son of the Reverend George Dickson, minister of Bedrule, Roxburgh. Entered the Navy in 1798, serving first in *Prince Frederick* and then in *Victory*. Appointed Surgeon 1799. Served 1805–8 in the Leeward Islands squadron and in 1813–14 with the Russian fleet in the Medway, receiving the Order of St Vladimir from the Emperor Alexander I for services during the fever epidemics. Physician and Inspector of Hospitals with the North American squadron 1814–15, after which in civilian service at the Clifton Dispensary, Bristol. In 1816 became Fellow of the Edinburgh College of Physicians, London. Physician, Naval Hospital, Plymouth, 1824–40, being knighted in 1834 for services in the West Indies. Inspector of Hospitals 1840.

ELLIOT, CHARLES (1801–1875), cousin of Admiral George Elliot (q.v.), was midshipman in *Minden* at the bombardment of Algiers in 1816 and lieutenant on the Jamaica station in 1822. In 1828 more or less retired from the Navy, being employed by the Foreign or Colonial Office. In 1830–3 was protector of slaves in Guiana, and in 1837 became Plenipotentiary and Chief Superintendent in the China Trade Commission, being superseded by Sir Henry Pottinger (q.v.) in 1841. Later Governor of Bermuda 1846–54, Trinidad 1854–6 and St Helena 1863–9. In 1865 made K.C.B. and Admiral.

ELLIOT, GEORGE (1784–1863), second of the first Earl of Minto, was present at the Battles of Cape St Vincent (1797) and the Nile (1798). In 1801 served in *San Josef* and *St George* under Nelson's flag, and in 1803 in the Mediterranean in *Victory* with Nelson, who thought highly of him. C.-in-C. Cape of Good Hope 1837–40, and C.-in-C. East Indies station and joint Plenipotentiary in the China Trade Commission with Charles Elliot (q.v.) in 1840, his poor health preventing any further service. Made Admiral in 1853 and K.C.B. in 1862.

ESTCOURT, JAMES BUCKNALL BUCKNALL (1802–1855), supervised magnetic experiments in Euphrates Valley expedition of 1834–6, the aim of which was to find a route to India from the Persian Gulf. Without previous experience of warfare, fought at the Alma and Inkerman and was made Major-General in 1854. As Adjutant-General was jointly responsible with Major-General Airey (Quartermaster-General) for administering supplies, both men being unjustly maligned for the suffering of British troops, the causes of which were manifold. His death from cholera was much grieved by Raglan (q.v.), who survived him by only a few days.

FRASER, ALEXANDER GEORGE (1785–1853), sixteenth Baron Saltoun, served in Sicily in 1806 and at Coruña (1808), Walcheren (1809), and in Spain and France 1812–14. Commanded the light company of the 2nd Brigade of Guards at Quatre Bras, and at Waterloo held the garden and orchard of Hougoumont and led the charge against the French Old Guard. In 1841–3 commanded the 1st or Right Brigade, which he led in the assault on Chin-kiang-foo, and then the entire military forces based in Hong Kong, being superseded by Major-General d'Aguilar in 1844.

FREMANTLE, CHARLES HOWE (1765–1819), second son of Vice-Admiral Sir Thomas Francis Fremantle, appointed as lieutenant to *Rochfort* (80) in 1820. After coastguard service in home waters, visited Mexico in the sloop *Jasper* (10). In 1826 appointed to command *Challenger* (28) in the East Indies. Admiral Superintendent at Balaclava in 1855 and C.-in-C. at Devonport 1863–6. Made K.C.B. in 1857, Admiral in 1864 and G.C.B. in 1867.

GIFFARD, GEORGE (1815–1895), third son of Sir Ambrose Hardinge Giffard, Chief Justice of Ceylon (1819–27), joined the Navy in 1827. Commanded *Vixen* 1843–6, being promoted Captain in 1845. Served subsequently as Captain of the steam frigate *Leopard* (12) in the Baltic and Black Sea 1853–6, and as Captain of *Princess Royal* (91) 1856–8. Made C.B. in 1855 and K.C.B. in 1875, retiring in 1870 as Vice-Admiral. In 1877 accorded the rank of Admiral.

GLYNN, JAMES (1801–1871), U.S. naval officer, entered the gunboat service at New Orleans about 1810, serving 1812–15 as acting midshipman in *General Pike* and

Superior on Lake Ontario. Made Commander in 1841. Served on the California coast in the Mexican War of 1846–7, and in 1848, commanding the sloop *Preble*, joined the East India squadron under Commodore Geisinger. His reports after the rescue of American sailors held captive in Japan in 1849 (Japan being closed to the West) helped pave the way for Commodore M.C. Perry's mission to Japan (1853–4) in the flagship *Susquehanna*, which led to a treaty of peace signed at Yokahama in March 1854, granting U.S. trading rights. In 1861 went to Pensacola in *Macedonian* and subsequently cruised in the Caribbean against Confederate raiders until 1862, when he retired as Captain. Made Commodore 1867.

GORTSCHAKOFF, PRINCE MIKHAIL DMITRIEVITCH (1795–1861), fought against the French in 1812–14, the Turks in 1828–9, and made General of Artillery in the Polish uprising of 1831. Became military governor of Warsaw in 1846 and commanded the Russian artillery in the invasion of Hungary in 1849. Led the Russian army in the Danubian principalities before succeeding Prince Mentschikoff as commander-in-chief in the Crimea in 1855, defending Sebastopol with great resilience, thus redeeming his defeat on the Tchernaya. Made Governor-General of Poland in 1856.

GOUGH, HUGH (1779–1869), became adjutant of Colonel Rochford's Foot at the age of fifteen. Served with the 78th Highlanders at the capture of the Cape in 1795 and was severely wounded at Talavera in 1809 when commanding the 2nd Battalion 87th (Prince of Wales's Irish) Regiment (later Royal Irish Fusiliers). Fought with distinction at Barossa and Tarifa in 1811, and was wounded at Nivelle in 1813. Made Major-General in 1830 and K.C.B. the following year. For services in China became G.C.B. and earned a baronetcy. Commanded the British at the defeat of the Mahrattas in 1843, and again during the Sikh Wars (1845–6 and 1848–9). For these victories was created in turn a baron and a viscount. In 1862 became Field-Marshal.

GREY, GEORGE (1799–1882), a grandson of the first Earl Grey (the second earl became Prime Minister in 1831), succeeded as second baronet in 1828. Called to the bar in 1826, later serving as Judge Advocate-General 1839–41. M.P. for Devonport 1832–47, and subsequently represented North Northumberland 1847–52 and Morpeth 1853–74. Among the ministerial offices he filled were those of Chancellor of the Duchy of Lancaster, Secretary of State for the Home Department under Lord John Russell as well as Lord Palmerston, and Secretary of State for the Colonies in the coalition ministry of Lord Aberdeen of 1854–5.

HALL, WILLIAM HUTCHEON (1788–1878), entered the Navy in 1811 and became a master in 1823. One of the first British officers to study steam, was given command of *Nemesis* in 1839 and in consequence of outstanding service in her, was procured an Order in Council to enable him to become a lieutenant in 1841. The Admiralty later arranged for him to count his time in *Nemesis* as if served in an H.M. ship and appointed him Commander in 1843 and Post-Captain in 1844. Inventor of Hall's patent anchor and of iron bilge tanks. Elected F.R.S. in 1847. In 1854 commanded *Hecla* in the Baltic, and in 1855 the blockship *Blenheim* at the bombardment of Sveaborg. Made Rear-Admiral in 1863 and K.C.B. in 1867. Published account of his voyage in *Nemesis* in 1849.

HAY, JOHN CHARLES DALRYMPLE (1821–1912), served on shore in the First Kaffir War in 1835, and then on the west coast of Africa in the suppression of the slave-trade, in South America and the Pacific 1836–9, and in 1840 as midshipman in *Benbow* (72) during operations on the Syrian coast. Present at the bombardment of Beirut and capture of St Jean d'Acre (both in 1840). Subsequently served in various ships in the Mediterranean and in the East Indies and China 1843–50, including *Vixen*, and as flag-lieutenant to Admiral Cochrane (q.v.) at Marudu Bay and on the coast of Borneo. Commanded *Wolverine* in 1846, and *Columbine* in 1849 at the destruction of the Chinese pirate fleets in Bias Bay and the Gulf of Tonquin. Flag-Captain in *Hannibal* 1854–6 in the Crimea. Commanded *Victory* (104) in 1854 and *Indus* (78) in North America and the West Indies 1857–60. Succeeded as third baronet in 1861. Made F.R.S. 1864; M.P. for Wakefield 1862–5, Stamford 1866–80, Wigtown Burghs 1880–5; Lord of the Admiralty 1866–8. Retired as Rear-Admiral in 1870, becoming Vice-Admiral in 1872 and Admiral in 1878. Made K.C.B. in 1885; G.C.B. 1902. His *Lines from My Log-book* (1898) includes reproductions of three water-colours given him by his former messmate Edward Cree.

HENDERSON, WILLIAM (1810–1872), homoeopathist, was Physician to Edinburgh Fever Hospital in 1832 and subsequently Pathologist to the Royal Infirmary and Professor of General Pathology 1842–69. By 1841 he used the microscope in the anatomy of the lung in pneumonia and other pathological studies. His adoption of homoeopathy in 1845 led to his resignation from the Royal Infirmary and to opposition from his former colleagues, including Professor Syme (q.v.), though in time he won back their esteem.

KEPPEL, HENRY (1809–1904), fourth son of the fourth Earl of Albemarle, entered the Navy in 1822, serving in 1830 in *Galatea* (42) and in 1831 on the East Indies station in *Magicienne* (24). Commanded the sloop *Childers* (16) in the Mediterranean and at the Cape of Good Hope 1834–8, and *Dido* (18) 1841–5, in which in 1842 he participated in the capture of Woosung and Shanghai and in operations up the Yangtse. In 1844, supported by the East India Company's steamer *Phlegethon*, destroyed a large piratical settlement on Borneo. In the war against Russia of 1854–6 commanded *St Jean d'Acre* (101) in the Baltic and Crimea, and led the Naval Brigade before Sebastopol. In 1857 in *Hong Kong* took an important part in the destruction of the Chinese fleet in Fatshan Creek. Made full Admiral in 1869, G.C.B. in 1871 and Admiral of the Fleet in 1877.

LIPRANDI, PAVEL PETROVITCH (1796–1864), served against the French in 1813–14, in the Russo-Turkish War of 1828–9 and commanded a regiment in the Polish uprising of 1831. Led a special detachment in Wallachia 1853–4 before transferring to the Crimea, distinguishing himself at Balaclava.

LYONS, EDMUND (1790–1858), served in East Indies 1810–11 and in the Mediterranean 1828–33, and then in various ministerial capacities. Created baronet in 1840 and made Rear-Admiral in 1850. C.-in-C. Mediterranean fleet 1855–8. Created Baron Lyons of Christchurch in 1856.

NAPIER, CHARLES (1786–1860), entered the Navy in 1799. In 1811–13 engaged in quelling the coasting trade on the west coast of Italy, and in 1814 served meritoriously in expeditions against Alexandria and Baltimore. Made C.B. in 1815. Commanded the Portuguese fleet in the service of Dona Maria in 1833, and was ennobled Viscount in the Portuguese peerage that year for his victory against the numerically superior fleet of Dom Miguel off Cape St Vincent. In 1834 raised the siege of Oporto (for which he was created Count), and by achieving the surrender of Ourem and Figuera brought the civil war to an end. In 1839–40 served as Commodore in the Mediterranean with Sir Robert Stopford (q.v.), and by ignoring orders to retreat, was responsible for the capture of Beirut by a land force (1840), for which he was taken to task. That year, nevertheless, was made K.C.B. Commanded the Channel fleet as Rear-Admiral in 1846, and the Baltic fleet as Vice-Admiral in 1854. His command of operations in the Baltic was unjustly criticised by the Admiralty, and he refused the G.C.B. offered him in atonement. In 1855 became M.P. for Southwark and in 1858 was made Admiral.

NEWCASTLE *see* **CLINTON**

OSTEN-SACKEN, DMITRI YEROFEYEVITCH (1789?–1881), fought against the French in the Napoleonic War and with distinction in the wars with Persia (1826–7) and Turkey (1828–9); also in the suppression of the uprisings in Poland (1831) and Vienna (1848). Organised the defence of Odessa against allied bombardment in April 1854 and took command of Sebastopol in February 1855, temporarily succeeding Prince Mentschikoff until Gortschakoff (q.v.) assumed overall command of the Crimean army. Made Count after his retirement in 1856.

PARKER, WILLIAM (1781–1866), entered the Navy in 1793 and saw considerable service until he retired to the country in the period 1812–27. Became Lord of the Admiralty in the years 1834–41. For his successful command in China 1841–3 he became G.C.B. and a baronet. Made Admiral of the Fleet in 1863.

PÉLISSIER, AMABLE JEAN-JACQUES (1794–1864), commanded the French 1st Corps at the outbreak of hostilities in the Crimea, succeeding Canrobert (q.v.) as C.-in-C. of the French army. For the successful attack on the Malakoff in September 1855, which achieved the surrender of Sebastopol, was made Marshal, and on his return to France created Duc de Malakoff and made a senator, as well as being granted 100,000 francs. French Ambassador in London 1858–9. Died serving as Governor of Algeria.

PENNEFATHER, JOHN LYSAGHT (1800–1872), third son of the Reverend John Pennefather of Co. Tipperary, commanded a brigade at the Alma and again at Inkerman, leading his men with vigour at the very centre of the second battle. Made K.C.B. in 1855, being invalided from the Crimea in July of that year.

PERCIVAL, JOHN (1779–1862), merchant mariner and U.S. naval officer nicknamed "Mad" or "Roaring Jack", went to sea aged thirteen and at twenty commanded vessels in the West Indian and transatlantic trade. Impressed into the Royal Navy in 1797, serving in *Victory* and then in a naval brig, escaping at Madeira two years later to the U.S. ship *Washington*. During the quasi-war against France of 1798–1800 served in *Delaware*. Sailing Master of the sloop *Peacock* (Captain Lewis Warrington) in her victory over the British brig-sloop *Epervier* in 1813. After cruises in *Porpoise* against West Indian pirates, sailed to the Pacific in Isaac Hull's flagship *United States*, and in 1825–6 commanded the schooner *Dolphin* in the South Seas. Made Commander in 1831 and Captain in 1841, commanding *Cyane* in the Mediterranean 1838–9 and the frigate *Constitution* on her Pacific/East Indies cruise of 1844–6.

PLUMRIDGE, JAMES HANWAY (1787–1863), served in *Defence* at Trafalgar and as flag-lieutenant to Sir Edward Pellew in *Caledonia* in 1810, seeing much service against the French. Superintendent of Falmouth packets 1837–41 and M.P. for Falmouth 1841–7. Appointed to the frigate *Cambrian* in 1847 for service in East Indies and became second in command of the station. Promoted Rear-Admiral in 1852 and commanded a squadron in the Baltic in 1854. Made K.C.B. in 1855 and Vice-Admiral in 1857.

POTTINGER, HENRY (1789–1856), served in India in the Third Mahratta War (1817–18) and in 1836–40 as a political agent in Scinde, for which he was created a baronet in 1840. That year appointed Plenipotentiary and Chief Superintendent of Trade in China, being made G.C.B. in 1842. In 1843 became the first British Governor of Hong Kong. Later Governor of the Cape of Good Hope 1846–7 and Governor of Madras 1847–54.

RAGLAN *see* **SOMERSET**

RAMSAY, JAMES ANDREW (1812–1860), succeeded his father as tenth Earl of Dalhousie in 1838. Governor-General of India in 1847, and at the end of the Second Sikh War in 1849 created Marquess. Introduced the railway system into India as well as the electric telegraph. In 1852 entered upon the Second Burmese War, which resulted in the annexation of Lower Burma, a policy which earned him much criticism.

REDCLIFFE *see* **CANNING**

ROBINSON-MONTAGU, HENRY (1798–1883), succeeded as sixth Baron Rokeby in the Irish peerage in 1847. In February 1855 took command of the 1st Division in the Crimea in place of the Duke of Cambridge, who had returned home physically ill and mentally shattered after the Battle of Inkerman. Became full General in 1869.

ROKEBY *see* **ROBINSON-MONTAGU**

SALTOUN *see* **FRASER**

SCHOEDDE, JAMES HOLMES (1786–1861), became an ensign in the 60th (Royal American) Regiment in 1800, served in Egypt in 1801 and in the Peninsular War (1808–14), receiving a gold medal for Nivelle (1813) and the war medal with fourteen clasps. Colonel 48th (Northamptonshire) Regiment 1830–3, and Lt-Colonel 55th (Westmoreland) Regiment 1833–45. In China commanded a brigade, which he led at the taking of Chin-kiang-foo in 1842, and was made K.C.B. that year. Became Major-General in 1854 and Lt-General in 1860.

SCOTT, FRANCIS (1808-1875), elder son of the Reverend Alexander Scott, Rector of Bootle, Cumberland, entered the Navy in 1822. Appointed Captain in 1848, commanding *Odin* in the Baltic in 1854. Made C.B. in 1857, then serving as naval A.D.C. to Queen Victoria 1862–6 and as Captain of *Victory* 1863–6. Retired as Vice-Admiral in 1873.

SIMPSON, JAMES (1792–1868), fought with the Grenadier Guards in the Peninsular War, and severely wounded subsequently at Waterloo. Chief of Staff in the Crimea in 1854, succeeding with much reluctance to the command of the British on the death of Lord Raglan (q.v.). Appointed General and made G.C.B. on the fall of Sebastopol in 1855, resigning his command in November of that year.

SIMPSON, JAMES YOUNG (1811–1870), physician, Professor of Midwifery 1839, and a pioneer in the use of chloroform for anaesthetic purposes. Created a baronet and made D.C.L. of Oxford in 1866. Contributed significantly to the science of obstetrics, anticipating the discovery of Röntgen rays. Published several books, including *Obstetric Memoirs and Contributions* (1855–6).

SOMERSET, LORD FITZROY JAMES HENRY (1788–1855), youngest son of the fifth Duke of Beaufort, served in the Peninsula as A.D.C. to Wellesley, and lost an arm at Waterloo. Created Baron Raglan in 1852. Commanded the British in the Crimea at the Alma, Balaclava and Inkerman, and was blamed for the maladministration, not to mention the suffering of the troops, that followed in the winter of 1854–5. Aloof as he had at first seemed to his men, came to be revered by them, and they mourned deeply his death from dysentery, as did the French C.-in-C. Pélissier (q.v.).

STAVELEY, WILLIAM (1784–1854), served with the Caithness Legion 1798–1804, after which entered the Staff Corps. Served in the Peninsular War and at Waterloo in 1815, when he was made C.B. In 1842 became acting Governor of Mauritius, and in 1846 was appointed Major-General. Commanded the British garrisons at Hong Kong 1847–50 and Bombay 1851–2, and then served as C.-in-C. at Madras 1853–4.

STEWART, HOUSTON (1791–1875), served at Walcheren (1809), on the Jamaica station 1817–18, and at the reduction of Acre (1840). Controller-General of the Coastguard 1846–50, and Rear-Admiral in command at the capture of Kinburn in 1855. Subsequently C.-in-C. North American station and at Devonport. In 1865 made G.C.B., and in 1872 Admiral of the Fleet.

STOPFORD, ROBERT (1768–1847), served in the West Indies, being decorated at the Battle of San Domingo (1806), and in the Rio and Copenhagen expeditions of 1806–7. Blockaded Rochefort in 1808 and commanded the naval forces in the Java expedition of 1811. Appointed Admiral in 1825 and made G.C.M.G. in 1837, commanding the Mediterranean fleet in the years 1837–41.

SYME, JAMES (1799–1870), surgeon, started a private surgical hospital at Edinburgh in 1829, and introduced a system of clinical instruction. Made Crown Professor of Clinical Surgery in Edinburgh University in 1833. The author of several surgical works, came to be recognised as the greatest living authority on surgery of his day.

TODLEBEN, FRANZ EDUARD IVANOVITCH (1818–1884), Russian military engineer, distinguished himself in the Crimea by his organisation of the defences of Sebastopol. Made General in 1869. During the Russo-Turkish War of 1877–8 planned the successful siege of Plevna (Pleven) and Bulgarian fortresses. C.-in-C. Russian army and created Count in 1878. Subsequently Governor of Odessa and of Vilna.

WILLCOX, JAMES (1812–1877), entered the Navy in 1826 and promoted Captain in 1850. Commanded *Fury*, mostly on the China station 1847–50, the steam frigate *Dragon* (16) 1854–5 and *Odin* in the Crimea 1855–6. Made C.B. in 1856 and retired as Vice-Admiral in 1873.

WOODFORD, ALEXANDER GEORGE (1782–1870), fought at Copenhagen in 1807, in the Peninsula (1811–14), and commanded the 2nd Battalion Coldstream Guards at Quatre Bras, Waterloo, at the storming of Cambrai, on their entry into Paris and during the occupation of France. Frequently decorated and mentioned in dispatches. Made C.B. in 1815, K.C.M.G. in 1831 and G.C.B. in 1852. Governor and C.-in-C. of Gibraltar 1836–43.

View from No. 1 Tehidy Terrace, Falmouth, Cornwall, the house occupied by Edward Cree and his growing family in the period March 1857–February 1860.

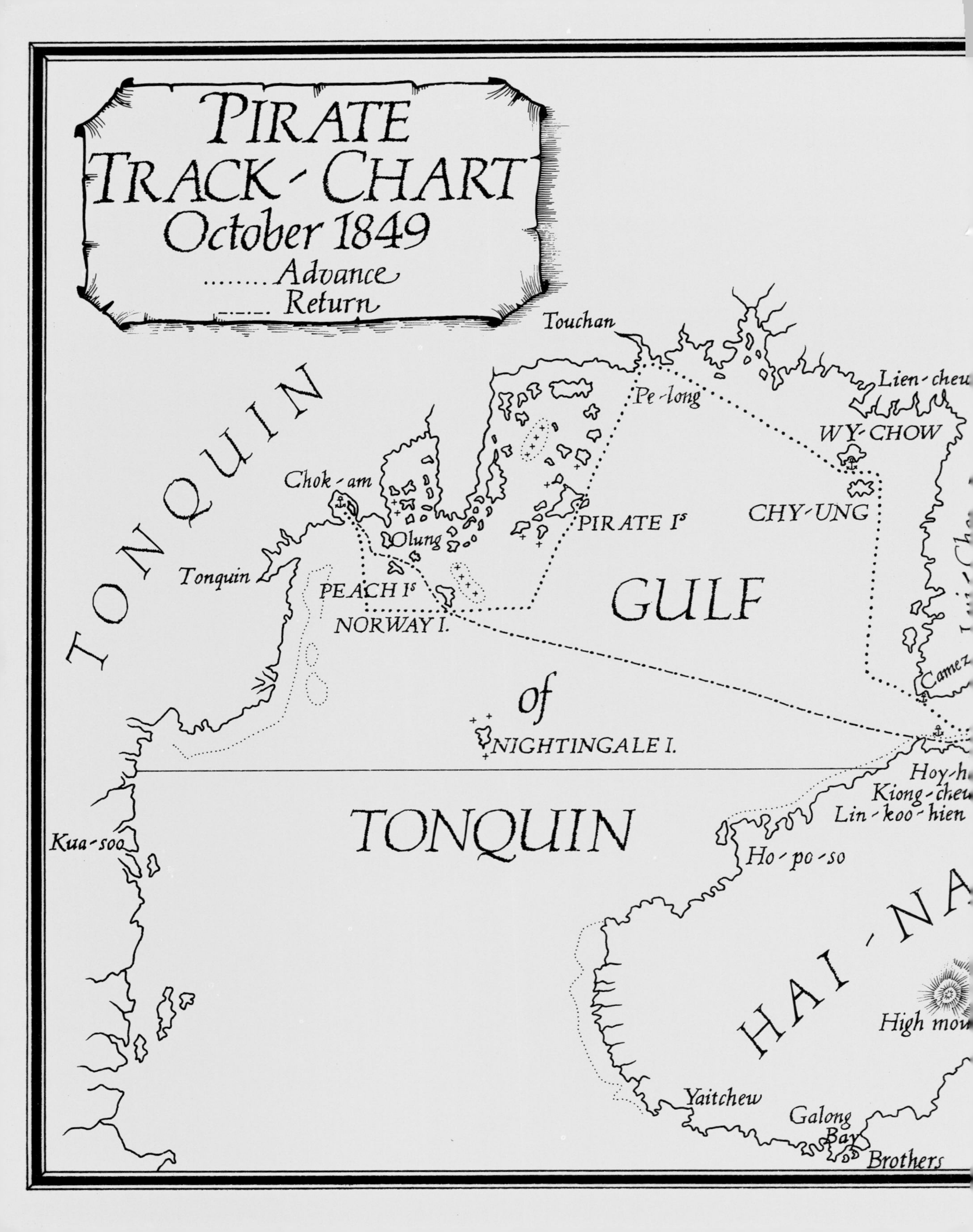
PIRATE TRACK-CHART
October 1849
........Advance
_._._. Return
TONQUIN
Touchan
Pe-long
Lien-cheu
WY-CHOW
Chok-am
CHY-UNG
PIRATE Is
Olung
Tonquin
PEACH Is
GULF
NORWAY I.
of
Camez
NIGHTINGALE I.
Hoy-h
Kiong-cheu
TONQUIN
Lin-koo-hien
Kua-soo
Ho-po-so
HAI-NA
High mou
Yaitchew
Galong Bay
Brothers